NO
MIRACLES
FOR
HIRE

NO
MIRACLES
FOR
HIRE

How to Get *Real* Value
From Your Consultant

J. Thomas Cannon

amacom

American Management Association

This book is available at a special
discount when ordered in bulk quantities.
For information, contact Special Sales Department,
AMACOM, a division of American Management Association,
135 West 50th Street, New York, NY 10020.

This publication is designed to provide accurate and authoritative
information in regard to the subject matter covered. It is sold with
the understanding that the publisher is not engaged in rendering
legal, accounting, or other professional service. If legal advice or
other expert assistance is required, the services of a competent
professional person should be sought.

Library of Congress Cataloging-in-Publication Data

Cannon, J. Thomas.
    No miracles for hire : how to get real value from your con-
sultant / J. Thomas Cannon.
     p. cm.
  Includes bibliographical references and index.
  ISBN 0-8144-5015-6
  1. Business consultants. I. Title.
HD69.C6C26   1990   90-55202
658.4'6—dc20   CIP

Printing number

10 9 8 7 6 5 4 3 2 1

To
Dorothy for her continuing patience and support

Contents

Preface

To the advice seeker:

Ladies and gentlemen, this book is directed to you if you are, or intend to be, a first-time user of consulting services, or, if you have used consultants with less than complete success and are wondering why. Hopefully, those consultants will be looking over your shoulder for suggestions as well.

No Miracles for Hire focuses on business/management consulting to corporations and other organizations and deals with my real-life experiences, as well as those of my colleagues, in both the for-profit and not-for-profit sectors. It endeavors to present the business client's point of view, not that of the consultant. However, the perspectives offered, and the "secrets" bared, come from one who has worked inside the consulting business for almost forty years.

The critiques and criticisms offered in the book apply mainly to my career in business consulting, which has involved strategic planning; marketing audits; new-venture evaluations, acquisitions, and divestitures; and a range of additional general management consulting assignments, including projects for clients in overall organization studies, field sales management and organization, market research, marketing policy, distribution channels, and sales compensation.

Such work has encompassed a diversity of assignments in over thirty industries, commencing with eight years with the firm of Cresap, McCormick and Paget, followed by six years as an employee of IBM, doing what I referred to as "captive" consulting. For the past twenty-three years I have enjoyed an independent consulting career specializing in strategic planning, marketing audits, managerial problem solving, new-venture evaluations, and new-business start-ups.

My motivations for writing this book are several. First, it hopefully will provide some perspective to business executives who use or are considering engaging consultants. It raises issues concerning whether and when to use outside advisers and offers ideas on how to screen and choose them. It is concerned with how to get results and bona fide productivity from them; how to help you avoid some of the pitfalls of bringing in a consultant; how to ensure the desired impact on your organization as the assignment proceeds; how to facilitate effective and timely implementation of the results of their work for you; and finally, how to get them off of your payrolls when you are finished with them.

A second reason for this book stems from the fact that the consulting business today is a growth business, with the quality problems such growth can invite. In the 1960s the then Big Eight accounting firms (now Big Six) began to discover the prolific opportunities in offering consulting services for their accounting clients, particularly integrated information systems planning. They have diversified aggressively into additional new service businesses for new clients and have reached a dominant position in the industry. Moreover, consultant rosters are swelling with each MBA graduating class and with each merger or acquisition that renders executives and professionals superfluous. From many years of activity and observation it is clear to me that new recruits could use practical advice on how to consult. I hope that both consultants and their clients might benefit from a realistic case-filled handbook on some of the hard lessons gleaned from over 130 client engagements and new-venture evaluations, with such lessons clarified from the client's viewpoint.

Lastly, this project enables me to try to clarify for my family just what I've been doing all these years. My in-laws have always struggled with this question, and particularly with the mystery of why I get paid for it. The questions from wives and children never end: "Tell me again what it is you do, Dad." "Oh, I see. You're an efficiency expert." "Do you mostly get companies to fire people? Or move them all over the country?" "How did it go? Is the project finished? Then, when will it be?" "What do you mean, we have to change our vacation plans (for a third time)?" Or, "Why are you bringing along the briefcase?"

No Miracles for Hire is an effort to clarify the consulting art and to develop useful generalizations with hindsight from consulting experiences. I must acknowledge up front my marketing viewpoint and bias toward focusing the client's efforts on his competitive marketplace. Also, while I draw on a number of cases from other consulting individuals and firms, most of my observations, analyses, critiques, and self-criticisms flow from my own first-hand work in a diverse array of assignments for equally diverse clients in both the for-profit and not-for-profit sectors.

Many of today's management treatises are primarily, if not entirely, compilations of dramatic success stories and cases. Unlike these, this book analyzes a mixture of assignments, discusses why some worked well and others faltered or failed, and, hopefully, draws useful generalizations and principles from them. It intends to use hindsight as a learning experience to contribute a little toward improving the state of the art of management consulting, particularly the effectiveness of clients in selecting and managing them. The post mortems on the cases are my own opinions.

Hundreds of people have contributed to my experience over the years, and it is impractical to acknowledge them all. Among my clients who have provided challenging opportunities and contributed most to my seasoning and to the legitimizing process I have gone through as a consultant under fire, the one who has been most patient and deserves most credit is Rowland Brown of Dorr-Oliver, Buckeye International and OCLC (Online Computer Library Center).

Other clients and friends to whom I am particularly grateful are Jake Carder of Transact International; Eric Ferguson, a most imaginative and venturesome entrepreneur; the late General Robinson of Carborundum; J. L. Eastwick of James Lees Carpets; Tom Lawson of IBM, EMI, and Ultronic; Herb Sand and Mort Schneider of Ideal Toy Corporation; and Guy Gabrielson, Jr., and Dr. Piero Modigliani of Nicolet Industries. Dr. Mo gave me one of my biggest lessons many years ago by falling asleep during my final presentation to his management. A very special acknowledgment is also due my many friends at OCLC, Inc., including Mary Ellen Jacob, John Shary, Larry Learn, Ken Harris, Tom Little, David Lighthill, Don Trotier, Tom Sanville, and others too numerous to acknowledge individually over a most stimulating eight-year strategic planning experience.

Outstanding shapers and influencers among my consultant associates include John Sargent, Bob Baumann, Charlie Wilson, Ralph Van Hoorn, and the late Bill Bokum and Willard McCormick from my CMP days; and many fellow IBMers, including Dick Bullen, Bill Simmons, Dick Warren, Warren Hume, Spike Beitzel, and Ralph Pfeiffer. I owe a special thanks to Warren Barker, both from our CMP duty and as a long-term freelance associate and periodic counsellor.

Finally, I am particularly grateful to Bill Souders and Tom Lawson for their patience and suggestions in reading and critiquing the manuscript at several stages.

J.T.C.

Introduction

Aims and Approach

To consult is to seek the opinion or advice of another; to take counsel together; to deliberate in common; to seek the opinion of as a guide to one's own judgment; to have recourse to for information or instruction.

Paraphrased from the *New Webster's Encyclopaedic Dictionary of the English Language*

Most definitions of consulting view the phenomenon first in terms of the seeker of advice, and second from the viewpoint of the advice giver. Consistent with these priorities, *No Miracles for Hire* offers the same emphasis, a guide to you, the client or would-be client, for selecting and using consultants productively and profitably.

The practice of consulting has undergone significant changes during the past thirty years, and it will continue to change as the needs of its clienteles change. However, certain fundamentals and dynamics will remain the same, and it is essential for the user of consulting services to recognize two that override all others.

The Two Overarching Characteristics of Consulting

First and foremost, the consulting function serves as an agent for change. It is an interactive exchange of information and ideas between insiders and outsiders, usually undertaken by a client to seek viewpoints and actions that differ from today's situation. It occurs between one party, the client, who seeks external wisdom, perspective, focus, and time saving, and the other party, the consultant, who clamors to give it.

Second, consultants inherently lack accountability as they perform their work for the client. They are unfettered by strict accountability for the results, good or bad, or by absolute responsibility to follow through.

The Consultant as an Agent for Change

In his traditional role, the consultant is never more than a facilitator or agent for change. In almost every instance, the client is seeking improved performance. He wants advice or assistance in making changes, correcting problems and their causes, refining basic managerial processes, and exploring new strategies or other opportunities for his business. Rarely does the client bring in an outside adviser merely to confirm that what he is doing should not be changed, although this role certainly is legitimate.

The consultant performs as an agent of change in a wide variety of ways and with different degrees of involvement in the client's business. Highly significant benefits can accrue to the client who selects and manages a consultant effectively. Such benefits can both help his managing process and improve results for his enterprise.

Lack of Accountability

If the client endows his consultant with accountability, then the latter becomes something different from the meaning of consultant as I use it. The significance is that the client can never duck the final accountability for the results of the assignment, and the consultant should not be relied upon to assume it, although the best ones often do with considerable conscientiousness and responsibility.

The emphasis on those being advised is fitting because it is the client who is accountable for seeking, then heeding or rejecting, the advice rendered, and living with the consequences.

Consultants can pack up their papers and leave at the end of the assignment, whatever good, bad, or indifferent things they may have done. However, most career consultants take a responsible approach to the trust placed in them, and by nature, take great pride in performing a helpful service. Most are unlikely to leave a client in the lurch; they would like job satisfaction, repeat assignments, and favorable endorsements to give other prospective clients.

Central Aims

This book has two principal aims:

1. To acquaint you with potential challenges to your successful selection and management of a consultant and to raise the questions and issues about that process that should receive your early consideration.
2. To provide you with a wide array of practical techniques, concepts, guidelines, and building blocks and to present these within the context of a tested framework for ensuring a satisfactory assignment.

This book is addressed to you, the client or would-be client, as you contemplate engaging your first consultant or awarding your next consulting assignment. My main intention is to give you useful insights from behind the mysterious curtain of the management consultants so that you can obtain greater practical value from your own endeavors with them. I offer insights to help you determine the up-front questions of *whether* and *when* to engage them, and demonstrate the pitfalls that can await the all-too-trusting or inexperienced client.

I also advise you on ways to make certain that a consultants' perspective and focus are what you really need. I clarify their *modus operandi* so that you may better control the pace of the assignment and be assured that their operating approaches and their staffing are compatible with your own people who must interact with them. I will suggest critical questions about the gaps that can develop between consultants' promises and their performances. And I will deal with perhaps the most critical question of all: How to be certain you will receive realistic and yet effort-stretching recommendations and action steps that are workable.

This book raises many questions and warnings, some of which you may assume are in poor taste and affronts to a reputable consultant. It suggests considerations that a client might take for granted or expect to be standard procedure. In brief, this book reflects on the experiences and observations of a management consultant who is saying, "Mr. Client, knowing what I do about the insides of my business and the businesses of some of my compatriots, you would be well-advised not to take us so much for granted or to view us with such awe!"

What then is to be learned that can significantly benefit you, the client, in your productive and timely use of the mysterious consultants? A useful starting point is to consider an array of potential challenges to superior consulting results that can confront you as client.

A Hierarchy of Potential Challenges

An underlying thread throughout this book is the identification and dissection of a hierarchy of key challenges that may be encountered by a client inexperienced in the selection and use of consultants. Such issues could be classified and presented in myriad ways. In the following chapters I review many problems within an overall structure of seven primary classes of challenges, and present a variety of principles, approaches, and actual case discussions for meeting them.

The seven challenges are:

1. Establishing a clear and stimulating purpose for your project together with sound and realistic timing while avoiding the problems first, of a fuzzy, overly ambitious, or ill-directed purpose statement and second, of the consequences of starting late.
2. Obtaining the best firm and people for your project, and

ensuring that they will be an outstandingly compatible match with you and your own organization.

3. Defining and establishing an accurate project scope, one that avoids such problems as being ill fitting, overly ambitious, too narrow to achieve the necessary perspective, or not focused directly on the critical aspects of your situation.

4. Making certain your consultant uses workable survey approaches and avoids those that are impractical to carry out or are unlikely to produce the required findings and recommendations.

5. Maintaining a sharp and relevant perspective and focus during the course of fact finding and development of conclusions and recommendations; keeping the findings consistent with the requirements of your external environment and your own resources, needs, and opportunities.

6. Keeping rigorous control of the project's schedule and quality throughout its life in terms of timing, cost, the impacts on your internal staff and outside constituencies; and perhaps most importantly, controlling the quality, relevance, and results orientation of the recommendations.

7. Achieving superior action and implementation plans, which are convincing to you and contain highly satisfactory preparatory steps, action programs, responsibility assignments, and guidelines for implementation and follow-through on the recommendations.

Your ability to achieve *superior consulting results* will be blocked if these seven classes of challenges, shown schematically in Figure 1, are not met effectively. To a considerable extent, your exposure occurs sequentially in the listed order as a consulting assignment progresses from recognition of a need, through screening and selection of a consultant, and on into and through the conduct, wrap-up, and implementation of the project. The seven sets of challenges and alternative approaches for meeting them are dissected within the context and sequence of the related parts of this book.

Figure 1. Challenges and objectives for superior consulting results.

Superior Consulting Results

Challenge Seven
Achieve superior
recommendations
and action plans.

Challenge Six
control project
quality and schedule
rigorously.

Challenge Five
Maintain sharp and
relevant focus
and perspective.

Challenge Four
Employ workable
project approaches.

Challenge Three
Define project
scope accurately.

Challenge Two
Seek and hire the
very best firm
and people for
the project.

Challenge One
Set clear and
challenging
purposes with
sound timing.

Client's Present Situation

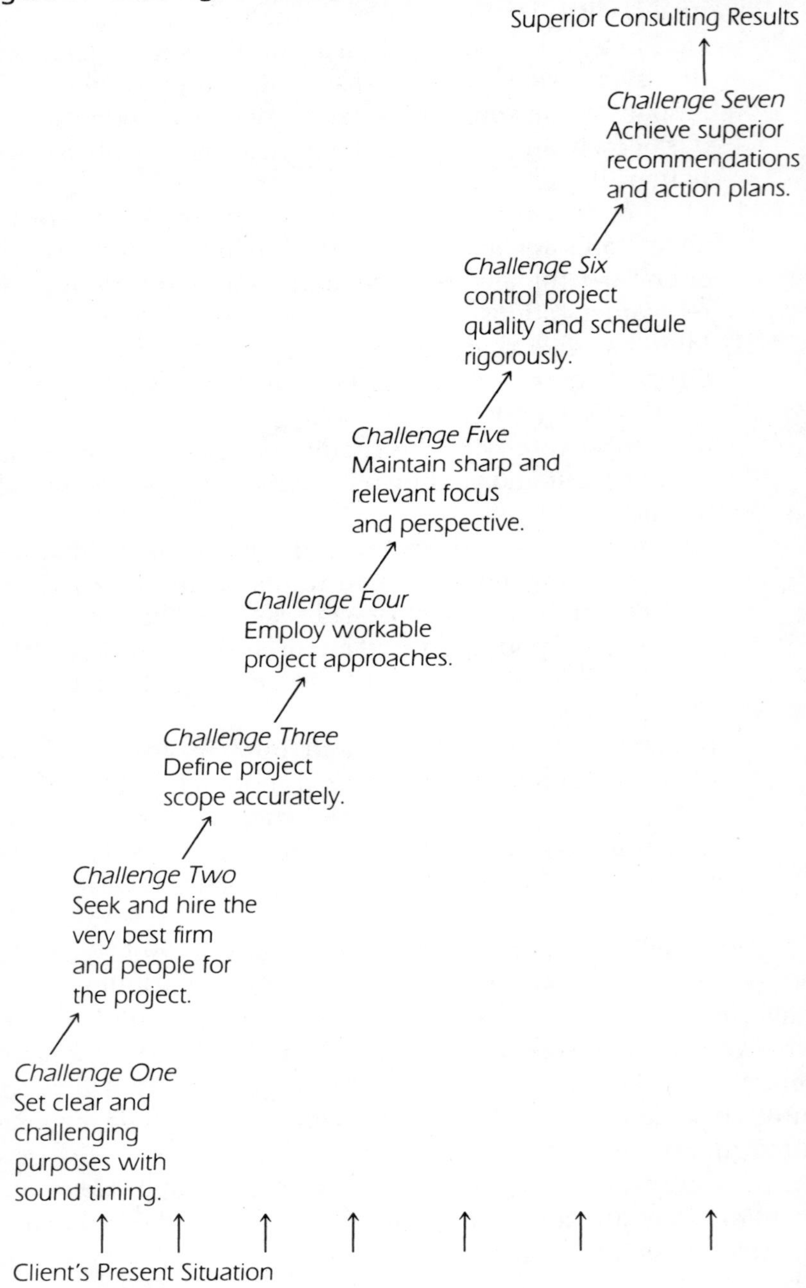

Approach: Dynamic Evolution and Flow of a Consulting Assignment

The seven parts and their twenty chapters are organized in a sequence that closely patterns the dynamics either a new or an experienced client might follow advantageously in considering and using consultants. The six major building blocks referred to throughout the book are depicted schematically in Figure 2.

Part One, Consulting Resources Available to You, lays a foundation for understanding what types of consultants you might consider using; what roles consultants can play for you; their potential benefits; and basic trends and issues you, the client, should weigh concerning the various types and sizes of consulting organizations available.

Part Two, Determining Your Need for Outside Help, defines the critical and formative starting point for a project. It addresses the first order of business, how you can determine whether you truly need to bring in a consultant. It presents suggestions for developing a situation analysis to define and clarify your basic needs and the objectives to be established for your project. It introduces timing considerations, including the very important question of whether you may already be too late in seeking outside help.

Further, Part Two, as well as all other parts, introduces several actual consulting-project experiences to illustrate some of the most pervasive dangers and lessons. Some are success stories; others were failures or encountered serious problems and cost overruns for a variety of reasons. All of the situations are presented from your viewpoint as a client, although several also give you hopefully useful insights into what goes on behind the consultant's hallowed walls, suggesting discreet inquiries and discerning questions you might raise with your consultant in order to short-cut serious slippages and other problems early in an assignment. Different aspects of some of the case situations are discussed in several chapters to provide continuity to the consideration of an overall consulting project.

Part Three, Choosing the Right Consultant, delves into the all-important *people* dimension, the issues concerned with careful selection of the right consultant to work closely with you and your staff. It helps you understand the many and complex reasons why people want to consult, so that you can provide maximum motivation for their performance in your behalf. It outlines the screening and selection process and presents guidelines for your choice.

A key aid to the selection decision is structuring the assignment through the formal proposal. Part Four, Structuring a Realistic Assignment, presents the essential elements, which normally include Objectives, Scope of Study, Approach (which outlines the basic survey plan), Staffing and Qualifications, Time and Timing Requirements, and Costs. The chapters in Part Four contain proposal examples, checklists, and common problems to avoid, supported by case or project illustrations.

The chapters of Part Five, Assuring Sound Perspective and Focus, address the fundamental question of how to achieve a high quality result in the substance or content of the project work. This part deals with critical requirements that heavily influence these aspects. Its chapters define, dissect, and offer solutions for careless problem definition, over-conceptualizing, the temptation to emphasize exciting new technologies instead of or to the exclusion of focusing on markets and what they really need, and flying in the face of, or ignoring, inherent or so-called natural strategic obstacles or strengths relative to your company's purposes and objectives.

Part Six, Controlling the Project, concerns suggestions for assuring effective *consultant management,* including the logistics, process, and quality of the recommendations being developed. This part includes issues, problems, and recommendations on study conduct, schedule control, and output quality; on potential impact on your staff; on the desired pattern of progress reports and ongoing communication with the consultants. It suggests ways of monitoring adherence to the project's purpose, scope, and timing; of stimulating innovative thinking where needed and appropriate; and of achieving realism and practicality with the recommendations.

The reason for all of the foregoing is *results,* high-quality, effort-stretching, action-oriented recommendations, and realistic and timely action steps. These aspects are the subject of Part Seven, Achieving Sound Implementation Plans.

In summary, *No Miracles for Hire: How to Get Real Value*

Figure 2. Building blocks for superior consulting results.

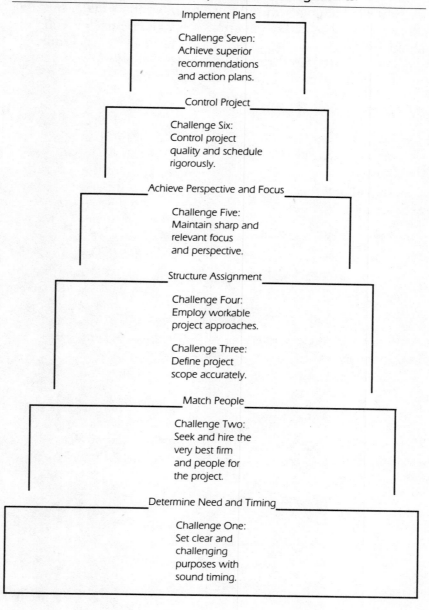

Implement Plans

Challenge Seven:
Achieve superior
recommendations
and action plans.

Control Project

Challenge Six:
Control project
quality and schedule
rigorously.

Achieve Perspective and Focus

Challenge Five:
Maintain sharp and
relevant focus
and perspective.

Structure Assignment

Challenge Four:
Employ workable
project approaches.

Challenge Three:
Define project
scope accurately.

Match People

Challenge Two:
Seek and hire the
very best firm
and people for
the project.

Determine Need and Timing

Challenge One:
Set clear and
challenging
purposes with
sound timing.

From Your Consultant is organized to cope logically with the hierarchy of challenges within the dynamics of six major building blocks that should be important considerations for you, the client or would-be client. The building blocks (see Figure 2), covered in Part Two through Part Seven, can help you achieve greater value from your consulting experience.

PART ONE

Consulting Resources Available to You

Question: Which of these professionals make a major contribution to the well-being of society and the economy?

Answer:

Manufacturing executives	47%
Clergy	44
Commercial bankers	32
Executives of service corporations	30
Accountants	18
Journalists	7
Investment bankers	6
MANAGEMENT CONSULTANTS	6
Executives of search firms	4
Stock analysts	4
Investment consultants	2

Survey of chief executive officers
undertaken for *Fortune*[1]

This survey of 206 major U.S. CEOs in late 1989 revealed a startling lack of regard for the value provided by a number of professional services to the economy. Industry leaders' less than enthusiastic perceptions of the contributions made by consultants are disappointing and puzzling in the face of an impressive continuing growth rate for consulting services over the last several decades. Some portion of the inconsistency between consultancy's growth and its perceived benefits to the economy (and individual companies) is real; part is the result of long-standing preconceptions and misconceptions, and part undoubtedly stems from inflated expectations that were not realized.

Every day truly outstanding consulting work is performed for satisfied clients, just as every day mediocre or unsatisfactory performances are registered. Unfortunately, the latter condition is believed to be in the majority, hence the limited regard many executives expressed for the general proposition of using consulting services.

Nevertheless, many consultants are qualified to deliver superior results, and in fact perform repetitively to the great satisfaction of their clients. Correspondingly, the growing complexities and heightened competition in industry make it increasingly advantageous for executives to seek outside assistance periodically to solve critical problems and take more timely advantage of new business opportunities.

One of the major contributors to inexperienced clients' misperceptions about the worth of consultants is an overly optimistic expectation that they are *miracle workers*. A principal objective of this book is to dispel that myth and to arm the client or would-be client with insights and techniques for finding the best consultant for his needs and managing his project effectively. The explosion of some common larger-than-life myths about consultants provides a beginning focus on more realistic perceptions and expectations.

Misleading Assumptions About Consultants

▲ *Consultants are outstanding managers of their own practices.* You should not assume that your senior consultant can always be counted on to manage his own team tightly and effectively. Competent career consultants are likely to be intelligent, resourceful self-starters, but also headstrong, difficult-to-manage individualists. Their confidence and self-esteem often make them quite opinionated about how best to approach your problems, and many are hesitant to take direction even from those who supervise them. The dangers in such instances can include missed project deadlines, misdirected efforts, excessive billings, negative impacts on your people, and any number of additional problems and shortcomings discussed herein.

▲ *Consultants can develop solutions for any problem.* A fairly prevalent misconception of first-time clients is that consultants can always find appropriate, generalized solutions for virtually any unique set of problems. You should not assume that your consultants' generalized skills and experiences can be applied readily to your specific situation. Although several decades ago management consultants were highly successful at imparting useful general management principles to their clients, today's managers and their competitors are better trained and more sophisticated and have access to far more information, all of which serves to require more specialized and better focused assistance from the consultant.

▲ *Consultants can readily convert concepts to actions.* Consultants shine at developing bold, innovative, and exciting concepts for your real-life problems and new opportunities. However, it is unsafe and frequently dangerous to assume that they can be counted on to convert such conceptions into workable actions. Individuals with a big-picture mentality often have difficulty translating their concepts from the wish list or dreaming stage to practical action steps.

Consultants' concepts may be visionary, far-reaching, and imaginative philosophical targets for the future, which can serve as useful stimuli and strategic directional signals for your organization. However, to be useful, such concepts should relate directly to specific strengths you now possess and to specific action programs your organization is capable of launching now or in the near future. Otherwise, you run the risk of your consultant leading you into impractical or impossible endeavors.

▲ *Smooth meshing of consultant and client staffs is a nonissue.* On the contrary, this aspect of the consulting project requires great thought and caution. The presence of outsiders can be highly threatening, and the issue deserves rigorous analysis before you commit yourself to a specific consulting organization. Negative internal client/consultant relationships can also spread to your company's outside constituencies: customers and prospects, suppliers, middlemen, bankers, and shareholders.

▲ *Your senior consultant represents the caliber of the entire team.* It is unsafe to assume without question that you will be getting the full impact of the brilliant, strong senior partner who impressed you so much during the selling, proposal discussion, and screening processes. Nor can you assume that the staff who will carry the brunt of the assignment has his savvy, intellect, resourcefulness, bearing, presence, depth of experience, and communication skills.

Reasonable and realistic expectations along the foregoing lines should enable you to establish and undertake consulting projects which have a high probability of yielding outstanding if not superior benefits to your situation.

Benefits of Using Consultants

Consultants can bring timely new insights and an outside perspective to bear on your problems and opportunities. They can give undivided and uninterrupted attention to a project, whereas you may be in a position to focus on it only intermittently as you cope with your dynamic, day-to-day responsibilities. They can serve as sounding boards or devil's advocates for new strategies and policies you may be contemplating. They can quickly bring new experience and expertise to bear on your situation, substantially cutting the time you might otherwise need to recruit new blood or train permanent staff. They can tackle unpleasant personnel and organizational problems for you and provide a host of additional services.

Achieving such benefits and advantages, however, rarely happens without careful advance planning and preparation. When engaging outside management consultants, the potential for unforeseen and unwanted problems is always present. Business history is filled with both the frustrations of clients who have experienced unsatisfactory consulting performances, and the satisfaction of a smaller number who have achieved superior results from outside advice and counsel. A number of representative experiences, both positive and negative, are probed herein.

Part One sets forth basic background information on the many types of consulting services and resources available to management and the benefits to be derived from them. Chapter 1 outlines the proliferation in classes of available services and highlights key issues relating to the types of outside assistance to seek. Chapter 2 discusses a variety of roles consultants can play for a client, and Chapter 3, potential benefits, which could contribute toward performance improvement.

Note

1. From a survey of 206 CEOs of *Fortune* 500 and Fortune Service 500 companies. See Terence P. Paré "Who Business Bosses Hate Most," *Fortune* magazine (December 4, 1989), page 107. A rating of eight or higher on a ten-point scale was a positive vote for the service.

1

Proliferating Consulting Choices and Issues

The Ballad of the Business Consultant

Of all the businesses, by far
Consultancy's the most bizarre!
For, to the penetrating eye,
There's no apparent reason why,
With no more assets than a pen
This group of personable men
Can sell to clients more than twice
The same ridiculous advice;
Or find, in such rich profusion,
Problems to fit their own solution.

Attributed to Mr. Bertie Ramsbottom,
from *The Economist*, October 18, 1987

Quite possibly, Bertie Ramsbottom engaged a consultant with good intentions and great expectations. If so, he obviously made an unsatisfactory selection and failed to manage the project effectively. The result is understandable in view of the rapidly multiplying types and numbers of consultants, and the great difficulty of predicting safely what differing experiences and expertise lie behind any given general label of consultant.

Bertie's glib poetry too often has the ring of truth and raises the issue of *quality* that should be of prime concern to all users and prospective users of outside consulting advice. This first chapter lays the foundation for your successful selection and use of consultants with a brief review of basic trends and consultant choices, along with several key implications for you, the client, as you begin your serious deliberations.

Consulting: A Growth Business and a Buyer's Market

The numbers and types of consultants available to you are growing at a healthy pace. This creates innumerable opportunities for you to locate and negotiate with just the right consultant for your need. More and more, consulting services are becoming a buyer's market. Heightened competition for your account enables you to gain fresh, varied, and contrasting insights as to just what type of assistance you really need. In fact, exposure of your situation to multiple candidates can help you determine whether you even need to bring in an outsider, or instead should undertake the project with your own people.

The Continuing Postwar Surge in Consulting Services

At least 100,000 consultants are estimated to be operating worldwide, of whom as many as 60,000 are consulting in the United States. Thousands of professors from the college and university campuses are consulting full- or part-time as individuals, offering an untold number of specializations. Several thousand more individuals have found themselves unemployed as a result of mergers, acquisitions, and dissolutions and are trying consulting as a new career or a stopgap until they find other employment.

In the 1950s the premier quality management consulting services were regarded by many to be McKinsey & Company; Booz, Allen & Hamilton; and Cresap (formerly Cresap, McCormick and Paget), in that order.[1] By the mid 1960s, over twenty U.S. firms were generating annual individual billings of $1 million or more. The industry was growing by 15 to 20 percent per year through the 1950s and 1960s, but growth began to level off in the 1970s. It proceeded to suffer from recessionary impact late in that decade. Consulting ultimately revived and began a growth surge, which has continued through the 1980s. *Consultants News (CN)* estimated the 1988 billings of management consulting at $13.5 billion for firms based in the United States, including $6 billion domestically.[2]

The Economist has estimated that three-fourths of the world's management consulting business is garnered by the fifty largest firms and that growth overall has been averaging 20 to 25 percent annually, with strategy consulting realizing 15 percent, and information technology as much as 50 percent growth per year.[3]

A consulting firm on a fast track for growth should be carefully scrutinized. The late John Main, then president of Management Practice Inc., contended that "focusing on maximizing growth is probably inimical to management consulting. It can only be pursued at the cost of internal chaos and a lowering of the quality of output. Quality control is a far more critical issue."[4]

It also should be of more than passing interest to the would-be client that one of consulting's senior spokesmen and "consciences," James Kennedy, editor and publisher of the previously referenced monthly *Consultants News,* has been admonishing for some time "Consultant, Heal Thyself." Kennedy's publications not only keep a finger tightly on the pulse of current events in consultancy, but also offer provocative insights on the problems this growing and rapidly changing industry is facing.[5]

Growth Factors Multiplying Your Consulting Options

At least four key factors are increasing the ranks of alternative outside advisers available to you. One of the most significant generators of new options since the 1960s has been the establishment of consulting divisions by the then Big Eight accounting firms (mergers have reduced the number to six), stimulated in recent years by their growing business in integrated information systems planning.

Second, corporate mergers and acquisitions continue to render competent and experienced senior executives unnecessary; such individuals often enter consulting either as a stopgap or to take advantage of their specialized expertise in an industry or major business function.

Third, the curricula of the prestigious business schools, coupled with high starting salaries, have stimulated MBA graduates to pursue consulting assignments fresh from graduation.

Fourth, individuals and small groups have been prompted to enter consulting by the lure of escaping the regimented corporate life and gaining the "independence" of being one's own boss.

One of your key issues as a client is how to exercise quality control and maintain or achieve high-quality performance with a firm that is rapidly growing and dispersing geographically. The economies of scale are difficult to realize in a complex consulting business whose major assets are talented, self-starting professionals. Management consulting is a highly individualized business, and the specific person or team working directly with you and your people should still be your major consideration, regardless of your consultant's size and growth rate.

Expansion of "Big Six" Accountants Into Consulting

In the late 1960s, the so-called Big Eight, who through mergers became the Big Six in 1989, began to develop significant consulting practices by trading on their established auditing relationships and their "running-start" knowledge of the client's business. They began to offer consulting services in information systems planning, general management, and strategic planning subjects. In 1979, following government investigations of possible conflicts of interest, an independent oversight board of businesspersons concluded that there were no conflicts between consulting and auditing.

A fundamental problem developed for some of the Big CPAs, however, in 1987 and 1988. Internal disputes and power struggles began surfacing between the accountants and consultants because of the consultants' dissatisfaction over their earnings. This led to some consultants' defections, to covert plans to pull key consulting staffs out and set up independent shops, and to some firings of the senior consulting partners. Seasoned industry watchers expected such difficulties and trends to abate gradually.

Continuing Mergers and Acquisitions

In the late 1980s, the English advertising giant Saatchi & Saatchi began aggressive acquisition of consultants, particularly of U.S.-based firms, but in 1989 announced intentions to liquidate all such holdings. Other firms have continued to seek acquisitions, and consulting firms of all sizes will continue to be merged and acquired, but probably at a slower pace while the internal conflicts are being sorted out. The Big Six survivors can be expected to continue their expansion moves through consolidations, mergers, and internal development.

Basic Issues of Choice

Your task of sorting out the particular advice to seek can be clarified by considering the principal differences in types of consultant services available. Four such dimensions are especially significant: (1) the wide overall variety of classes of services; (2) the issue of using specialists versus generalists; (3) domestic firms versus those with an international or global scope; and (4) special considerations with strategic planning services.

Wide Array of Choices by Class of Operation

If you are a seasoned user of consulting services, you undoubtedly have acquired dossiers on companies or individuals you would like to use again. You also may have a list of those you would never reconsider for future assignments, based on past disappointments.

On the other hand, as a new prospective client, you may well be in a quandary as to your choices and even confused as to how to begin the hunt. Your problem is compounded by an almost unbelievable proliferation of options for many consultant types and quality levels. One classification by type of operation reveals at least ten distinct approaches:

1. National general management firms
2. National CPA firms with consulting units

3. Functionally specialized firms
4. Industry specialized firms
5. Public sector firms
6. Think tanks
7. Regional and local firms
8. Sole practitioners
9. Turnaround consultants
10. Conglomerates with consulting units

The Appendix, Information Sources, defines and describes these classes of services. It references several of the more important consulting associations and directory publications that constitute excellent sources of information to help you clarify and locate candidate firms.

Historically, the title of "consultant" most commonly referred to "management consultant" and the services mainly were managerial practices: objective setting, planning, operations, control, leadership, organization, management development, and so forth. Today the title is applied to an unbelievably wide range of practitioners throughout the for-profit and not-for-profit sectors, and it is possible to find a specialist in every industry and organizational endeavor, in every function of an organization, and for all types of product and market categories. Making a sharp distinction of a consultant's capabilities beyond a label or a superficial clarification is important to every would-be client, if he is to achieve a sound match-up.

Key questions that should be raised to delve beneath the general label are "Consultant of or in what" "How long have you been doing it?" and "With what results?"

Further, how does the individual candidate describe his expertise and experience? What types and caliber of results has he or she produced in these areas? Has he or she had enough different experiences to offer a broad and seasoned range of suggestions? Is his or her particular package of talents convincingly relevant to the client's needs?

Your best solution to the confusing use of consultant titles lies in intensive, face-to-face confrontations and discussions prior to making a commitment. You should then reinforce such effort with suitable references from satisfied clients. This entire subject of matching consultant and client is explored fully in Part Three.

Shifts From Generalist to Specialist Consulting

Traditionally, much of the earlier management consulting work had been focused on organization studies, the client's planning process, management practices, marketing audits, personnel policies and practices, control, and other classic managerial functions. Consulting firms applied their expertise in these functional areas across diverse industries, for example, moving readily from fabricated steel products, chemicals, and heavy machinery to toys and games, drugs and pharmaceuticals, textiles and apparel.

As generalists, the major firms customarily did not accept assignments with competing clients in the same industry. They were quick to argue that useful generalizations of management practices could be applied with full effectiveness across diverse industries. In their view: Executive direction was executive direction was executive direction.

The strong counterargument is that significant *content* differences among industries deserve specialized consulting expertise, although working for directly competing companies can be a touchy issue. The client should seek consultants qualified to give careful consideration to the unique conditions of a type of business and its competitive environment and to the content of its strategic requirements in each case, not just generalized advice on management processes. Major projects may well need a blend or balance of consulting attention to managerial processes and unique strategic content.

Post-World War II consulting in specialized areas received its initial impetus from the college and university campuses. Professors in large numbers found they could take advantage of their specialized and deeper subject expertise and supplement their incomes significantly through part-time assignments in industry. Many operated alone, but some became affiliated with off-campus consulting firms on a somewhat regular basis. Others left in groups to offer specialized new services.

This issue of generalist versus specialist consultant is a perennial debate in the industry. The arguments do not clearly favor either extreme, but rather a mix of the two. It is a case-by-case decision for the client. The larger the project and the staff it justifies, the more likely an ideal balance can be achieved on the consulting staff between specialist depth in the client's business and generalized expertise to bring outside perspectives to bear.

When a generalist argues in such cases that he has an outstanding contrary record, it is revealing to query whether he brought specialist skills and focus to the assignments and whether they were indeed a major contributor to success. In many situations where management already has demonstrated a reasonable degree of managerial acumen, it is a decided advantage for the consultant to bring with him some measure of historical involvement with the client's industry and marketplace. When such specialization is teamed with broad, generalized management expertise, powerful benefits can be realized.

On the other hand, smaller companies with few management positions, as well as others that may not have made use of manager development programs, often can benefit from generalized guidance in management processes, particularly in entrepreneurial ventures, high-tech start-ups, and new, low-technology situations.

Consultants who specialize successfully by industries or market segments, sell their services on the basis of the in-depth understanding and historical perspective that come with having been involved in an industry for years. On the other hand, others have considered it unethical to serve multiple clients in the same industry. Some major consulting firms have been highly successful following such a policy strictly, usually limiting this restriction to a five-year period following the assignment. Bain & Co., for example, and many others before them, have made much of this noncompetitive policy.

The recent trend seems clearly to be moving in the direction of specialization by type of business and/or by function. However, there are sound management principles that should continue forever to apply across totally foreign situations, and competent generalist consultants will continue to be available for clients who can use that approach to an advantage. You should select your consultant in terms of the mix of generalist/specialist expertise most appropriate for your unique situation.

Domestic-Only Versus Global Consultants

John Main, in the previously noted reference, cautioned that two divergent courses are underway which "no user of consulting services can afford to overlook."[6] The majors are aggressively pursuing one path, which Main called "high-tech globalization," while he made a strong argument for the other route, "high quality, personalized services." Main conceded that globalization and the drive for growth shouldn't matter so much if the consultant can maintain high quality service *on your assignment*. He contended, however, that this becomes harder and harder to do as a consultant stretches his business scope geographically and functionally while pursuing major growth.

The major consulting firms have had multinational offices for many years, but the impending unification of the European Community plus the added dimension of the Eastern European countries and a recent surge of acquisitions and expansions has accelerated this trend. Proponents of global expansion cite several factors as advantages. They include economies of scale, the ability to match a major multinational client's dispersed organization, and the increased leveraging of senior consulting partners' and specialists' talents across a vast pool of professional talent that they hope can be made available flexibly worldwide.

John Main contended that there appear to be few advantages of globalization, however, except in rare instances. One exception could be corporate-wide information systems planning for a global company. In many respects, however, a client's foreign operations often are anything but global in perspective, rather tending to operate autonomously and parochially, country by country. This argument is supported by IBM's outstanding success with its international business.

As early as the 1920s, Thomas J. Watson, Sr., put together his highly successful IBM World Trade Corporation, based on country-level companies. He opted for locally managed and locally staffed national organizations throughout the world, rather

than establishing limited agency arrangements or worldwide
functional management. His approach proved eminently successful.

In view of the highly personalized nature of consulting and
the importance of the particular staff assigned directly to the account, the burden should be on those consultants who argue the
global consulting approach to prove its merits to the global
would-be client. The global argument is undeniable if the consultant has the right type of superior staff "everywhere" needed.

Trends and Issues With Strategic Planning

Among the most significant specializations that emerged in the
1960s was strategic planning for the corporation as a whole, beginning with a variety of "formula" approaches. A number of
large and small firms ultimately embraced this concept, but one
of the earliest successes was The Boston Consulting Group
(BCG), which had been formed in the early 1960s.

Bruce Henderson founded BCG, and one of his initial strategic approaches was his development and advocacy of *the experience curve*. This led the industry into more sophisticated
"formula" strategic planning approaches, including the numerous variations of *portfolio planning*. These included: the *growth/
share matrix*, pioneered at General Electric; the McKinsey/GE
nine-box matrix; the concept of *strategic mandates;* and *PIMS*
(Profit Impact of Market Strategy), developed by the Strategic
Planning Institute.[7]

Many graduates of BCG launched their own variations of
the pioneering portfolio planning services and amplified them
with more sophisticated and comprehensive services to meet the
criticism of superficiality leveled at the earlier portfolio analysis
approaches. The best of these have been built on a concept of
differentiating a company's discrete profit centers or results centers into strategic business units (SBUs) or line-of-business
units (LOBs). This approach has been particularly popular
among the larger conglomerates and other multibusiness corporations, who frequently reorganize their corporations along
the lines of the SBUs, in order to decentralize accountability and
focus management attention on discrete subbusinesses.

Recently it has become the vogue for the business press to attack strategic planning as an outmoded fad or a failure, but this important class of consulting service will survive. The practices being challenged are not the fundamental need, but rather, some of the particular formula approaches referred to above.

Every active organization generates a degree of strategic direction either deliberately or without plan. This happens by design or by default, and the strategies are either explicitly developed, documented, and pursued, or they remain implicit. Strategic directions for a business always exist, whether based on total opportunism, informal reliance on past experience with "what works," response to the current competitive situation and perceived market needs, or the drive of an intuitive entrepreneur.

The more opportunistic and unfocused such directions are, the greater is the likelihood they could be deficient in some respects. One must acknowledge and applaud the intuitive success stories, but there is always a risk of serious problems when the company does not fully realize or focus on the strategic implications of its major decisions and actions. Laying aside the faddish approaches, strategic planning consulting can assist you with astute, realistic, and action-oriented recommendations for your strategic directions. It will continue to be an area of specialization where you can benefit significantly from the objective viewpoint an outside consultant can bring to your situation.

Implications for the Client

As a client or prospective client, you should keep several implications of the foregoing trends and characteristics in mind.

Growing Need for Outside Advice

Business growth of the newer high-tech companies will continue to outpace the ability of their entrepreneur founders to cope with increasing strategic and managerial complexities. Growing and mature companies in many industries will face increasingly intensive competition in the free marketplace from both domestic and foreign organizations. In many instances, the impending "unifications" within the European Community and the addition of Eastern Bloc countries to EC will contribute to such a need.

Increasing Relative Demand for Specialized Consulting

The growth factors will create more demand for expert outside advice and counsel on specialized product/market strategies and niche marketing. Mergers, acquisitions, takeovers, leveraged buyouts and the indigestion from junk bonds, and the October 19, 1987-type debacles will increase the difficulties and challenges for the surviving CEOs and their boards.

More Confusing Choices for the Would-Be Client

Consulting, by its nature, has always been one of the more intangible services a company is likely to consider. The choice is complicated by the increasing number and types of new consultants, with their resultant proliferating options for prospective users. Perhaps more than any other business product or service a client purchases, the specifics to be delivered will continue to be well hidden from view at the time of the "purchasing" decision.

Consulting Is and Will Be a Buyer's Market

The growth of consulting makes this inevitable in terms of both the number available and the types and levels of expertise and quality needed. You will have greater opportunities than ever to obtain superior consulting services, but your selection task also will be more difficult.

Elusiveness of Quality Results Is an Overriding Issue

Achieving consulting results of superior quality should be your number one concern. But this is far easier said than done and involves the total process of selecting and managing your consultant. Like avoiding weak links in a chain, the level of quality is influenced successively by every one of the six building blocks

around which Part Two through Part Seven of this book is structured. Your continuing involvement is required through each
stage.

Naturally the almost geometric increase in options height-
ens your odds against obtaining high-quality and dependable
advice. *The Economist* magazine contended that "the Anglo-
Saxons have turned in the West's worst management performance in the past 30 years. Cynics say this is because too many
brains are advising and not enough doing."[8]

Convincing proof of this hypothesis would be difficult to
marshal. Consulting, in its many, many forms, is not a precise
science with comfortable standards against which it can be mea-
sured. It has no well-established body of historical quantitative
or qualitative information on which to draw for such an analysis.

Consulting has no universal accreditation procedure, although several industry associations have been working toward
that objective for some years. In the eyes of some, it is not yet a
profession, and thus lacks the performance criteria and accreditation requirements of the true professions. Profession or not, it
is still an art, and appears destined to remain so. In the absence
of established criteria related to experience levels, expertise, and
quality, the first-time client may have difficulty determining
those consultants likely to be most appropriate to address his
problems.

Consultants and the industry have been the subject of criticism from the very early days of the first management science
practitioners, which included Henri Fayol, Frederick W. Taylor,
Frank and Lillian Gilbreth, and Charles Bedaux, among the dis-
tinguished pioneers. The stigma of efficiency expert was one of
the first critical labels to be applied, and that connotation pre-
vails in the minds of many disbelievers. Such public generalizations and perceptions should have a very small influence on your
choice, if you have identified that one very best firm or individual
who gives you a high comfort level for your particular assignment and situation.

One of the essential considerations that must become comfortable for you is your conviction that the consultant understands your needs, has the credentials to meet them, and, most
important, has a solid and communicative *people match* with

you. Careful searching and screening should enable you to find several candidates to fit this requirement.

In brief, the likelihood of obtaining a high level of quality starts with your framing a clear and well-timed project objective and continues with a well-structured and realistic proposal for the assignment from a consultant who will mix and match well with your people. Then conducting the project must lead to achieving effort-stretching recommendations that have a sound perspective and focus and are in tune with your company's external marketplace, competitive environment, and internal situation. The final determining ingredient is a workable results-oriented action plan.

Notes

1. See "Management Consultancy—the New Witch Doctors," a special section of the February 13, 1988 issue of *The Economist*, for a definitive discussion of the history of consulting, its leaders in the United States and abroad, and a survey of the issues surrounding the industry in the 1980s.
2. *Consultants News* (May 1989), a monthly publication of Kennedy Publications, Fitzwilliams, N.H.
3. "Management Consultancy—the New Witch Doctors."
4. John Main, "Management Consulting: The Fork in the Road," *Management Practices Quarterly* (Winter/Spring, 1988), page 1.
5. Kennedy & Kennedy, Inc., Fitzwilliam, N.H. 03447.
6. Main, "Management Consulting: The Fork in the Road," page 1.
7. Two excellent treatments of these strategic planning approaches are Richard G. Hamermesh, *Making Strategy Work* (New York: John Wiley & Sons, 1986); and John J. Pendray and Ernest E. Keet, *Strategic Development For High Technology Businesses* (Wilton, Conn.: Value Publishing, Inc., 1987).
8. "Management Consultancy—the New Witch Doctors."

2

What Consultants Do for You

Traditional CEO—"I hear Jim has brought in a consultant. If he has to do that, he must be hurting."

Contemporary CEO—"On the contrary. Many progressive and successful firms are using consultants these days. I happen to know Jim's pulling some exciting new programs together, and he's enlisted a top-notch firm to help him."

Not too long ago the need to bring in an outside adviser often signalled trouble—loss of market share or markets, severe competitive weaknesses, declining revenues and profits, problems with personnel or the managerial process, impending bankruptcy. This still happens, but using a consultant should not be assumed categorically to be an indication of weakness today. More often than not, the decision to employ a consultant is considered a sign of strength and a warning to competitors that the client is on the move. He may be squaring up to problems and meeting them head on. He may be undertaking to add significant new competitive value to his current products and services and the benefits his customers can derive from them. Or he may be on the track of exciting new opportunities for diversification.

Principal Consultant Roles

Whatever specific role is called for, the adviser usually begins with an indoctrination to the client's business. He starts with an orientation designed to prepare for critiquing what is or is not being done and applies an outsider's perspective to what he sees and hears. This then enables him to stimulate innovative thinking about corporate purpose or mission, objectives and goals, strategies and policies, business offerings, the operating process, managerial practices, and whatever else the client has asked him to focus on—all areas of the business are fair game. He facilitates review of these new ideas and their comparison with the established.

This agent for change develops alternatives, works with the client to determine what new directions, if any, are appropriate, and makes recommendations. He then may be asked to assist in implementing accepted changes in the client's business scope and processes and in the roles of its key participants. Lastly, he may be called upon to help audit the changes and their results.

Over the last few decades, this classic role for the management consultant has evolved into two major approaches: (1) consultant in the managerial processes and (2) content strategist.

Managerial-Process Consultant

A significant debate among management consultants and clients alike concerns the balance the effective consultant needs to strike between *process* and *content*. Here *consulting in the management process* refers to the functions of managing: *how* to run your business more successfully. *Content* refers to your specific objectives, strategies, policies, and programs, or *what* you should be doing: what products and services, in what markets and geography, with what distribution channels.

The how-to-manage role is acknowledged to have begun with Henri Fayol and Frederick W. Taylor, and perhaps even earlier. So-called efficiency experts were brought into a company to upgrade the productivity of an operation, such as bricklaying or a product assembly process. The idea of increasing efficiency and reducing the size of the work force spread to virtually all functions of the business. Over many years, advice-giving evolved into broader and broader scopes of assignments on the basic processes of managing the enterprise. By the early post–

World War II years, major management consultants had built
thriving practices advising clients on the full array of organizational and managerial aspects that addressed the issue of how to
manage a business successfully: objective setting, planning, organization, personnel development, and control.

In 1957, the Association of Consulting Management Engineers, Inc. (ACME) published its knowledge requirements for
professional consultants. It stressed eleven generic elements of
managing:

1. Gathering information
2. Synthesizing information
3. Planning
4. Decision making
5. Organizing
6. Communicating
7. Motivating
8. Directing, guiding, or counselling
9. Measuring, evaluating, and controlling
10. Developing people
11. Promoting innovation[1]

Consultants developed and offered their expertise in these
how-to-manage fundamentals for the organization as a whole,
as well as for its major divisions and functions, at times specializing by discrete industries.

Then came the strategic planners to help develop and establish orderly processes for setting basic objectives and strategies
for a company. They developed a host of schemes or frames of
reference for classifying what stage or cycle of a corporation's life
the client might be experiencing. Such work frequently also
evolved into a what-to-do role as a consultant recommended new
product diversification, acquisitions, divestiture, or dissolution
of parts of the client's business.[2]

In the latest wave of how-to-manage consulting, one authority labels the foregoing as traditional, or mechanistic, approaches, which must give way to a more dynamic concept of
"organic" management consulting. Consultant Robert O. Metzger outlines what consultants should be doing to modernize

their services in keeping with the more sophisticated needs of the new managers.[3]

Metzger argues that today's and tomorrow's clients will need sharper problem-solving skills, more expertise in developing innovative approaches, and proven facilitative skills. Clients will want how-to help with the dynamics of their businesses—establishing new values among their staffs, getting them to accept "ownership" of their problems, helping workers to adopt more productive methodologies and changes in beliefs and values, not just learn new technology-based skills. They will expect their consultants to bring broad industry knowledge to the assignment and be comfortable with global marketing strategies, information management, and cost containment principles that pass added value on to the consumer.

Content Strategist

The what-to-do roles a consultant can perform for you address the substance and content of your business and are as pervasive as the how-to. What new business opportunities exist or lie latent in your marketplace? What should your objectives be? What should be your major strategic directions and basic strategies in terms of your product lines, your markets in total, and by specific niches or segments?

Where should you be operating geographically? Should you be marketing domestically or globally? Should you be sourcing your components and finished products offshore? What basic policies should you be employing to improve your growth rates and market share and gain a stronger competitive edge?

Should you be expanding and diversifying your scope, or should you be contracting in order to concentrate just on the most profitable growth areas? And what should be the timing for all of these considerations?

In the post–World War II era, and particularly since the ascendancy of strategic planning services, consultants have been playing an expanding role in advising clients what they should be doing and what types of business enterprises they should be building. With the continuing increases in management sophistication, this trend is certain to continue. You should expect the consultants you enlist tomorrow to have the capability to help you more definitively with *what* you are trying to accomplish, not just *how.*

Process vs. Content

What should the basic emphasis of your potential consulting project be? It could be 20 percent content and 80 percent putting the process of managing in order, counting on the strategic content to materialize with the right people as your new processes of managing emerge and season. Or instead you could be going for: "Damn the textbook form and the principles of managing, just tell me *what* I should be doing. Identify the competitive forces at work and the opportunities in my marketplace; then recommend the strategies and programs that will be key to my success. If I agree, I'll delegate and assign accountability, and we'll run hard to the target."

Peter Drucker has been eminently successful over many years as perhaps the leading example of the philosophy-of-managing school; even so, his work also reflects crystal-clear insight into the important "what" strategies and content for those he has served. But relatively few consultants can perform outstanding service in both camps. Client situations differ markedly as to which emphasis they most need for a given problem.

The Silicon Valley phenomenon has shown us that an outstandingly successful high-tech startup almost always grows beyond the capability of its founder-entrepreneur to manage a surging growth situation effectively. To survive, he needs an infusion of professional management and perhaps the assistance of a consulting firm with a high success record in managing and developing new, high-tech enterprises.

At the other end of the argument, many situations call for the *content strategist.* You may feel reasonably comfortable with your organization for strategic planning and your managerial and business development processes, but want fresh ideas, stimulating new alternative "what" strategies and policies to evaluate. A number of the major firms are particularly well-positioned to perform strategic content work in their respective areas of deep expertise, as well as attend to your managerial processes.

Beyond these two broad consultant roles of *process* and *content* are several complementary and/or supplementary types of approaches that could be valuable to you depending on your situation.

Information Provider

Usually the chief role of the neophyte consultant cutting his teeth on a field survey assignment, or of the free-lance market researcher or broader-scoped market*ing* researcher is to provide information. A number of highly qualified marketing research firms and focus groups are available to size markets, ferret out new market opportunities, and provide direction on product positioning and marketing strategies to corporate strategic planners. Often specialists from industry who have started consulting while looking for gainful re-employment in industry begin as information providers.

You can always get information at an affordable cost level and on a suitable time schedule either with existing staff, by hiring or acquiring permanent new personnel, or by engaging a qualified outside consultant. The latter route buys time utility and often greater objectivity. The right choice of consultants can yield broader insights into your marketplace and competition. An outside consultant or focus group can be invaluable to research market demand and define requirements for new product concepts and programs where it is essential to preserve secrecy and anonymity. In such cases, your main and most difficult challenge is to *believe and accept the unpleasant things you may learn.*

Listener and Therapist

Astute consultants can make excellent objective and confidential listeners for people throughout an organization who don't have normal access to top management or whose good ideas become diffused or distorted as they are communicated up through channels. At times the very act of unloading to a sympathetic and interested outsider vents pent-up frustrations and provides a bit of corporate therapy.

Top executives of both large and small organizations often have great difficulty maintaining meaningful and objective communications where layers of supervisors and managers separate them from the first line of the company's sales and operations functions. This problem can be severe, not only internally but also externally in relation to the company's marketplace and key accounts.

An outstanding "corporate listener," Doug Williams has had a highly successful professional consulting career helping management learn and understand the states of mind and morale of its constituencies. Doug brings to a client a thorough understanding of organizational dynamics and what does or does not motivate people. He combines superior skills as a nondirective interviewer, an unfailing discipline to ensure and protect individual confidences, and sophisticated and finely honed analytical powers about what he is hearing and observing. To cap all this, his recommendations for the people dimension of managing are invariably realistic and timely. He is particularly strong in showing clients how to address the negative attitudes and convictions that often block effective organizational teamwork.

With his nondirective style, Doug has performed valuable services to many organizations by talking confidentially throughout an organization, in one-to-one or small-group sessions. In the process, he releases pent-up steam and frustration, and identifies surprising perceptions about supervision, management, and corporate directions or employees' lack of identification with them. He invites and stimulates grass-roots thinking about the business, its problems, and opportunities.

Doug also aids in clarifying individuals' ambitions and careers and suggests to management how it can identify more closely with such individual aspirations for greater cohesiveness and teamwork. Doug was working to help executives understand their corporation's "culture" before culture-type consulting became a popular professional service.

You won't always like what you hear from Doug, but you would be wise to listen carefully and take heed. Most types of organization and management practices consulting projects should include communications as one of the principal study approaches. More clients—*and consulting firms*—could use the rare Doug Williamses of the world. Being a good listener should be a criterion for every consultant you select.

Innovator, Devil's Advocate, and Persuader

In this role, a consultant critiques and tests a project you are seriously considering. Or, he may relate to your business an array of carefully selected but entirely foreign strategies and tactics that have worked in totally different situations. The adviser sends up trial balloons to obtain both internal reactions and outside opinions and to stimulate alternative thinking where, perhaps, historical approaches have become stale, shopworn, or mature.

An independent devil's advocate can intensify new debate and evaluations and can test management's conviction about current ways of doing business. You should expect and encourage this type of consultant to hang tough in the debate of innovations until he is certain your people have come to the nub of any challenges to the status quo he might be raising. At times the seasoned devil's advocate gets to be linelike in his persistence to make new things happen. Hopefully, he or she is totally objective and retreats when your counterarguments to innovative proposals have become conclusive.

Coach and Educator

By instinct or because it just comes naturally, career consultants often exercise the role of educator or coach, whether or not they have been requested to do so by the client. This role may involve random coaching on the job as needed or it may mean taking on full-scale reeducation in management practices subjects. One of the more recent popular refinements is in strategic planning workshops, where some consulting firms have become adept at combining coaching in the strategic planning process with the real-time development of strategic objectives and plans for a client, as discussed in Chapter 1.

The Consultant as Change Agent

Most "authorities" on the subject describe the "compleat" consultant as an *agent for change*. This agent, first of all, promotes information and idea exchange—exchange within the client organization and between the client and his external business environment.

The broadest role a business/management consultant can play is as agent for change or facilitator of decisions and action steps leading to performance improvement and to discernible and measurable results. The role involves the other six roles of managerial-process consultant; content strategist; information provider; listener and therapist; innovator, devil's advocate, and persuader; coach and educator, and more.

In relation to the role of the listener, the facilitator has additional functions of stimulating and fostering interactive communications and exchanges of information, opinions, and suggestions. Through communication, he or she seeks to find common ground and consensus, and to help bring conflicts, issues, and hidden agendas to the surface for resolution. The facilitator may be expected to extend this role across departments and functions, up and down organization levels, with the client's field marketing organization, and with distributors, suppliers, and key accounts.

Somewhat analogous to the annual physical, certain situations may occur when you bring in a consultant to confirm that you are on the right course. If you are, then no change should be made and the fees should be considered well spent. Similarly, although you may think you require change, a rare consultant may conclude otherwise and urge you to stay the course.

Most of the time, however, consultants are engaged with the expectation that they will be agents for productive and profitable change, facilitators of new and different strategies, programs, and processes, or even innovators.

Consultants' Pervasive Roles in Change

Virtually all of the reasons for bringing in a consultant can be thought of within the context of change in any or all of the principal managerial areas of an organization, as Figure 3 suggests. The heart of the work of effecting change concerns the assignment of responsibilities and the allocation of your human and material resources. With most broad-scale projects for a going concern, this means both reassigning responsibilities and resources and applying new personnel and other resources to your operations. Both propositions invite problems, disruptions, and changes in the signals that guide the everyday activities of at least some of your people.

All of the consultant's primary and complementary roles have one common denominator; they are used to develop significant ideas that can assist you in achieving certain specified results. Your determination of the particular role or combination of roles you need makes a difference in the type and caliber of consultant you should consider employing.

Relatively few consultants or consulting firms either perform all of the above roles well or operate outstandingly in all of

Figure 3. Consultants' pervasive roles as agents of change.

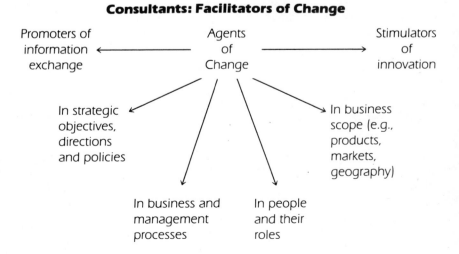

Consultants: Facilitators of Change

Figure 4. Basic functions and emphasis of change.

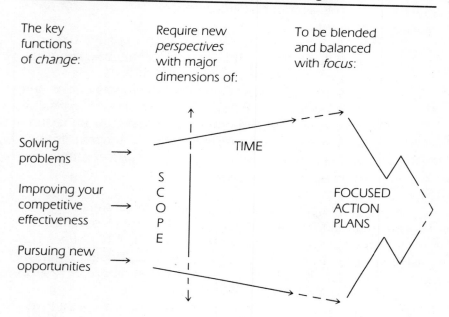

The key
functions
of *change*:

Require new
perspectives
with major
dimensions of:

To be blended
and balanced
with *focus*:

Solving
problems

Improving your
competitive
effectiveness

Pursuing new
opportunities

TIME

S
C
O
P
E

FOCUSED
ACTION
PLANS

the company's managerial functions shown in Figure 3. In fact, few clients want them to play such a pervasive role. But there are a number of less all-encompassing and different ways in which the right consultant can make a significant contribution to your organization. Such differences represent special and distinct emphases, styles, or approaches in which particular consultants specialize and excel.

Determining which of these combinations will be most needed in your assignment is very much an art and depends totally on your particular situation. It becomes an iterative process as you determine precisely what need you have; proceed to the consideration, screening, and selection of a consultant for the job; and begin to structure the right proposal for your situation.

Basic Functions and Emphasis of Change

Change has three key functions (schematically depicted in Figure 4), each of which, in turn, requires changes in *perspective* and *focus*. In brief, consulting is all about change. The goal of most consulting assignments is to effect change in one or more of three broad patterns:

1. Change in situations that pose problems in current operations and processes
2. Change to gain greater competitive advantage from your current strategies and programs
3. Change to take maximum advantage of new opportunities, for example through expansion of current product lines and markets, diversification, or vertical integration of functions and resources

Figure 4 also introduces two principal dimensions essential to effecting significant change, namely the aforementioned companion concepts of perspective and focus. While these pervasive aspects are relevant to your consulting project from the outset, the most critical opportunities for their abuse or neglect occur during the conduct of an established study. Therefore, I consider them separately as the fourth building block and treat them in some depth in Part Five.

Notes

1. ACME, *Common Body of Knowledge Required by Professional Management Consultants* (New York: Association of Consulting Management Engineers, Inc., 1957), page 15.
2. For more detailed discussions of the trends and issues with these types of services, see Chapter 1.
3. See Robert O. Metzger, *Profitable Consulting: Guiding America's Managers Into the Next Century* (Reading, Mass.: Addison-Wesley, 1989), Chapter 3.

3

How You Can Benefit
From Using Consultants

Clients' Aspirations

Innovative strategies
Profitable change
Significant performance improvement
Miraculous solutions

Managerial Benefits

Time saving
Objective problem analysis
Fresh, new perspectives
External intelligence
Internal communications
Sharper focus on plans
Personnel evaluations

Performance Results

Increased profits
Added customer value
Profitable growth
Greater cash flow
Renewed workplace
Faster implementing

By choosing the right consultant you can achieve most of the
above aspirations, benefits, and results, and more. However, it is

unwise and dangerous to assume that consultants represent *miracles for hire*. Change, although tempting and easy to recommend, is inordinately difficult to implement and takes considerable time, courage, and patience, especially where the collective mindset and culture of an organization should be changed.

Generally, consultants at their best bring little more than outside perspective, time saving and improved communication to bear on your problem. However, such factors can be most advantageous. Since consultants' point of departure is different from yours, they may be able to apply lessons or ideas from entirely different situations. Also, they can devote uninterrupted extra time you may be hard pressed to spare to address a problem.

In addition, consultants can offer a confidential ear to involved people both inside and outside your company. Some members of your staff may have valid alternative or contrary views as to what your internal operations or your competitive environment require but for various reasons may not care to express their ideas directly to you.

As you seek consultants who can help you with superior recommendations and their expedient implementation, you should be assessing the potential benefits from two distinctly different viewpoints. First, are you convinced they can supplement your own managerial functions and processes on a more timely and complete basis than you could presently do with your own staff? Second, are you confident that they can produce superior *results* and in time? This chapter discusses selected benefits from these two key vantage points.

How Consultants Benefit Your Managerial Processes

There must be valid reasons for the growing use of consultants and their ability to obtain repeat assignments in firms of all sizes throughout both the for-profit and not-for-profit sectors. Some of the reasons are suggested by a look at several of the more prevalent ways business/management consultants can augment your managerial processes and enhance your executive effectiveness.

Benefit: Saving Time

A significant justification for hiring consultants is an urge or a need to save time. The consultants are not burdened or pinned down by management's day-to-day pressures and can devote concerted full-time effort to the problem at hand. Using them may be, at times, the quickest and most cost-effective method for assessing new and unfamiliar markets. Perhaps you would bring in a consultant as a stop-gap to cover your needs until you have had time to employ permanent staff with the appropriate expertise or establish and develop your own in-house capability later.

Saving time may be important for accelerating the momentum and competitive dominance of a winning strategy or for planning business diversification or new product/market strategies. Time might be needed for fighting some expedient and major problem, be it internal organizational and operating processes or a significant competitive crisis. Or, new markets may appear with just too small a window of opportunity for a firm to develop the needed capabilities inside the organization.

Benefit: Avoiding Permanent Overhead

You can often effect potential long-term cost savings through short-term use of a consultant in lieu of establishing a permanent staff. Or, employing a consultant with new skills without a long-term commitment can help you decide whether you will want to develop such a function on your staff or even employ that individual later.

A prime example is the growth of firms specializing in strategic planning services, as discussed in Chapter 1. Suppose a conglomerate of unrelated businesses or a multiproduct, multimarket company needs a comprehensive review of a large number of its discrete product/market segments. The objective is to develop separate strategic plans for each distinct business segment and a cohesive plan for the corporation as a whole. If the company staffed up on its own to do this completely, it could find itself saddled with excess market research and planning personnel once the first round of broad, marketplace audits and plans was completed.

A competent strategic planning consultant can provide the needed surge of effort, giving your line executives engrossing hands-on training in putting together business plans and then departing, having put into place a dynamic process that you can repeat internally. You then maintain the function with a considerably smaller staff, whose work has been focused by the consulting project. Perhaps the greatest advantage of the approach is that it integrally involves your line executives in strategizing and thus, "buying into" the developed plans. Your principal caveat is to make certain you do not grow so dependent on the consultant that you never get around to asking him to leave.

Benefit: Gaining Outside Perspective

Often at or near the top of a client's list of goals is the desire to obtain fresh, objective, outside perspective. This perspective might pertain to a tough problem, to a significant new opportunity in unfamiliar areas, to heightened or new competition that threatens a company's market share, or to an audit of the overall state of the company's business. A CEO may lack confidence or conviction as to what moves he ought to make. Or, he may just call in the "expert" to seek confirmation or to be indulged with a little hand-holding. Perhaps he considers that his management team lacks the needed expertise and objectivity and should get a refresher management course while working with a consultant on a difficult problem.

Benefit: Gaining External Information Incognito

This benefit is a variation of gaining outside perspective. Anonymous consulting projects are commonplace in industry, particularly for purposes of marketing research, evaluations of innovative new products and research developments, audits of competitive standings, and assessments of new technologies. The consultant's interviews are obtained and conducted in the "blind," meaning that the client's name is never revealed. Concealing the originator of the query is not a particular problem when soliciting ultimate consumers' opinions and reactions to an unannounced new product or product concept. Both individual surveys and focus groups can yield quite useful findings in the hands of competent consultants. Most interviewees will be reasonable about respecting the proprietary interests of the client in such situations.

In-the-blind surveys that border on industrial espionage are another matter, and quality consultants will shy away from accepting missions with questionable ethics or requiring devious or dishonest fact-finding approaches. However, it continues to be amazing that business interviewees of all types often will respond openly and fully to blind requests, whether legitimate or not.

Incognito consulting works because of human nature: Most people like to talk and to be considered authorities or experts. With the right structuring and preliminaries, skilled interviewers can get them to reveal previously ill-formed or latent opinions, discuss trade and corporate practices openly, or even share proprietary information with the outsider.

The blind approach doesn't always work, and generally is a practice that you should neither insist nor rely upon nor should the consultant undertake it. The exceptions are those instances where it is absolutely essential to obtain marketplace feedback while preserving the utmost secrecy. A straightforward request with clearly stated reasons for the anonymity invites cooperation more often than one would expect. Deviousness is ill-advised, and the approach can backfire for both parties.

Benefit: Facilitating Internal Communications

As touched on in discussing the listener/therapist role and the work of Doug Williams in Chapter 2, sooner or later many managements of medium- to large-size companies experience a feeling that they are not getting an objective or realistic story on morale, on what is happening down through the ranks, or on what is going on in the marketplace. Independent "listeners" can be useful to discuss the state of the business confidentially through all levels of the company in cases where it has become difficult or impossible for the CEO to learn what the "troops" are really thinking.

Throughout their entire tenures at IBM, the Watsons maintained healthy internal communications through their emphasis on people and their practice of visiting at any level without first clearing the visit through the reporting channels. Also, the senior Tom Watson's Open Door Policy, which his sons Tom, Jr., and Dick continued, was a most effective communications device. Watson's door was always open to anyone with any grievance, but the visitor had better first make certain that he or she had exhausted all possibilities in discussions with his immediate superiors, or the open door could well have an icy blast. This policy not only kept the Watsons in touch, but also maintained pressure and incentives for open and straightforward relationships among supervisors, subordinates, and peers throughout the company.

Independent "listeners" can be useful in discussing the state of the business confidentially through all levels of a company in cases where it has become difficult or impossible for the CEO to learn what the "troops" are really thinking or where bottled-up feelings and opinions are rampant.

Benefit: Assessing and Testing a Prior Decision

At times, companies are forced to take risks, meet competition, and seize opportunities before having the chance to thoroughly research the situation. This situation might be a case of prematurely putting a new product onto the market or introducing a major, new pricing policy. Or, management may need to move quickly to make an opportune acquisition. Assuming some critical aspects of an acquisition always remain hidden and the buyer never learns all he should until after the purchase, a consultant often can be useful to ferret out booby traps or add more objective insights and perspective for future planning.

In other cases, corporate acquirers have brought in outside counsel in the hopes of blessing or validating a *fait accompli*. The experience of a major commodity firm illustrates the importance of timing in using consultants for confirming a decision.

Commodity Traders: A Case of Late Decision Review

Commodity Traders, Inc., a large company involved in trading agricultural commodities, decided to diversify by purchasing a successful regional manufacturer of packaged food products. To run the new operation, they hired an outstanding food products executive who immediately was chartered to bring in strong brand managers, upgrade merchandising, add to the product lines, and aggressively expand to national advertising, marketing, and distribution.

The acquirer's objective was to achieve a significant national market share by astute merchandising, establishing a national salesforce, and using national media for advertising, which would spread the otherwise prohibitive media costs over the total U.S. market.

A consulting firm was then brought in to audit the acquisition and assist in developing plans and strategies for exploiting the national markets. The consulting team, as it developed background understanding of the new client's business, concluded that the risk of going national was extremely high and recommended against such a move. The client took exception to this conclusion, feeling too deeply committed to turn back. They proceeded with the national strategy, only to return to a regional scale several years and several million dollars later.

This client had been too late in calling in outside counsel and then had not listened seriously enough to the advice to stay regional. The consultants also contributed to the mistake in judgment by not making a forceful enough case for their position.

Benefit: Implementing a Predetermined Action

This reason for using consultants has two primary versions: (1) implementing a decision that has already been made and is known to the organization; and (2) undertaking a *directed study* with a concealed prior executive decision.

In the first version, a new venture may have aspects foreign to the client's experience and he wisely chooses qualified outside assistance to expedite the action. Normally a consultant would not like to start at this point; often, as he gets into the implementation, he differs with the client as to what should be done and how. This is not all bad for the client if the consultant's suggestions stand up to critical scrutiny. It becomes a case of better late than never.

The second version, the *directed study,* is to hire a consultant to produce a recommendation the client has already decided to adopt but has not made known to his people. For various reasons, the client does not want to be identified as the author. He expects the consultant to project an independent, objective viewpoint while working through a study that will produce the predetermined result. Most quality consultants consider the hidden, directed study unethical, but a few like the revenue, even though their objectivity is compromised.

The systems and technology group of a major electronics conglomerate had five subsidiaries in an array of high-tech businesses. Two subsidiaries were consistently profitable with most promising growth prospects, but the other three were losing money badly. The group executive brought in a reputable consulting firm to consult with senior managements of all five subsidiaries on how best to improve the group's business prospects. What the subsidiary heads did not realize was that their superior had already decided he wanted them consolidated into one corporate entity, spreading the profitable units' performances over the others, thus hopefully de-emphasizing their deficiencies.

The consultants proceeded with the study as planned, conducting multiple interviews with the senior managements of all five units. In each case, they solicited concerns and opinions about the problems of the business and ideas on future directions, organization, and management processes. There were some common threads to the five units, particularly in related technologies. However, the markets and competitive requirements were quite different in most cases. The majority opinion was to retain separate, profit-centered units to continue the entrepreneurial drive and autonomy in each, as well as retain on-site control since the units were widely dispersed geographically.

The group executive persisted in his original intention and carried out his consolidation. The head of the most successful subsidiary resigned rather than accept a higher-paying, senior staff assignment in the new group's organization. Morale declined rapidly and the centralized, functionally organized headquarters lost control. The parent company eventually sold or liquidated all of the units. This result probably would have been inevitable for some of the subs but could have been considered more straightforwardly without the cost and negative people impact.

Benefit: Evaluating Key People

Consulting assignments initiated for an announced variety of purposes may have an additional objective of evaluating the effectiveness of senior executives and management development needs of the key managers.

In numerous instances, the board of directors engages consultants for general organization and management audits. The broadest scope of such studies might include all operating and staff functions, the managerial processes, and the structure of the corporate organization. During the course of the audit, informal progress reports are made to the CEO and the board's executive committee. Additionally, and unknown either to the CEO or the consulting staff, the senior consulting partner reports separately to the board's executive committee.

The board's use of a consultant in such situations has two benefits. It accomplishes a much-needed overall audit of the business while the CEO is still on board to provide helpful input and insights. Also, it helps the board confirm its own judgments and shift the onus of a possible dismissal of its CEO to an outside party.

Benefit: Shifting Responsibility for Unpleasant Action

A new face with no corporate entanglements may aid the chief executive in transcending political infighting and shifting the balance of power blocs among factions or key executives. As just suggested above, a recommendation from the consultant can transfer to a third party at least some of the onus of unpleasant

actions, such as key demotions, firings, transfers, layoffs, department reorganizations, or spinoffs.

Benefit: Facilitating Change

McKinsey & Co. has stated that its mission is "to help our clients
make positive, lasting and substantial improvements in their
performance." D. Ronald Daniel, a senior McKinsey consultant
and its recent managing partner, explained, "We're not selling
time and answers, like law or accounting firms. We're selling a
benefit called change. Change is where the value is."[1]

Facilitating change, the prime function of most consulting
assignments, teams with virtually all of the other benefits discussed above. The CEO of a leading company in a mature area
of the branded food products industry found complacency
throughout his organization, even as others started chipping
away at his dominant market share. The company had almost
stood idly by as others came in to wrest leadership away from
key brands, which the company had introduced to the market
years before. This company was trapped in the status quo and
sorely needed some outside challengers to explore with them
how to regenerate sales and profit growth. A consultant gave
them new ways of looking at their strengths and instituting
strategies for capitalizing on them which, like "not seeing the
forest for the trees," had eluded them for some time as market
share deteriorated.

In another instance, the head of a fast-growing firm whose
drive and success had been based on technological prowess concluded that his people had lost touch with the changing needs of
their markets. The product managers and engineers were periodically making proposals to market brilliant technologies and
clever products born in the lab but without clear reference to
compelling needs of users. The CEO of this company took advantage of the fresh perspectives of a competent outsider to
dislodge a widespread, false assumption that his key people
understood their marketplace.

Boards and managements in numerous similar situations
have not clearly appreciated the dangers of complacency bred of

success, technologies in search of markets, not-invented-here attitudes, and failure to establish common visions of what the company is after. These are not isolated cases, and they often dictate a common need—to change. They may need to effect fundamental changes in competitive strategies, in corporate philosophy, or in fostering teamwork throughout the organization through a shared vision of the company's mission. The process of change may well take a third party, an objective outsider, to discover the roots of such problems and to assist in establishing the foundations for change.

The preceding discussion has illustrated some of the principal ways in which consultants can aid or complement your own managerial processes. Depending on the situation, the benefits can be significant in terms of saving time, avoiding false starts with questionable projects, and of exposing your staff to the analytical consulting process. However, the payoff that makes the temporary disruption of your routines all worthwhile is what results can accrue from acting on the consultant's recommendations.

Desired Consulting Results

The prime result you should be seeking and demanding with the aid of your consultant is *superior performance improvements* over time. This result requires a combination of superior quantitative and qualitative targets, with the former often more easily set than the latter. Several generalizations are in order.

Hopefully, the quantitative side translates (in varying degrees depending on the individual assignment) into improved profitability and the definitive results that should flow therefrom, for example higher return on investment, enhanced shareholder equity, reduced fixed debt, stronger cash flow, and more funds for investment spending.

Underlying the hoped-for quantitative results are the functional and programmatic improvements you must make to accomplish them. One comprehensive way of defining such qualitative results is by using Michael Porter's pervasive concept, the *value chain,* as a managerial discipline for planning and achieving *competitive advantage.*[2] In addition to its overall utility as a basic strategic tool for performance improvement, the concept can serve as an excellent model for envisioning and specifying the functional-improvement results you may seek from the consulting assignment.

In brief, Porter identifies opportunities for competitive advantage within a dynamic process flowing from your suppliers to your own enterprise, on to your channels of distribution, and then on to your buyers. He introduces value-chain analysis "to separate the underlying activities an enterprise performs in designing, producing, marketing, and distributing its product or service." The analysis discretely examines improvement opportunities within each of nine generic categories of activities and then integrates them into an overall improvement package. The first five are *primary activities*—inbound logistics, operations, outbound logistics, marketing and sales, and service. The four *support activities* are procurement, technology development, human resource management, and firm infrastructure.[3]

Within Porter's broad framework and given the total scope of any enterprise, an oversimplified starter list of classical performance results targeted for a particular project might include:

- ▲ Manufacturing productivity improvements contributing to reduced product costs, including concurrent engineering
- ▲ Installation of just-in-time procurement and manufacturing processes to reduce direct and overhead costs
- ▲ Distinctive, differentiated product features capable of winning greater market share
- ▲ Improved performance, serviceability, and servicing of products, reducing the users' cost
- ▲ Development of new product/market programs that increase channels' support, raise visibility with the buyers, and establish positions in new niche market segments
- ▲ Successful adaptation of new technologies to your lines leading to superior product features, lower product cost, and improved productivity in the buyers' use

Newer dimensions of industry also suggest new types of results to be targeted, a small sample of which might include:

- ▲ Establishing global joint ventures and marketing and distribution capabilities, positioning your operations to compete effectively with the European Community as it approaches its "moment of truth" in 1992
- ▲ Developing integrated information systems to network your operations and resources on a corporatewide scale, manage the burgeoning external information flows pertinent to your planning and operations, and interconnect your internal departments and divisions to maximize their information interchange
- ▲ Renewing your company's working environment, refocusing your driving force, accomplishing more positive work design to take advantage of group motivation and teamwork, and reshaping your corporate culture to more effectively relate people to their roles in your overall mission

Such incomplete benefits lists as the foregoing are presented to stress two points primarily:

1. Your need, in advance of committing to a project, to focus sharply on the results you are seeking, in terms of both quantitative and qualitative results; and
2. The importance of probing for evidence of consultants' *ability to produce results* for you. You need to establish early, preferably before selection, that they are not just proficient in consulting processes but have proven that they can deliver meaningful results from their efforts.

As with the virtually unlimited roles consultants can pursue for you, the potential benefits to be gained from them are legion, both in the various ways they can augment your own managerial processes and in the types and quality of results you should expect.

Notes

1. John Merwin, "We Don't Learn From Our Clients, We Learn From Each Other," *Forbes* (October 19, 1987), page 126.
2. Michael E. Porter, *Competitive Advantage: Creating and Sustaining Competitive Performance* (New York: The Free Press, 1985), pages 33ff.
3. Ibid., pages 36–45.

PART TWO

Determining Your Need for Outside Help

> When considering the use of consultants, my entry point *always* has been to figure how I could make do without them. This has the greatest chance when I have constructed a thoroughgoing *Situation Analysis* and *Statement of the Need* in advance of any commitment.

The seasoned client, a multidivision manufacturer of industrial products, went on to say that his approach did not always result in a do-it-yourself program, but he felt he was the winner either way. His own perceptions of his needs were clarified in the process, his managers always expanded their understanding of their problems, and he got tighter proposals and more relevant performances on those assignments that were undertaken.

This client practiced a sound and thorough approach to clearing the first of the seven challenges to superior recommendations and action plans:

CHALLENGE ONE: SET CLEAR AND CHALLENGING PURPOSES WITH SOUND TIMING

Building Block Diagram A outlines key considerations covered in the next three chapters.

When determining whether to bring in a consultant and then searching and screening candidates, consider some preliminary pitfalls that are commonplace when setting up a consulting project.

Each possible exposure deserves careful advance consideration and planning if the potential benefits are to be maximized, and each one focuses on the front end of the process, the critical formative stage of determining the purpose and objectives of the project, and its timing.

- *Starting with a fuzzy, carelessly designed declaration of a project's purpose.* This can expose you to wasted time and money, to confusion on your staff, to "fishing" expeditions by the consultant, and to ambiguous or idealistic recommendations.
- *Defining the "wrong" purposes, usually stemming from an inadequate or erroneous definition of problems and their underlying causes.* This may start the effort down blind alleys and leave insufficient flexibility in the consultant's assignment to adjust or retarget in midstream.
- *Embarking on directed studies and hidden agendas without preparing for and safeguarding against the potential exposures.* This can result in loss of confidence and trust among your people and possibly damage your reputation with the trade or your customers.
- *Writing into a consultant's proposal an aim or purpose that is overreaching, idealistic, unreasonable, or impossible to achieve.* This could result from an overly ambitious result you hope to achieve. Or it could reflect a consultant's loose or grandiose promises, which he offers to make his proposal stand out from others under consideration, in order to win the job.
- *Procrastinating or otherwise delaying consideration of outside help.* This can cost time and advantage. It could cause you to miss a "window of opportunity" in your market, to lose a competitive advantage, to allow an unattended personnel or procedural problem to cause internal dissention or defections, or to create any number of other harmful and unprofitable conditions.
- *Acceding to a consultant's unsolicited "pitch."* This can be wasteful, particularly when you had no idea you were experiencing problems needing outside help.
- *Perceiving objectives differently.* Even a clear and well-

Building Block Diagram A.   Summary factors: determining need and timing.

Implement Plans

Control Project

Achieve Perspective and Focus

Structure Assignment

Match People

Determine Need and Timing

Key Consulting Roles:	Problems Determining Need:	Clarifying the Need:
▲ Solve problems.	▲ Fuzzy, unclear purpose.	▲ Situation analysis.
▲ Seek current competitive advantages.	▲ Wrong problem focus.	▲ Needs definition.
▲ Pursue new options.	▲ Myopic aims and options.	▲ Matching needs and opportunities.
▲ Facilitate change.	▲ Differing perceptions.	▲ Go/no-go criteria.
▲ Improve performance.	▲ Hidden agendas.	▲ Project objective.
	▲ Missed market window.	

constructed written statement of a consulting project's objectives can have serious problems if the client and consultant perceive it differently.

▲ *Taking on outside advice without first reexamining your organization's basic objectives and strategies.* This is the cardinal sin. It is still a critical first step for *you* to determine whether your company's aims and strategies have remained attuned to your markets' and your customers' needs and what you are striving to be. You should do this prior to any discussions with candidates, even if such an examination is to be the subject of the consultant's assignment.

Suggestions and actual case situations are presented in this part to cope with the foregoing concerns. Chapter 4 deals with clarifying your company's needs and aims. Chapter 5 concerns timing considerations, including the all-important question of whether it is already too late for outside counsel to be helpful, as well as some of the dangers in accepting unsolicited proposals. Chapter 6 presents guidelines for determining whether you have a valid purpose for proceeding, and for structuring a realistic and effort-stretching proposal.

4

Clarifying Your Company's Needs and Objectives

How did you make money five years ago?
How are you making it now?
How might you be making it five years from now?

Or

Who were your customers five or ten years ago?
Who are they now?
Who might they be five years from now?

Or

What products did you rely on five or ten years ago?
Which ones do you rely on now?
Which new products might have to be developed
within another five years?

Robert O. Metzger

Metzger finds these nonthreatening questions useful in helping a prospective client focus on what business planning and consulting needs he may have.[1] The well-structured assignment should begin with a careful deliberation on your company's mission and objectives and your assessment of where you stand in achieving them. It is critical that you take stock up front as to whether your market, your competition, your customers and prospects, and the trends in their needs are still what you thought they were. Most importantly, you should be self-critical about whether you are establishing the foundations now to meet future needs.

You also should inventory your pertinent resources, strengths, and weaknesses, and develop a preliminary statement of the basic needs you perceive at the outset. These elements should be assessed in light of your mission for the company as a whole, and also for any division, subsidiary, department, program, or strategy on which you may be focusing. This assessment is an essential first step, and you will find that your perceptions about your business grow and change with each consultant screening session.

Almost every successful executive has experienced situations where intuitive business judgment calls produced better results than overconsulting or overplanning. When pressed by a client, I once defined a consultant as "One who is conservative, negative, and disappointed with unplanned success!" It behooves you to deliberate long and hard as to whether you have a bona fide need for management consulting advice.

On the other hand, as a prospective client, you should not hesitate to reach for outside help with the tough problems, and you should try to avoid bringing in the consultant too late. You should not expect the impossible when defining your expectations for the proposal. Do not insist on totally unrealistic objectives; just make the assignment a bit more effort-stretching than you think the consultant is capable of performing. Do not accept or be unduly influenced by pie-in-the-sky promises, even if accompanied by a money-back guarantee.

Unless you are confronted with the rare dire disaster, emergency, or great opportunity that will not wait for preliminary study, you are well advised to develop a *situation analysis* and a *needs definition* and review your marketplace, corporate purposes, objectives, and strategic directions. Initiate these evaluations in advance of talking with consultants and let them be the basis for deciding to investigate a consulting project more seriously.

The Situation Analysis

Normally, your best point of departure is to review your basic aims and purposes for your organization, your objectives and goals. What are you trying to accomplish? What have you already stated in writing—to your organization, your shareholders, and others—that you are and want to be? A relatively small not-for-profit service organization, Online Computer Library Center, Inc. (OCLC) provides an outstanding example of the formalized corporate mission statement as a guide to its internal management and professionals and to its consultants.

OCLC: A Clearly Articulated, Market-Oriented Mission

OCLC is a small not-for-profit membership organization whose prime orientation to the needs of its users, with the aid of a succession of consultants and market research firms, has kept OCLC in the forefront of technology for library and information applications.

OCLC was established in 1966 and developed by the brilliant scholar, librarian, and researcher, Frederick G. Kilgour, under the sponsorship of a consortium of Ohio college and university libraries, who became participating members. Initially, the library consortium was seeking labor cost savings from the pooled production of library catalog cards, and they commissioned Kilgour on a consulting arrangement to proceed. After a short time, he was made president and served in that leadership capacity for a number of years. The teaming concept he initiated has proved eminently successful over the years because OCLC and its member libraries kept their sights focused on changing needs of the users and adopted new information technologies only when they became feasible and economical.

By the late 1960s the vision of Kilgour, his OCLC associates, and the founding members had led OCLC into expanding the business to include an online electronic card catalog service to each member library via OCLC's private telecommunications network. Each member's database became available to it in real time through computer terminals in the local library. The next step was an online interlibrary loan service (ILL) because the central files on each registered book and magazine contained a record of every library member who owned that item. Kilgour also extended OCLC's scope to a national consortium of members.

Kilgour's successor in the 1980s, Rowland C. W. Brown, spearheaded expansion of OCLC to include foreign members and other participants who would add to the international collections referenced in the bibliographic database. Brown and his associates and

consultants also initiated projects for diversification into selected information services to supplement the original bibliographic-only library card records. These new programs were aimed at a more
comprehensive information service to libraries and information end
users.

As a foundation for making such moves—global expansion,
services for the information end user, and electronic publishing—
Brown had concentrated initially on making OCLC more service-
oriented. He improved system performance and economic viability,
changed the pricing structure, and made higher and more consistent
allocations of revenue to R&D.

The OCLC statement of its mission, which has been its driving
force throughout its years of growth, emphasizes service to the library
and information user and the benefits to be provided to them:

> The purpose or purposes for which this Corporation is
> formed are to establish, maintain and operate a comput-
> erized library network and to promote the evolution of li-
> brary use, of libraries themselves, and of librarianship, and
> to provide processes and products for the benefit of library
> users and libraries, including such objectives as increasing
> availability of library resources to individual library patrons
> and reducing rate-of-rise of library per-unit costs, all for the
> fundamental public purpose of furthering ease of access
> to and use of the ever-expanding body of worldwide
> scientific, literary and educational knowledge and infor-
> mation.

Witness to the success of this emphasis is the fact that
OCLC after the first year, has never had an annual deficit. Its
member service revenues doubled in the five years through fis-
cal 1988/1989, when the total reached almost $95 million, with
a staff that had grown to about nine hundred employees, serving
more than ten thousand libraries in the United States and
abroad.

As a prelude to determining your consulting need, you
should commit to writing not only your company's objectives but
also its strengths and weaknesses, its assets and liabilities, its
position in the markets you serve, its financial performance

against objectives. Such an assessment can take many forms, depending on individual circumstances, but a comprehensive situation analysis should include a review of the following eleven elements:

1. Statement of purpose or mission
2. Supporting objectives and goals
3. Strengths
4. Weaknesses
5. Financial performance and resources
6. Market and competitive position
7. Strategic position against objectives and plans
8. Natural strategic advantages and disadvantages
9. Critical problem summary
10. Agenda of opportunities
11. Key personnel inventory

The purpose of such a checklist is to help you and your key managers make a thorough and complete evaluation of your situation from a variety of viewpoints. Your goal is a clear and comprehensive understanding of your status today as a solid foundation for future accomplishment and what parameters you should establish for your consultant.

Completeness, quality, and brevity are the keys for each element of the checklist, as illustrated in Figure 5 by a statement of resources and strengths from the 1988 strategic plan of OCLC.

A frequently neglected facet of a situation analysis concerns natural strategic advantages and disadvantages. Chapter 16 addresses this concept in some detail with case illustrations. Briefly, it is a "water seeks its own level" principle, which refers to inherent advantages or disadvantages of your business that can be expected to prevail in your competitive environment, unless offset with significant counter actions.

Such natural advantages might be a strong patent position, a status as the low-cost producer, or a brand loyalty franchise with consumers. Conversely, natural strategic disadvantages could include such virtually insurmountable conditions as hopelessly outmoded plant and processes, products that have reverted to commodities, or union complications that reduce the

Figure 5. List of OCLC resources and strengths.

Strengths in Bibliographic and Information Technology

- ▲ Database management and database capacity
- ▲ Telecommunications: leased lines, large-network management, diagnostics, software, hardware, value-added network contracts, critical-mass price leveraging
- ▲ Testbed and benchmark testing capabilities
- ▲ Offline production capacity
- ▲ Full-service maintenance services at local site
- ▲ Technical standards activity and leadership
- ▲ Credibility in operating large online systems

Expertise in Library Applications, Markets, and Marketing

- ▲ Library, information science, and computer professional competence
- ▲ Pricing and membership policy
- ▲ Direct and network sales, user support, promotion and exhibition management
- ▲ Application training
- ▲ Market research
- ▲ International hands-on experience in the above

Financial and Administrative Expertise

- ▲ Accounting, data collection, and billings
- ▲ Legal, purchasing, RFP preparation, and response services
- ▲ Documentation and publishing
- ▲ Significant financial resources
- ▲ Adequate credit resources
- ▲ Established track record for performance and credibility in operating large and complex online systems on a financially sound basis

Source: Online Computer Library Center, Inc., Dublin, Ohio. Reprinted by permission from the 1988 OCLC Strategic Plan, 1989.

flexibility to compete. Early recognition of the natural forces that influence your business always adds a sharpened focus to your structuring of a consulting assignment, and, in fact, can help you determine whether a project seems worth the expenditure of time and money.

The Needs Definition

A thorough situation analysis constructed as above should confirm that you indeed have a justifiable need for a consultant. Such a need might spring from:

- An unusually tough problem you and your staff are having difficulty defining and solving
- A market opportunity for which you lack the resources and knowhow, or do not have time to mount the necessary effort
- Unsatisfactory financial performance trends
- Or even a general lack of clarity or confidence in "what your company is now and is trying to be"

The possibilities are numerous, and prior to seeking outside counsel, you should make a concerted effort to define sharply your understanding of your basic need. The specific elements will vary from industry to industry, but many times should fall somewhere within the generic listing shown in Figure 6. Virtually every line item of the figure, and combinations thereof, could be the subject of a consulting project. The Appendix shows that there are consultants around for almost every recognized and unrecognized business need.

Seeking More Precise Definitions of Your Situation and Needs

On occasion you may be confronted with an extremely complex and confused competitive situation or with a most elusive problem definition. In such instances, you may wish to employ highly disciplined and comprehensive soul searching as a prelude to discussions with candidate consultants. Porter's previously noted concept of the *value chain* (see Chapter 3), is quite well suited to amplifying your situation analysis and needs definition where you face stubborn and pervasive competition in your present business.[2]

The discipline of the value chain approach forces you to dissect and challenge every key aspect of your business process and its vertical interrelationships with your suppliers and users. Analyzing against Porter's structure of five primary and four support activities should cause you to focus on your traditional business approach with entirely new perspectives. The chances are great that you will look differently at such issues as:

- ▲ The linkages and relationships among your functions and how they can work more effectively together
- ▲ Your key cost elements and how they may differ from competition
- ▲ Which of your product and service characteristics differ significantly from competition and whether such differences are essential
- ▲ How and whether you are using technology to compete effectively

The development of the situation analysis and the needs definition are an iterative process related intimately with your corporate purpose and objectives. The process almost always helps you sharpen the definition of your basic mission and the intended consulting project. Not redefining your mission at the outset can lead to false starts, wasted time for you and your key people, and cost overruns.

Defining What Your Company Is and Wants to Be

The statement of corporate mission and objectives should be the most encompassing and effort-stretching set of goals or purposes that can be agreed upon as being reasonable and practical to pursue. It would be impossible to categorize all of the types of objectives a management should include, but consideration should be given to the following questions when framing the corporate statement.

What is our company and what is our mission? What is our vision of what we want it to be?

What are we endeavoring to do for our customers? Do we clearly understand their newest needs, and how we can hope to meet them?

Where are we on our industry's experience curve? What are our competitive strengths and weaknesses? Can we hope for a satisfactory market share?

Are major opportunities yet ahead of us in our present venue, or can we make new ones materialize? If not,

Figure 6. Alternative consulting needs checklist.

What corporate environmental situation?

- ▲ Your market share and your market's trends and prospects
- ▲ Your customers' current and expected needs
- ▲ Basic trends and changes affecting the applications for your products and services
- ▲ Customers' satisfaction levels with your products, their reliability, and servicing
- ▲ Competitors' relative standings, advantages, and disadvantages regarding the above
- ▲ Technological trends affecting your marketplace

What corporate objectives and directions?

- ▲ Redefinition of your mission, purpose, objectives, goals
- ▲ Strategic directions by major units, products, markets, and applications
- ▲ Your corporate vision, driving force, "culture" of the organization
- ▲ Financial goals: revenues, profits, return on investment, market share, common stock share values
- ▲ Turnaround requirements and objectives

What business scope?

- ▲ Your range and mix of products by markets
- ▲ Types of services: geographic coverage, domestic and international
- ▲ Methods of operation: manufacture, subcontract or buy, just-in-time, license to or from, concurrent engineering
- ▲ Growth alternatives through internal R & D versus acquisitions, joint ventures, partnerships
- ▲ Need for divestiture or liquidation of business areas

How manage and operate the discrete business processes?

- ▲ How-to studies of specialized functions and activities, e.g., production processes, R&D programs, marketing audits, information systems, distribution studies, sales compensation, marketing policies

How staff, organize, manage, and lead the overall business?

- ▲ Human resources requirements, policies, and programs
- ▲ Organization structure
- ▲ Personnel training and career development, management development
- ▲ Performance incentive programs, and risk/reward/penalty policies
- ▲ Managerial processes for planning, operations, and control: strategic planning process; annual and longer-term budgeting; information systems planning; key-personnel succession planning

What problems, causes, and solutions regarding the above?

- ▲ General studies to clarify and resolve problems of profitability, cash flow, growth, competition, perceived value to the investment community, and a host of other factors stemming from both known situations in the foregoing areas and unknown causes

should we consider diversification? What are the avenues
of diversification best suited to provide synergy with and
leverage from our existing strengths?

What is the net of what we are trying to be and do? What is
our driving force for getting there?

What are our financial performance requirements? What
profit levels will satisfy shareholders? Other owners? The
financial markets?

The importance of the earliest possible definition or redefinition of an organization's basic mission cannot be overesti-
mated. Witness the experience of Bache & Company as it
embarked on a general management study. In this case, neither
Bache nor its consultant challenged the basic objectives in the
preproposal stage. However, the need became apparent and was
addressed almost immediately upon launching the study. The
result was a highly significant and critical early change in the
direction and scope of the study.

The Bache Partners: Where's the Consensus?

Some years ago, Bache & Company, a large Wall Street investment house, engaged a management consulting firm to study opportunities for strengthening the business by reorganizing and
overhauling the firm's management processes. After individual intro-
ductory sessions with key partners, the senior consultant became un-
easy that the proposal's survey purposes might not be well matched
with the facts of the situation. The partners were not voicing consistent views as to the basic mission of the partnership.

To test this concern, the consultant obtained the senior investment partner's permission to expand the scope and take a step that
had been unforeseen in the proposal. He asked all partners to respond separately in writing to twenty basic questions dealing specifically with Bache's strategic aims. These concerned segments of the
investment market to pursue, types of services to offer, guiding policies, financial performance criteria, and the broad timing of future
objectives and strategies.

While the responses revealed expected differences in specific in-

vestment policies and goals, types of markets to exploit, and personnel philosophy, the most striking disparity was found in relation to
the partnership's basic mission. Some variations were explained
readily in terms of the relative size of individual partners' investment
stakes, differences in the sources of their capital, and personality variations that contributed to a number of the partners' differing priorities for the business.

On a tactical level, these findings were neither surprising nor
undesirable to either the partners or the consultants. Most disturbing,
however, was the absence of a common strategic thread to bind the
partnership together. It had been functioning as a loose confedera-
tion of investors rather than a compatible and coordinated partnership entity, and as a result was not taking full advantage of the firm's
combined financial power.

What had been initiated as a straightforward organization and
management study, was refocused via the questionnaire on a much
more fundamental initial need. With the questionnaire inputs as a
base, the consultant negotiated a basic-missions agreement with all
senior partners. Through this exercise, he was able to preserve considerable flexibility to accommodate most individual aims of the partners as well. Only then did he get on with the organization and
management process work, which, not incidentally, was completed
to the considerable satisfaction of the senior partners, largely because
of the new set of shared goals.[3]

Except where the major purpose of an engagement is to
evaluate and redetermine strategic directions, the issue of what
a company is striving to be should always be clarified early. The
early redefinition of perspective and focus was essential to the
success of the Bache assignment.

Maintaining Objectivity and Avoiding Myopic Mindsets

Another problem with framing basic corporate missions is the
ever-present threat that a management becomes obsessed with
a technology and with its own subjective convictions as to what
the marketplace needs.

Many years ago, Ted Levitt's classic article, "Marketing

Myopia," postulated "Are we in the railroad business or the transportation business?"[4] A company may be experiencing a can't-see-the-forest-for-the-trees syndrome, or pursuing technologies in search of a market, or facing a not-invented-here block to taking advantage of what has already been learned and proved by outsiders. Or, the myopia may be a highly subjective bias born of personal experience or subjective feedback—"My mother-in-law thinks it's the greatest thing since the microwave oven."

A high-tech startup situation demonstrates the problems of achieving perspective and focus in the strategic development of a business. Its lesson for you, the client, is to consider only consultants who will bring a counterbalancing objectivity to the situation.

Radio Technology: Blinding, Subjective Motivations

"You and I, both having lost dear ones to cancer, need no convincing on the market potential for my low-cost procedure for burning out malignant tumors."

The speaker was the owner of licenses and patent rights to a system employing low-frequency radio waves to target an identified tumor and reduce it to harmless matter without requiring incisions. The occasion was the entrepreneur's enlisting of a consultant in a speculative investigation for his company, Radio Technology Inc. (RTI), without front-end fees, which hopefully could lead to a business plan and new financing.

Both the CEO of RTI and the consultant had recently suffered tragic losses of loved ones due to cancer; both had experienced the intense frustrations of trying one new approach after another, each offering some early encouragement only to fail.

For the consultant, the venture was largely a speculation of his own time and expenses, which could lead later to an investment opportunity for himself and an investor associate. It was only after he got out into the marketplace to solicit a range of independent opinions and visit medical centers that had tried prototypes, that the consultant was able to penetrate his highly emotional veil of hope that colored his view of the project.

The method had been sanctioned for limited and carefully monitored experimentation and had produced some positive results, so it was not pie-in-the-sky. However, it had significant practical limitations as a business risk: some questions of patent infringements, heavy up-front capital and working capital requirements, and the expectation of a painfully long period of restricted use before governmental approvals and clearances for expanded market introduction could be expected.

After this counterbalancing input, the consultant bit the bullet and persuaded his investor associate to decline the project along with him. The entrepreneur found some initial markets in certain countries with looser restrictions on testing but continued to limp along for some time in the United States without major success.

It is difficult enough when a client's perspectives are blinded or diverted by subjective feelings about the project or problem at hand. When his consultant's views are similarly subjective, the chances of an unsatisfactory engagement are increased geometrically.

In such instances, you should seek out consultants who will be able and willing to challenge you with complete objectivity and will exercise independent perspectives to identify significant natural strategic disadvantages early. In highly subjective situations, you need a consultant who will exercise an aggressive and steadfast devil's advocate role.

Notes

1. Robert O. Metzger, *Profitable Consulting: Guiding America's Managers Into the Next Century* (Reading, Mass.: Addison-Wesley, 1989), pages 80, 81.
2. Michael E. Porter, *Competitive Advantage: Creating and Sustaining Competitive Performance* (New York: The Free Press, 1985), pages 33ff.
3. J. Thomas Cannon, *Business Strategy and Policy* (New York: Harcourt, Brace & World, 1968), page 262.
4. Theodore Levitt, "Marketing Myopia," *Harvard Business Review* (July/August 1960), page 45.

5

Timing Considerations

I had a great opportunity to acquire a small business that ought to fit in with ours, but I had to move fast to avoid losing it. Now I'm not so sure just what we've bought. Could you come talk with us about a study?

This executive was confronted with a classic timing conflict. He could consummate a deal that might not be available for very long based on more limited information than that with which he felt comfortable, or, he could take a calculated risk of having a consultant look over the proposition and possibly lose the opportunity.

Assuming that you have determined to seek outside assistance, the question of timely initiation of the project remains. One frequently recurring issue is whether an outside party would be able to help you soon enough. The obvious, but not specifically helpful, timing answer is "We appear to have enough lead time to reach credible conclusions by the time action should be taken."

Accepting this principle still leaves the executive short of a comfortable answer to the question. Ultimately, it is a trade-off between the risks of not seeking outside counsel on one hand, and, on the other, the risks of time constraints, costs, and organizational problems that may result from bringing an additional perspective to bear on the matter. A number of timing issues could be determining factors.

Timing Issues

- ▲ Does it appear that the "best" expert in the world on the subject would have time to focus the problems and their causes and develop possible solutions?
- ▲ Would there appear to be time to achieve the assignment's purposes, given the best possible conditions, on-schedule performance, and action plans? Would there be time under the worst conditions?
- ▲ Are financial resources and credit likely to be exhausted before a reasonable period of time needed to identify and take remedial action? Does it seem realistic that you could fund the resulting recommended actions?
- ▲ In an acquisition or joint venture, are there likely to be so many critical unknowns hidden behind the seller's or proposer's facade that there would not be time to discover and evaluate them all prior to the deadline? Will you have to close before obtaining definitive external inputs?
- ▲ Is the project timing consistent with the life cycle of the end proposition involved? Can any research or product-development life cycles be undertaken within the window of opportunity for the proposition? Will competitive responses be required prior to completing preparation of new facilities, retraining, start-up activities?

Too often a company does not bring a consultant in soon enough; consequently problems may have gone too far, marketplace opportunities may have been missed, or key decisions may have been made that could have benefitted from some objective prior study. This timing squeeze often occurs when acquisitions and mergers are being considered.

Paper Specialties, Inc.: Timing the Use of Consultants

Paper Specialties, a manufacturer of a line of specialized paper and paperboard products for a variety of industrial and commercial applications, brought in a consultant for a comprehensive four-phase assignment. The project was to involve: (1) a study of markets for the existing product line; (2) a diversification study; (3) evaluation of the company's organization and management operations; and (4) recommendations for a research and new product development program.

The objectives of the first-phase market study were to assess the long-term outlook for the existing lines and identify new applications to augment declining volumes in the traditional businesses. The consulting team launched a broad-scale field market study to assess the future viability of the established products and applications and to explore a wide range of new opportunities under consideration by the client. The client also expected the consultants to identify entirely new market potential.

Near the end of this highly productive engagement, the client CEO informed the consultants that he had been negotiating for the acquisition of a small, new company with some relatively untested but complementary products and, in fact, had agreed to buy the company. Upon completing the initial paper market study, the consulting firm was asked to conduct a similar exercise for the acquisition in lieu of the previously planned broad diversification study for the second phase.

Unfortunately, others had been negotiating for the purchase and the CEO had to complete the deal before a thorough study and evaluation of the markets and new product concepts could be made. For reasons not revealed to the consulting team, management had chosen not to ask them to study the candidate prior to purchase. Unfortunately, the consultants' subsequent market study of the acquisition revealed quite mediocre prospects for the new line, and significant sales revenues never materialized.

This situation illustrates the high risk of buying a concept based on a product that has yet to be well tested in the market and the importance of timing in bringing outside perspective to bear on an acquisition assessment. From the viewpoint of Paper Specialties, they might have lost the purchase to others if they had waited for the outcome of a thoroughgoing market study. On the other hand, this study might have saved them considerable funds and diversion of management effort.

Another prevalent timing problem concerns getting help for internal operating problems before it is too late. When companion problems of late timing and failure to focus on the fundamental weaknesses are combined, it can mean the difference between continuing success and failure of or the need to divest a venture, as in the situation of the VanityWare Products Corporation.

VanityWare Products: Get Back to Basics Early

An entrepreneur was confronted with significant losses with one of his investments, a small eastern fabricator of a line of high-quality molded plastic, marbleized countertops for bathroom vanities and kitchen counters. Their principal applications were in single-family residences, new apartments, hotel complexes, and commercial buildings.

Soon after acquiring VanityWare, the owner brought in a new general manager who had been a highly successful sales executive with a major paper company. In a very short time, he established a large order base from the commercial and apartment-house markets.

Sales were clearly no problem. However, losses continued because of a high rate of rejects and missed order delivery commitments; also, production output was substantially below the plant's rated capacity. The performance claims of the production-system vendor were not being achieved. After sustained losses, the owner sought outside technical and plant engineering help without success; he then brought in a management consultant for guidance.

The consultant concluded that the fundamental problems not only resided with technology, raw materials, and the production layout, but also with supervision of the work crew, plant scheduling, and overall management. He worked with the VanityWare management to define breakeven output levels, sharpen cost standards and material measurements, and more tightly monitor order processing, production scheduling, and shipment control procedures.

In the area of management practices, the consultant recommended that the plant supervisor, who had had no previous related experience, be trained in more aggressive supervisory practices or be replaced. The general manager's natural bias had previously led him to concentrate in his area of greatest experience and expertise, hence his very high sales and marketing productivity. Both he and the entrepreneur were given guidelines for more balanced attention to other key managerial and operating functions.

Some improvements began to materialize, but not at a rate the owner was willing to support with prolonged working capital infusions, and the technical problems of the manufacturing process could not be resolved completely. He sold the business and took his investment losses. The new owners brought in management experienced in the type of rough-and-tough day-to-day direction the operation required. They reportedly began to improve financial performance, but the business was extremely competitive, the system's performance claims could not be fully met, and profitability was slow in developing.

On hindsight, the entrepreneur might have turned the business around if he had focused earlier on identifying the root causes of the unsatisfactory performance, addressed the gaps in his manager's *modus operandi,* and replaced the plant supervisor. It is a common occurrence to define one's problems in external terms, such as "It's the competition," or in inanimate terms, "It's the technology," without delving deeper into all key causes. The other major lesson is one of timing, recognizing the need for outside help before it is too late.

Another timing issue with considerable risk for the prospective client arises when a consultant initiates the subject. Over the years, many CEOs have been persuaded to engage a management consultant when they had not known or realized they needed one.

Timing Cautions for Unsolicited Initiatives

Historically, the quality firms have relied mainly on building a record of effective performance to generate additional billings from an established client, and on word-of-mouth from board room to board room to gain new clients. More recently, a number of the major firms, and thousands of smaller ones, have begun to use typical product marketing and promotional initiatives to seek new business. Through the years, however, a few particularly aggressive consultants have endeavored to generate work

from firms that had never focused on, or realized they had, a
need for consulting services.

SBCS: You Didn't Know You Needed Us

One of the most successful at using aggressive advertising,
sales, and promotional methods was Small Business Consulting Services, Inc. (SBCS), founded prior to World War II. This consultant
served any kind or size of business, including manufacturers, resellers,
and service companies. Its stated interest was to help businessmen
solve their problems such as methods, markets, organization, or
profits.

Numerous consultants invest in direct sales, advertising, and
promotion programs, or employ public relations firms to help spread
awareness of their services. SBCS's promotional budget from its earlier years was a significant percentage of annual billings. One of its
unique promotions was an annual sponsorship of a major sporting
event for professionals where the winner received a first prize in five
figures plus a contract to perform exhibitions for the next twelve
months all over the world!

The dozens of such exhibitions at private country clubs each
year brought the SBCS people into direct contact with literally thousands of business executives, most of whom were at least theoreti-
cally potential clients. Often such prospects were proprietors of small
businesses in the area who found themselves committing to consulting studies when they had never entertained the thought, nor realized they had significant problems to be solved. A number of such
projects turned out to be beneficial to the client, and SBCS has continued to grow.

As a general policy, it is never sound to rush into an externally initiated study without careful and unhurried deliberation
of the question whether you have a valid and significant need or
are being asked to consider a "consulting assignment in search
of a problem."

Another dimension of timing and the aggressive consultant
phenomenon relates to the perennial client who becomes known
to spend megabucks for outside services, not always on his own

timing. Such a client becomes a frequent target for both direct
and indirect promotion by competing consultants. This has been
the experience of a major U.S. conglomerate, almost continually
active in acquisitions and divestitures and involved in as many
as fifty or more separate businesses at any one time.

Associated Industries: Have Fees to Spend, Will Hire!

Associated Industries had employed several different strategic
planning firms from the early days of SBU planning with considerable
success. The process was ably managed by its vice president of planning who had honed the SBU approach to fine precision, adapted it
to the particular needs of the company and its CEO, and established
it as a completely in-house program. Moreover, the line executives
had become sophisticated at spearheading their respective strategic
planning and decision-making responsibilities.

Although the internal planning approach worked well, the CEO
continued to be pressed periodically by new consultants to discard
the established process and try something new. Fortunately, the
planning VP was usually able to quickly defuse such new initiatives,
arguing cost savings and avoidance of tampering with a well-oiled
and smoothly working mechanism that the senior executives understood and accepted.

Determining Consulting Need at Your Initiative

Whatever the type or source of pressure that may originate from
the outside, it behooves you to determine most carefully whether
a bona fide need exists and whether taking on new consulting
services can be justified. The unsolicited proposal usually is a
fishing expedition that should be viewed with considerable
skepticism. Its proponent may well have outstanding new insights to bring to a company, and if this appears to be the case,
the proposition should be considered. However, it should be put
to the same test as the client-initiated need, applying the rigorous analyses and soul-searching described in Chapter 4.

Segments of the consulting industry are putting on the

hardest "sell" in its history. The newer types of firms have established dominant market positions, and, driven by intensive competition for their new types of services, they must market their wares aggressively. The surge of highly effective new managerial processes, philosophies, and technologies has opened opportunities for which virtually every organization has an application. In some instances, the prospective client must adopt the new approaches to stay competitive. The older professional firms and individual consultants have not always stayed attuned to what is new that works.

Your first caution is not to undertake a project you did not realize you needed without a thorough examination of whether you truly have such a need. Proceeding with a study that has risen entirely at the initiative of an outsider can be wasteful and diversionary. In such situations, as well as those at your own instigation, your first priority should be to determine whether and when a bona fide need in fact exists and, if so, how you might manage to do it yourself rather than bring in outside assistance.

The go/no go and timing issues are iterative with the consultant screening process. These issues should be kept alive until you have become fully involved in the process of considering alternative consulting approaches and firms and are negotiating with them. At any point in the discussions, you may find warnings not to proceed. The proper time to close your consideration of both the timing issue and the decision whether you should proceed at all is when you have resolved what your project objective is to be, the subject of Chapter 6.

6

Establishing the Project Objectives

Consultant's Perception: "But you accepted my written proposal, whose first objective was to define strategic objectives for you and redefine overall strategic concepts and themes for I/U."

Client's Reality: "Yes, but what I want are specific acquisition prospects who fit the characteristics and criteria I gave you."

The stated objectives of the consulting assignment set its entire tone, provided you and your consultant have an unmistakable meeting of the minds. The quandary posed by the foregoing situation is reviewed below. In the most desirable situation, you must be convinced that you have a solid and realistic objective before deciding to undertake a particular consulting project. You must also be certain you and your consultant are communicating on the same wavelength.

The decision to proceed with a project becomes easier when you have done the homework advocated in Chapters 4 and 5 to clarify your situation and need and exercise debate on your timing issues to your satisfaction. Even after taking these steps, some of the critical go/no go and timing conclusions are likely to remain unclear until you are well into the study. You often must make a decision while still lacking some of the key facts and insights. In such cases, the stated objectives need to include an aim of clarifying those issues that remain uncertain. At the risk of being repetitive, it is most helpful to redefine your basic corporate mission prior to making a consulting commitment, even though a redefinition of that mission might be a goal of the project.

The statement of consulting objectives could be as simplistic and broad-brush as McKinsey & Company's basic aim "to help our clients make positive, lasting, and substantial improvements in their performance." More specific objectives are the norm: They must contain no ambiguities and be effort-stretching, yet realistic.

Given so many different areas for a consulting project and the uniqueness of every client and his problems, it is easy to envision how a poorly constructed or misunderstood consulting objective can start a project on the wrong foot. Failure to clarify the intended assignment with crystal clarity can have negative consequences, such as those experienced by the chief executive and his consultant in the following situation.

Info/Universe: A Case of Misunderstood Objectives

Info/Universe provided an array of both printed and electronic information services and library publications to several highly competitive growth markets. The information industry was experiencing increasing popularity of computerized, online databases accessible via telephone networks nationally and internationally.

The client had adopted aggressive growth and profit objectives, which called for programs of acquisitions and internal product development, to be confined to related products and markets. His aim was to take greater advantage of Info/Universe's considerable expertise in database production, marketing, and information distribution, and to increase profitability by adding new database products that would fit in with established markets, overhead, and capacity.

The president received a carefully constructed written proposal that included the following specific objectives a consultant had reviewed with him prior to submission.

Project Objectives

1. Define and develop strategic growth objectives, criteria and profiles for profitable expansion of Info/Universe's informa-

tion services. This will include redefinition of overall strategic concepts and themes for I/U.

2. Identify and screen potential acquisition candidates and types of services fitting I/U's growth and profit objectives, service profiles, and strategic themes, and fitting I/U's specific set of criteria concerning candidate revenues, customer base, and information database characteristics.
3. Develop a target list of acquisition possibilities, both generic types and specific organizations and/or services.
4. Assist I/U management by initiating and participating in discussions and negotiations with the targeted acquisition candidates.

The client expressed great urgency for the study to proceed, but left on a business trip before authorizing it. When the consultant received word from a VP that a go-ahead was authorized, he plunged into the initial work.

On the phone following the client's return, objective 4 was eliminated; any such work would be performed by the client. The president promised to forward some additional studies on his markets and competition, which he did. The consultant and an associate reviewed this material, conducted a few initial field interviews, and made a preliminary progress report to the president.

The consultant, on the strength of what he had considered a reasonably satisfactory discussion of progress, submitted his first monthly statement covering the work to date. The client called a meeting to review the bill before authorizing its payment. He considered it unfair to be charged for time reviewing reports with which he, the client, was quite familiar. He also was uninterested in the generalized work done on the first study objective, particularly the starter strategic concepts.

The consultant concluded that the client only wanted to be billed for work directly involved in finding specific unfamiliar acquisition prospects about which he had no prior knowledge and expected such names almost instantly. Although the consultant and his associate both had prior experience in the industry as consultants and information users, the uniqueness of the client's business still required some initial background gathering and orientation, which had been specified in the written proposal.

The consultant sensed a no-win situation and resigned from the job, settling for half payment of the fees and out-of-pocket expenses to date. The client seemed not to have accepted the front-end investment of consulting time to which he had committed. The consultant had failed to ascertain that the client was not focusing on and accepting the specific terms to which he had agreed, particularly the need for initial orientation activities.

The Info/Universe situation is a common case of misperceptions and incomplete communications, even when included in writing. The I/U president knew what he wanted from the project, namely objectives 2 and 3. He was uninterested in the conceptual objective 1, so he ignored it. He failed to perceive that the consultant assumed it appropriate because it had been left in the written game plan for the project. Info/Universe was the loser of the president's time and the fees paid, without receiving any benefits.

The issue of suspected hidden project goals—concealing some purposes of the assignment from the consultant or one's staff—is another kind of problem that can pose major complications and consequences for both client and consultant if not handled carefully.

Majestic Mills: A Case of Suspected Hidden Agendas

Majestic Mills was a manufacturer of woven textile products, mainly fabrics to be fashioned by others into sheets and pillow cases, shirts, blue denim jeans, and sportswear. A few major retail chains, including Sears, Penney, and Montgomery Ward, were the main customers. These chains wielded great influence over pricing, scheduling, product planning and specifications, and other Majestic policies, working through the latter's sales agency. Independent sales agents traditionally had been dominant forces in many segments of the textile industry, but were gradually being taken over or phased out by most mills or in some instances becoming integrated businesses by acquiring their mills.

Through the initiative of several Majestic directors, a management consulting firm was engaged for a multistaged assignment to commence with a review of sales, marketing, and distribution policy, strategies, and programs. This first stage was to be followed by a series of general organization and management studies that would examine all of Majestic's other key functions.

As expected, the initial stage revealed that Majestic was almost completely dependent on the sales agent for all product design, marketing plans, and sales. The agent also exerted significant influence on Majestic's overall strategic objectives and decisions. Another concern of the consultants was that the big chain customers were accounting for an increasing proportion of total revenues, and their pressures on and through the agent for margin-squeezing price concessions were relentless and successful.

The slow growth and shrinking profits were considered to be totally unsatisfactory by the consultants, whose partners also generally regarded full-function sales agents as passé. They did not believe that the agents could exercise sufficient objectivity and balance, operating as such influential participants in Majestic's strategic and managerial direction and decision making. At a very early stage of the initial study, they recommended terminating the agent and establishing Majestic's own product planning, marketing, and direct sales organizations.

Before long, accusations of a hidden agenda and a directed study were leveled at the consultants, at the particular directors who had brought them in, and at the Majestic president. Charges and countercharges of incompetency went back and forth between the consultants and the agent. The agent threatened legal action against the consultants. Different factions of the board entered into the dispute, and the overall timetable of key project milestones was upset. The situation was particularly disruptive for the agent's ongoing dealings with the mills' major accounts.

The project turmoil turned into an unplanned second-stage study when the sales agent unexpectedly proposed that the consultants audit the agent's activities with the hope of making changes to enable him to serve Majestic more effectively. However, this soon deteriorated into a sequence of seven lengthy registered letters from the agent methodically attacking every key element of the consultants' findings and recommendations. Copies were sent also to all of the board members.

After surviving the onslaught of these memos and somehow

dissuading the agent's few board supporters, the consulting team was successful in convincing management and the board to fire the agent. They then proceeded to the next stage, a general organization and management study, which included assimilation of the functions formerly performed by the agent.

From your viewpoint as a would-be client, the Majestic experience suggests some of the sticky problems, exposures, and traumas for corporate boards and managements who enlist the aid of outside consultants to assess the need for, or to effect, fundamental strategic change. On the positive side, it dramatizes one way to ease the process of recovering corporate control in adversarial or conflict situations, that is, shift as much of the onus as possible to an independent third party.

Majestic Mills also underscores some of the pitfalls that can accompany hidden agendas, directed studies, and the political problems of coping with warring board factions. At times such approaches are duly warranted. However, they almost always raise unusual exposures that should be fully understood in advance. The Majestic sales agent was taken completely by surprise, otherwise he might not have cooperated so fully with the consultants in the initial fact-finding stages.

An outside consultant can enable you to pursue new opportunities more objectively and aggressively than you may be in a position to do with your own staff. A case in point is Richard J. Reilly, Jr., Inc., which made good use of a consultant to test a bold new concept beyond the traditional approaches responsible for its initial growth and profitability.

Richard J. Reilly, Jr., Inc.: Setting Effort-Stretching Consulting Aims

In the late 1970s Reilly was exploring a number of new directions due to recessionary conditions that were adversely affecting its traditional business of building and servicing platform tennis courts. The president and his associates considered a number of diversification alternatives, one of which was a bold new, high-reaching concept that had significant risks but a fighting chance to succeed.

Reilly was considering building a chain of platform tennis courts on leased space atop department stores in major suburban shopping centers around the United States. The president envisioned a center providing ample parking in a concentrated market within a ten- to fifteen-mile radius and the appeal of quick exercise at noon, before or after work, evenings and weekends. This combination could offer a natural draw of additional shoppers for the department stores for both daytime and evening store hours.

Platform tennis is a high-energy, outdoor doubles game played in a wire-encased rectangular court with a tennislike net. It has a raised deck of specially seasoned and treated, granular-coated wood timbers for nonskidding (later aluminum and heated for rapid snow melting and removal). As in squash, all four walls are used.

Platform tennis, or paddle, is a cool weather and winter sport with courts installed at country clubs, tennis and racquet clubs, private homes, and commercial platform tennis centers. It is a fast, competitive game, and often in mixed doubles is the occasion for social events after the game or tournament. In recent years, it has experienced significant competition from similar games played indoors, particularly racquetball, but has continued to grow in popularity with new installations at country clubs and private homes.

Reilly, the dominant builder and maintainer of the courts, presently accounts for 75 percent of the U.S. courts, and most of those built elsewhere in the world. In the late 1970s, Reilly, with only a 50 percent market share, found that its small and labor-intensive business had been entered by local contractors who instigated severe competition and price-cutting in both new construction and the ongoing court maintenance business.

In efforts to stimulate the growth of commercial platform tennis centers, the Reilly president called in a consultant to study the financial situations of the few such centers in existence. They concluded that, to be viable, a center needed at least six to eight heavily used courts in order to support the staffing overheads and amenities, such as warming hut, nursery, and refreshments. Moreover, eight active courts dictated location in a heavy population area concentrated within a thirty-minute drive at the most from the players' homes or offices.

The proposition of placing centers on the unused rooftops of major department stores seemed like a winning strategy to the CEO and his venture team—the paddle center entrepreneur, a sporting equipment company, and the consultant. Funds were spent obtaining architect's renderings and drawings and using his consultant to help prepare a business plan and proposal for a prime store unit of a major department store chain.

The meetings with the retailer were discouraging and the negative reactions so convincing to the president that he abandoned the idea. It had been an exciting and fun concept, with many theoretical arguments why it could sweep the country. He had invested time and dollars as a reasonable way to augment the growth and profit prospects for his traditional business, and he considered the rooftop idea well worth a shot.

Unfortunately, department store reaction to the idea was unmistakably negative. In response, Reilly refocused its efforts on strengthening and enhancing its traditional approaches. By the late 1980s the company had put together a succession of profitable growth years in building new courts for country clubs and private homes, and continued to be the dominant factor in servicing established courts. Among the most promising recent diversifications was the development of a paddle-tennis dude ranch in the northwest, with luxury vacation accommodations for enthusiasts of paddle, skiing, hiking, and other mountain activities. On hindsight, the earlier rooftop project had served Reilly management well by forcing a refocusing on the principal markets and user patterns which had been the basis for their initial dominance in the sport.

Determining Whether You Have a Worthwhile Objective

Hindsight provides guidelines for understanding problems of feasibility and timing and determining that you should proceed with a specific consulting project. The decision whether to proceed can be supported in a number of judgmental ways. One of the most comfortable is your own organization's past experience with consultants in similar situations. Lacking that, some of the following positive signals can reassure you to proceed.

▲ *Your situation analysis is convincing.* Your situation analysis and reexamination of your corporate mission and objectives clearly convince you of the need.

▲ *Your need for outsiders is persuasive.* Your reasons for bringing in consultants argue persuasively for using them to address your problem. You have become convinced that you cannot accomplish the result with your own staff or at least need to augment your internal capabilities with outside assistance.

▲ *Comparable situations paid off for others.* You have identified other companies that have used consultants successfully in similar situations, and the results they achieved are persuasive.

▲ *Natural strategies are favorable.* Your problems do not appear to be fundamental and insurmountable. The strengths of your situation appear to meet the natural strategic and competitive requirements of your business. You have identified no natural strategic disadvantages that argue against success from the outset.

▲ *There is room to improve market position.* The dominant market positions of others can be challenged and do not constitute overwhelming odds against your achievement of a satisfactory market share.

▲ *Requisite leadership is on board.* You and your key executives possess the leadership qualities and managerial skills that are likely to be required.

▲ *Your window of opportunity is adequate.* You probably will not have to commit a new concept and product to the market before you are able to acquire new expertise internally. Your window of opportunity appears large enough to give you time to meet your requirements for successful entry.

▲ *You still have enough resources.* You have ample funding. Or, you are in a critical loss situation, yet your declining profits, cash flow, and borrowing power have not yet eroded to the point where your only resort is to file under Chapter XI or fold the business. You possess an entrepreneurial optimism that refuses to give in, and the odds appear favorable that a consultant, even a turnaround expert, has a good chance of helping you work out of your problems.

Having met the test of such tough questions and issues as those above, a precise statement of the intended purposes of the assignment is still required. At least one more important hurdle stands in your way, namely a problem of perceptions, which manifested itself in different ways in both the Info/Universe and Majestic Mills situations.

Problems of Perceptions and Polite Head-Nodding

The relevance of the project purposes to your needs and their clarity to both you and your prospective consultant are essential conditions. But you also must guard against the Info/Universe kind of problem, where at least part of the difficulty was a case of polite head-nodding. Both client and consultant assumed they understood what the other meant; unfortunately their perceptions differed about what was to be done, or at least what each expected the project to accomplish. Similarly, differing perceptions about what the Majestic Mills project was all about created great confusion and disruption, although there might not have been a better alternative way to deal with the overriding issues involved.

This matter of misinterpretations and imperfect communications is so common a problem that consulting can almost be called a game of matching and aligning perceptions. It is most critical at the formative end of the project, its starting objectives.

Chapters 4 through 6 have considered the first building block toward superior consulting results and have addressed approaches for meeting the first challenge, setting clear and challenging purposes with sound timing. Preparation of a situation analysis and a needs definition can help you determine what need you may have for outside consulting assistance and with what timing, and also, can assist in establishing an effective project purpose.

PART THREE

Choosing the Right Consultant

He told the bench that Burbridge had to take anti-consultant drugs and tranquilizers.

From *Punch,* in its "Country Life" column

Assuming Burbridge had a bona fide need for consulting assistance, it is highly possible that his misfortune began with an unsatisfactory selection. Countless business executives have been known to share his disappointment and anguish. A smaller number have been highly pleased, and the skillful selection and use of consultants can be highly rewarding.

Citing Burbridge's plight is intended to emphasize the great caution and care needed in the screening and selection process, with the expectation that the present trend of mergers, acquisitions, and dissolutions will continue. As a would-be client, you will discover larger numbers of consultants. You should hope and expect that at least several are likely to have specific skills and experiences in business subjects relevant to your areas of interest.

Experienced managers and specialists from industry represent a pool of talent steeped in the practical experiences of business, which clearly can be of great immediate advantage to you. Specifically, they can provide you with instant capabilities, if they are already familiar with your business environment, competition, and marketplace. Thus, you can avoid the learning time that many consultants need

93

Building Block Diagram B.   Summary factors: matching client and consultant staffs.

Implement Plans

Control Project

Achieve Perspective and Focus

Structure Assignment

Match People

People-Matching Problems:

▲ Staff mismatch with client.
▲ Poor communications skills.
▲ Motivations lacking.
▲ "Unknowns" assigned to job.

Key Screening Steps and Criteria:

1. Identify potential consultants.
2. Screen several firms in depth.
3. Test against selection criteria.
4. Seek multiple formal proposals.

Determine Need and Timing

at the outset of an engagement and typically build into the cost of the assignment.

Conversely, you may need how-to consulting as much as, or more than, expertise in the content of your business. With a seasoned, professional consultant, you are much more likely to be assured that you are buying expertise in how to perform a consulting assignment and the advice you may need in how to manage. Your challenge is to become convinced that your candidate has such analytical skills as problem definition, ability to perform resourceful, confidential interviewing of your staff and customers, clarity in oral and written communication and presentation of findings, and thinking conducive to achieving sound perspective and focus. If this is your situation, an established and qualified consultant who also has on his staff competent individuals with experience in your type of business can give you the best of both worlds. '

Part Three concerns the second of the seven major categories of challenges clients face:

CHALLENGE TWO: SEEK AND HIRE THE VERY BEST FIRM AND PEOPLE FOR YOUR PROJECT

This issue, which cannot be overstressed, starts with picking the best firm for your needs and becoming convinced that the senior account executive who will be working for you is a person with whom you can communicate and are completely comfortable. Then you must assure yourself that you will get solid staff assigned to your project. One of your objectives should be compatibility of the project leader and consultants with all of your key client people who will be involved. Frequently, these considerations cannot be clarified easily at the outset.

Part Three presents a number of guidelines and considerations that can help you to match the best possible consultant with your situation. Chapter 7 outlines steps in the screening and selection process, and Chapter 8 discusses a number of guidelines for making the final selection. Both chapters also include situations illustrating some of the causes and consequences of client/consultant mismatches. Building Block Diagram B outlines a number of considerations discussed in this part.

7

Screening and Selection Steps

1. *Identify qualified consultants.*
2. *Initiate screening discussions.*
3. *Focus on people compatibility.*
4. *Request a formal Proposal.*

In this chapter I discuss the steps in undertaking the search for a consultant. I consider ways to identify and screen them, the importance of their compatibility with your organization, and the case for obtaining a formal proposal.

Initiating an effective consulting assignment can be as simple and uninvolved as contacting a known entity, outlining your needs and objectives, asking for his terms, and authorizing him to proceed. However, most situations will benefit from a search for two or more qualified firms or individuals and one or more informal screening sessions with each. Then if it still makes sense to bring in a consultant, request at least two front-runners to submit formal proposals, picking firms or individuals who differ the most in qualifications and approach. This routine helps you test your own perspective of what you are after; and contrasting views and approaches to your situation tighten your definition of your purpose and scope.

Step One: Identify Qualified Consultants

The first step is to identify several of the most highly qualified consultants for your need. As a general rule, it is much more satisfactory if you initiate the search and contacts rather than respond to firms who have solicited you "cold." Except for the obvious leading-name consultants in the industry, you will need to do some careful digging to find the best candidates for you.

Historically Low-Key Promotion by Consultants

Quality management consultants have traditionally been most discreet and low-key in their promotional activites. In most cases, their direct marketing still is confined mainly to professionally toned brochures and newspaper space advertising for recruiting new staff.

The most successful management consultants have historically depended largely upon indirect methods of obtaining new business. They rely on such practices as publishing learned articles, making presentations at professional and industry conferences, participating in or conducting seminars, reprinting speeches, and maintaining and cultivating old-school ties, advantageous city and country club memberships, and well-orchestrated social and recreational contacts.

Word-of-mouth references from satisfied client board members and executives and repeat assignments from the old clients because of outstanding prior performance have perennially been most important in obtaining new business. Cresap, McCormick and Paget, acquired in the early 1980s by Towers, Perrin, Forster & Crosby, Inc. (TPF&C), was founded after World War II by two prewar Booz, Allen & Hamilton partners and a third seasoned consultant, all of whom had been wartime associates in the U.S. departments of the Army and Navy in Washington.

CMP's early years of growth were dominated by continuing assignments from two highly satisfied clients, Westinghouse and American Cyanamid, by referrals through those clients' boards, and by the three partners' wartime contacts. They were also aided by similar networking that capitalized on the consulting reputations and contacts of additional partners who joined them from other consulting firms as they grew.

CMP's business thrived because prospective clients were tapping directly into the experiences of satisfied clients who had been there with them and did not need to mince words about benefits or problems resulting from the assignment. The intangibles and uniqueness that serve to differentiate one consulting project from another make it imperative that you talk with your candidates' other clients as some of the most reliable input for your choice.

Shifts to Consultant-Initiated Marketing

Increasingly, some of the newer consultants have adopted more aggressive business-seeking initiatives, particularly the large accounting firms and other specialists who are putting together impressive teams with new planning and consulting approaches to subject disciplines. Some such approaches include just-in-time manufacturing services, information systems planning, and telecommunications systems development.

These consultants aggressively seek out cold-call prospects, assuming that major companies with significant activities in such areas must need help with problems or growth plans related to technology, the surge of information to be managed, and other new-wave developments.

Identifying Prospective Candidates

In seeking the right firm, consider first any consultants you already may have used. If they seem to fit your new needs, you can take good advantage of their established knowledge of your business, particularly their understanding of how you and your people strategize and manage your operations. They will not need as much of the costly and time-consuming front-end educational process that first-time consultants almost always need in order to learn your territory. Orientation activities normally are priced into the fee structure of the proposal.

If you have not already done so, ask your board members for suggestions. Solicit input from your legal counselors and accounting firm, unless the latter are in management consulting themselves in areas you are seeking. If your CPA is a candidate for your assignment, check out his management consulting performance and qualifications independently before approaching him, to make a more objective assessment.

Other sources of candidate leads include several associations active in management consulting. ACME, the long-established Association of Consulting Management Engineers, and the Institute of Management Consultants are two of the more prominent domestic organizations, and it is of interest that they agreed to merge in 1989. The monthly trade paper, *Consultants News,* publishes a comprehensive directory of consultants, which is updated annually.

The Appendix provides information on some of the associations, publishers, and other sources to which you might turn for potential consultants. These only scratch the surface of the more generalized sources. Virtually every industry has association people and publications that can provide you with additional leads. Also check media that carry recruiting advertising for consulting staffs; these can give you a feel for some of the firms on the move who are aggressively seeking new personnel.

Step Two: Initiate Screening Discussions

The best way to start a tricky consulting proposition is to initiate a lot of talk. Talk the needs over with your own key people. Talk out the problems with several different outside consulting firms or individuals. Talk with their references and with others who may have differing viewpoints about their work. Talk with other CEOs who have experienced similar situations.

In your initial consultant contacts, start in-depth probing of your concerns, needs, and issues with them, getting their input on how they would undertake to help you. Most quality firms will spend this time with you at their own risk, without any fees; it is a regular part of their business development activity. Begin narrowing your choices to the two or three firms who seem closest to understanding your needs, who project the best match of perspectives and approaches with your own situation and perceptions, and who can communicate with you.

In these early discussions, a prospective client often may reorient his thinking significantly about his needs and what he should be trying to accomplish, just as a result of talking with an enlightened third party. He may even decide he doesn't need a consultant after all and instead end up getting very useful insights on how to solve a problem or take advantage of a new opportunity without outside help.

At the very least, these initial screening sessions need to accomplish important information exchange on both sides. One author has expressed the requirement in this way:

> Reaching a mutually beneficial agreement is made difficult by ignorance. Both sides are missing information. The client doesn't usually know enough about a consultant. The consultant isn't brimming with knowledge about the client. That's not a pleasant feeling for either party entering into complex negotiations in which cost is only one determining factor.[1]

One of the safest ways to ascertain what level of expertise your candidate represents is to screen him on your own territory. The following case illustrates the experience of a prospective client. The screening did not progress very far for obvious reasons.

Computrol: Specialist Expertise Desired

"You're asking what twisted pairs are? You're looking at them. By the way, have you had any experience with wideband coaxial cable transmission systems?"

"No."

"Have you done anything in computer-based systems for communicating data and information?"

"No."

"Well then, have you done anything at all in telecommunications?"

"No."

[Pause] "I see."

This lopsided and very superficial technical discussion occurred during a preproposal briefing a CEO was giving a consultant. The founder of Computrol Incorporated, a small high-tech company that designed, manufactured, and installed computer-based monitoring and supervisory control systems, was taking the consultant on a plant tour. Computrol had installed a number of sophisticated telecom-munications-based security systems for nuclear power plants and was working with NASA on high-speed data communications appli-cations. It was also involved in joint ventures with IBM, Lockheed, Perkin-Elmer, and others using Computrol's related technological knowhow.

A referral from a Computrol lawyer, had brought the consultant into the picture. Based on briefing materials the founder had for-warded prior to their first meeting, the consultant had done some homework and preliminary speculative market research. From this briefing and from discussions with his lawyer friend, he surmised that the company might need help in marketing and business planning and in obtaining new financing. He reviewed this homework with the founder at their second meeting.

The Computrol CEO had a seasoned marketing man on his small staff who was well-grounded in his applications. The CEO chose not to proceed with the consultant. The obvious Achilles heel in this case was that the consultant was a neophyte in the company's technologies and, in the opinion of the founder, needed a lot of sub-ject orientation. The founder was not about to invest time and money educating someone before he could become productive either as a consultant or as a board member, which was an option the lawyer had suggested. He very quickly learned what level of start-ing expertise in his business the consultant possessed.

Step Three: Focus on People Compatibility From the Outset

As stressed previously, it is most important that you determine early whether you and your candidates can communicate on the same plane. Discover whether you feel comfortable sharing your corporate secrets and concerns with them. Once you have vali-dated your need to bring in an outsider, your choice of the spe-cific finalists should be based on the expected *people fit* between client and consulting staff. The client/consultant relationship depends more on personal compatibility in consulting than in just about any other outside service a business seeks, virtually as much compatibility as an outstanding marriage. Communications is perhaps the first hurdle to an effective people fit.

The Importance of Translatable Communications

One of your first rules should be, *Make your consultants speak your language*. Often they tend to use "buzzwords" and to think and write in scholarly or school-of-management styles. Such approaches can be quite powerful in helping to clarify your problems and opportunities and reach innovative solutions for you. However, the key word is *translate;* insist that your advisers communicate on the same level your management does. Wherever it is useful to introduce new management concepts, they should do so sparingly, developing and using the necessary bridges for your staff's understanding.

It is fair game for a consultant to use all the conceptual tools and management theories that can help the client. However, they should be kept invisible where they do not fit the situation, as New England Propane's consultants learned the hard way.

New England Propane: Make the Consultant Match Your Lingo

An entrepreneur assumed control of New England Propane, a regional propane gas distributor/dealership that delivered the product in pressure cylinders and tanks from one central base and several branch locations to residential, commercial, and industrial customers throughout New England.

The new owner had no prior experience in this industry and felt the need for an overall audit of the company's management and operations in order to understand better what he had bought. He engaged a consulting firm that had been recommended highly by his legal counsel. The lawyer was on a board of directors the consultant had served effectively.

A partner and a senior consultant met with the entrepreneur to define the desired objectives, scope, and approach to be proposed. At that time, the two consultants were enthusiastically developing a generic analytical package to use in proposing and conducting over-all business audits. They felt that this prospect would be an ideal candidate and guinea pig. So they talked with the prospect about their new package for some proven management precepts, which they had named OOPPS. OOPPS stood for Opportunities/Objectives/Policies/Plans/Strategies, which represented their steps in analysis and the preparation of a basic business plan.

The entrepreneur seemed to be intrigued with OOPPS—at least he nodded his head politely. He gave the consultants the go-ahead to audit his new company, requesting that they document the under-standing with a written proposal.

A description of OOPPS was not written into the proposal; nor was it introduced or explained to the client's management team as the assignment got underway with the traditional orientation and fact-finding exercises. These activities included requests for additional information; preparation of a survey plan; examination of product and sales literature; financial statement review; key management in-terviews; visits to facilities; and demonstrations.

An additional junior consultant was assigned to carry the brunt of the field work, which he commenced following a brief orientation to the business. Upon approval by the client, an outside market re-search firm also was engaged to conduct a phone survey of the com-pany's propane users, prospects, and competitors' customers throughout the client's area of operation. At no time during this study phase or the first two progress reports was the OOPPS package as such presented to management.

For the final chart presentation of findings and recommenda-tions to the client and his staff, however, the consultants recast the report into the OOPPS framework. They embellished it with the most learned management practices verbiage they could construct. Need-less to say, as the presentation unfolded, the client's staff began reg-istering confusion as to its relevance to their operations. Some dozed, some stayed awake only with difficulty.

The partner and the senior consultant, intrigued with their bril-liant conceptual framework and tutorial, had totally misread their sit-uation. They had failed to think through from the client's viewpoint what form their presentation should take or how they could com-municate most appropriately and sell a basically sound set of conclu-sions. They failed to recognize what would constitute down-to-earth, practical action statements this particular management could feel comfortable implementing. They did not see the need to attune their recommendations closely to the management style and vernacular of the propane distributor or his dealers' competitive world. The consultants had given virtually no conscious thought to such questions.

All of this became embarrassingly obvious before the end of the session, and the consultants were not surprised when the client told them to redo their report in a form all of his managers could relate to and understand. They did this, but salvaged the job with only modest client satisfaction because they had not concentrated enough on the grass-roots characteristics of the propane service industry or the tough-minded strategies and tactics required to be competitive in such a commodity business. Thereafter, they used the OOPPS conceptual package only as an invisible guide or internal checklist for testing conclusions and for sanity checks on their recommendations.

You must make certain that your consultant can develop a communication bridge into the same real world your management and your competitors are addressing. A management may need the tutorial to strengthen and sharpen its business practices, but a dialogue at a common level of understanding is essential to acceptance, motivation, and action. In this situation, the client did not focus on the issue at proposal time, and he failed to stay close to what the consultants were developing as the study proceeded.

Step Four: Request a Formal Proposal

The efforts of the first three steps should lead you quickly to the point of asking for at least one or two formal proposals from the best candidates. Several arguments prevail for requesting a formal, written proposal; yet many consultants are engaged on the strength of a verbal understanding of what is to be done. In any but the simplest assignments, misconceptions and misunderstandings can easily come into play with wasteful, if not disastrous, results.

Yogi Berra once said that "an oral contract isn't worth the

paper it's written on!" Printed agreements move the two parties much of the way toward common ground on the purposes and conditions of a project. Informed third parties—trusted board members, your legal counsel, other key executives—then should be asked to examine the draft and critique it for clarity, relevance, meaning of terms that could be interpreted differently by the two parties, and other potential dangers or vague specifications.

Another advantage of the documentation is to be able, when a go-ahead has been given, to communicate the conditions consistently to all persons in your organization who have a need to know and will be expected to participate and cooperate in the endeavor.

The written proposal also makes it much easier to compare the "apples and oranges," which can always be counted on to appear when multiple proposals or bids are sought. In much government work, this problem is reduced by the use of a request for proposal (RFP), but most management consulting proposals in the private sector are not solicited in this fashion.

Still another powerful benefit of the formal proposal effort occurs in the process. You inevitably gain better insight about your needs as you think through your problems more clearly while reviewing the written documents. At times the formal proposals contribute to much clearer insights into your problem and may even give you the confidence and ideas as to how to proceed with their solutions without outside counsel. This clarification seems to be more difficult if the discussion and negotiations have been left on the verbal level.

Consultants hate to make the investment in a proposal they have researched, often with considerable expenditure of staff time, and then have you inform them you have decided to do the work internally. But this is a risk they know they must take, and it is fair game and perfectly ethical behavior for you. Keep in mind the consultant who retires gracefully from such a situation and go back to him when you have another serious need that could clearly benefit from an outsider's participation.

With one or more well-constructed and thoroughly negotiated proposals to choose from, you are ready to proceed with your final deliberations and selection. Part Four contains a number of illustrations from actual practice to give you a better feeling for proposals and their elements. First, however, I have reviewed some additional guidelines for the screening and selection process in Chapter 8.

Note

1. "Taking the Big 8 Into Account," *Information Week* (July 6, 1987), page 32.

8

Guidelines for Your Choice

People Match:

Take advantage of the buyers' market for consulting services with an exhaustive comparative search

The proliferation of alternative consulting services has created a growing buyers' market for those seeking outside help. You have an unprecedented opportunity to be discrimininating in your selection. Consider as many alternatives as you need to be completely comfortable with your choice. Do not favor either the lone consultant or firms of large size and scope per se, and do not equate mere numbers of assigned consultants with a quality result. *Emphasize the direct people fit.*

Your compatibility with and confidence in the relatively few people who will carry the direct workload for your account should basically determine your choice. The growing body of experience and expertise a firm is accumulating in the new approaches certainly is valuable. However, the highly personalized nature of most assignments renders a firm's backup capabilities secondary in value to the services of the qualified team who will become directly and intimately familiar with your situation.

Arrive at your decision through intensive sessions of talking, listening, communicating, and probing. Do all this to ensure that you are finding the consultant with the qualifications and motivations that most match your needs and are compatible with your staff. Also, whenever other factors are relatively equal, opt for a blend of generalist and specialist talent whenever it appears to be fully relevant to your strategic requirements.

Consider each alternative as a temporary implant who will interact well with your personnel. Much as you might approach a trial marriage, assess each candidate for his or her potential fit as a permanent employee, even though you may have no intentions in that direction.

Hindsight is wonderful, but how indeed can you foresee fully the characteristics and capabilities of potential consultants in the screening stage? You cannot, of course, but you can consider a number of problems and guidelines for selection in advance. This chapter presents some of the most important issues.

Consultant-Selection Problems With People-Matching

Chapter 7 stressed how vital it is to have a positive, workable people match between client and consultant, and suggested several of the problems you should be alert to avoid. To summarize the earlier arguments and add to the list, people-matching problems generally seem to follow several patterns or combinations thereof.

- ▲ Your choice of the wrong firm in terms of types of experience and expertise that are directly applicable to your needs.
- ▲ Your choice of a fine firm with a reputation for the requisite experience and expertise, but a lack, or at least current unavailability, of specific project leaders and or staff with such requisites.
- ▲ A mismatch of staffs between you and your team and the consultant for a wide variety of reasons. These might include deficiencies in the consultants' levels of expertise, experience, and sophistication about your business; in their maturity and judgment levels; individual personality conflicts; and tendencies by the consultant to rely on or overemphasize generalizations, concepting, and high levels of abstraction.

▲ Consultants' motivational problems; lack of results orientation; poor sense of urgency about accountability for results.

▲ Deficiencies in the consulting staff's communications skills, verbal and written. Can they think and write clearly? Are they persuasive? Some of this is basic in the individual, and some involves difficulty in adapting to or interpreting findings, conclusions, and recommendations in your language, as witnessed in the New England Propane situation.

▲ Making the assumption that the level of quality you have enjoyed from a consultant will automatically be forthcoming from his "unknown" associates. Consultant One is not Consultant Two, is not Consultant Three, and so on. Although you may have obtained consistently high quality performance from a consultant, you should not assume you will continue to get the same from others in the same firm.

▲ Other inadequacies in consulting skills: in interviewing and eliciting free discussion with individuals and groups; in inviting and protecting confidences; in knowledge of information sources; in logical abilities, defining problems and differentiating between problems and their causes; in distinguishing and focusing on significant information from the mass; in "netting down," in determining and expressing "the big picture," in judgment and perspective.

Some of these potential problems can be identified readily in advance through the preliminary discussions with the consulting principals and by following up with reference checks. It is always a good idea to insist on meeting representative associates who will be assigned beforehand, but this usually is difficult with a successful firm, because their working staffs are likely to be heavily scheduled or busy winding up the previous engagement.

The "expert" connotations of a consultant title or label need careful verification before hiring; much of the *real* human being in the prospective consultant remains hidden until later. *Know the consulting staff beforehand.* When selecting consultants, do not "buy a pig in a poke," and above all, do not buy on "hype."

Do not assume, after successful use of a consultant, that the new (to you) staff he might bring in to work on a following assignment will do as well for you. That old axiom "Let the buyer beware!" fits the choice of consultants, and it is a very personal decision most of the time, as the following situation attests.

City Museum: Hidden Dangers in Using Unknowns

Some years ago the not-for-profit services department of a major consulting firm performed a series of highly satisfactory assignments on organization, managerial processes, and control systems for the board of a major metropolitan museum. Consequently, when some assignments arose outside the not-for-profit department's areas of expertise, the museum board commissioned the consultant's marketing department, which had a fine reputation for serving industrial clients, to undertake them.

The first project involved its monthly subscription magazine. The consultant was to perform subscriber interviews, conduct an editorial review, and recommend strategies for increasing circulation. Studies of the museum's public relations and fund-raising activities were to follow.

Neither the marketing partner in charge nor his working associate had had direct experience with such aspects of a not-for-profit organization, but both individuals hoped to generalize effectively from their experience in industry. The findings and recommendations for the magazine were only modestly helpful, and the work ran well over the upset cost; the consultants absorbed the difference.

Next, the consultant hired a public relations person from industry to join the marketing associate on the public relations and fund-raising assignments. The new hire knew his subjects quite well and was a highly personable and outstanding interviewer. However, when it came time to prepare chart presentations and written reports for the client, the project fell completely apart because the PR man could neither organize his thoughts logically nor write! He was released, and the marketing associate, still a duck out of water in the new areas, struggled through many days and nights to complete the proposal commitments.

When the reports were finally ready for delivery to the museum, the prose was clear, concise, and of generally high level. But the contents were unimaginative and minimal. The museum's board chairman, a seasoned business executive, authorized payment of the upset cost but terminated the marketing consultants, canceling their planned implementation phase. Not surprisingly, their not-for-profit associates were awarded very little additional work from this client.

The marketing consultants had a quality performance record in the for-profit assignments where they had specialized knowledge of the functions and business content; but they started with virtually no understanding of City Museum's magazine business or the subjects of public relations and fund raising. The museum board had assumed erroneously that they naturally would be outstanding, because that was what the museum was accustomed to getting from this consulting firm. The tough lesson for both client and consultant was that each new situation with unknown people needs new communication, screening, and validation.

Consultant-Selection Criteria and Guidelines

If there is a definitive and comprehensive set of guidelines for selecting consultants, it should include nine significant considerations: (1) consulting credentials, (2) compatibility, (3) communications skills, (4) commitment, (5) objectivity, (6) state-of-the-art awareness, (7) availability, (8) motivation, and (9) results orientation. Consider all of them as you conduct face-to-face screenings of consultants for your project.

Consulting Credentials

What relevant experiences, qualifications, and intellectual resources will be brought to bear on your situation with these particular people? Is the firm known for solid, reliable experience, expertise, and performance in your areas of interest? In the management and operational functions? In the subject matter—products, markets, technology, applications? Or in all of these? Has it had experience relevant to your particular type of business? Or if not, do you feel that it could readily adapt?

As you choose from among your few best alternatives, critically evaluate their respective consulting attributes and credentials. Which firm possesses the most solid, relevant expertise and strongest motivations for consulting and for your assignment? Does your candidate already know how to consult? How well? Does he or she understand how to favorably affect the bottom line of the P&L and the stockholder equity item of the balance sheet?

For a relatively straightforward and specialized assignment of limited scope, your best choice could be someone who has just come from industry. In such a situation, your need for expertise in *how* to consult should be considerably less important than fresh, new experience on *what* other outstanding businesses have done to solve your particular type of problem. Broader and more complex projects, however, normally will benefit from a seasoned consultant who is highly skilled in the following six generic arts of the consulting process:

1. Problem definition and solution
2. Fact finding and analysis
3. Listening, questioning, and communications skills
4. Ability to develop imaginative alternatives tempered realistically and pragmatically
5. A results and action orientation
6. Motivation to perform well

If your direct observations, reference checks, and other sleuthing bear out that your candidate has all these skills, including a very strong motivation to produce, then any direct experience he or she has in your industry is an extra advantage and should resolve your decision favorably.

In evaluating and accepting evidence on the foregoing, a practical caution is in order. Credentials lend themselves to crisp and positive presentation in resumes, dossiers, and the curriculum vitae, but with all of these forms it is difficult to read between the lines. The problem is compounded when the con-

sultant assigns new staff midway or late in the project. This potential problem is commonplace, as illustrated by the experience
of an industrial machinery manufacturer who had employed a
consultant to research its sales, distribution, and field service
functions.

The consultant had experienced slippage in his schedule
and brought in an additional team member to help with the report wrap-up stage. This individual was assigned to summarize
and analyze a large number of distributor interview reports and
completed questionnaires. The client inadvertantly discovered
that the new man was on his first assignment in consulting, had
no requisite experience in his business, and had performed none
of the essential field work. Needless to say, the distributor section made virtually no contribution in a key problem area, and
the client was most dissatisfied with that part of the final report.

You can never be certain what level of experience is being
applied to what aspects of your assignment unless you are able
to establish a very close and continuing liaison with the team
working on your project.

Compatibility

Have you met all of the consulting team's key people? Are you
comfortable in face-to-face discussions with the project leader
and staff? Do your people who will work with them feel the
same? Do the consultants reflect basic business views compatible with your own or with the assignment objectives? Are you
completely comfortable and able to communicate freely with the
individual who will be in charge of and accountable for the assignment? And with his principal associates?

Communications Skills

Have the prospective team leader and staff demonstrated their
communications effectiveness to you, both verbally and in proposals or other written communications? Are they speaking in
academic concepts and idealistic management principles? Or
can they communicate to you and your staff in down-to-earth,

meaningful language? When they talk principles of management can they relate them to your industry and your company?

How often have the conversations lagged while you both struggled for a common basis of understanding? Are their responses to your questions specific? Are you completely comfortable in your exchanges with them? In group screening sessions, does the senior consultant monopolize the floor, or is there a healthy interchange with all of the team in attendance? Have you been allowed adequate opportunities for free individual exchange with all of the key staff who would be assigned to your account?

Commitment

What reasonable indications have you that each consulting staff member's allegiances and other obligations will assure a relentless application to the problems at hand? Are the key consulting staff members already coming to grips with the gut issues in your proposition? Are they assimilating the facts that you have presented to them and developing insights about their ramifications?

Objectivity

Do they call a spade a spade? Or, do they seem to give you what they feel you want to hear? Are they likely to provide their own candid assessment of your situation and needs? Will they completely avoid trying to second-guess what they think you want to hear? Do you feel they will call it like it is, particularly in relation to what both your outside marketplace and your own people are saying?

State-of-the-Art Awareness

Is your consultant familiar with industry's changing ground rules and new business approaches?

New Ground Rules

Does your consultant understand the increasingly complex ground rules under which today's and tomorrow's business enterprises must operate? And can he make the connection to your own requirements?

Depending on the nature of your project, he may need to be conversant with such classic issues as environment and ecology, fair employment practices and equal rights, ESOPs, government and legislative regulations and compliance procedures, tax and accounting rulings and changes, and business ethics considerations. If he is not proficient in such areas, can he guide you to those who can be helpful? Discerning questions during the screening can clarify how qualified your candidate is with the compliance and regulatory factors applicable to your assignment.

New Business Approaches

Is your consultant knowledgable about the latest innovations in managerial and leadership concepts, the functions of business, and how they might apply to your situation? About the new global considerations related to your ability to compete in and with the EC? Does your consultant have experience in the formation of joint ventures and other strategic alliances to collapse time in the marshalling of new global capabilities, market bases, and marketing capabilities?

You may already have instituted, or have a serious opportunity to consider, such approaches as just-in-time manufacturing and procurement, concurrent engineering, integrated information systems and telecommunications networking of your operations, expert systems and artificial intelligence for decision making or your R&D programs, new concepts of work design and self-design in your operating functions, or progressive compensation policies and practices that depart from the traditional industry pay structures to favor so-called performance-based systems of compensation.

Where applicable, your consultant should have some understanding of which of these are as yet too new to have been well tested; which have been successfully employed, by whom, and with what results; which are likely to be strongly applicable to your situation. You should not expect to find someone proficient in all such areas, or even any of them, unless your project is targeting in precisely on them. However, your consultant should be able to tell you if you need or should investigate the new approach and should steer you to those who could help you.

Availability

Have you met and checked out to your satisfaction the specific staff individuals who will be assigned to your project? Can you be assured that staff changes during the course of the assignment will be unlikely? Or, if changes should become necessary, does the consultant appear to be backed up with highly qualified substitutes capable of meeting your needs?

Motivation

Do the candidates exhibit a strong motivation toward your problems and your need? Even though you have concluded that you are comfortable with the first seven selection criteria, is the candidate's motivation to perform for you also among his or her strongest factors?

The issue has two dimensions. First, how strongly motivated does he or she seem to be toward your work, and how earnestly and aggressively is he pursuing your account? Second, what particular motivations appear to be driving him the most as a consultant? Beyond what the candidate directly represents to you, your answers to both questions are judgment calls and you will get clues as you reflect upon the other seven criteria. How enthusiastically and conscientiously he performs will depend greatly on what factors have and are motivating your candidate to consult in the first place.

A brief review of some of the principal reasons why people consult can help you, not only with your selection decision, but also with how to mesh and stimulate their efforts with your own people. According to Charles Shultz's Charlie Brown, "Half the world desires to serve in a consulting capacity." Just why do people want to consult rather than manage?

Intellectual Curiosity

Many consultants have insatiable and scholarly curiosity about everything and are idealistic about making the business world more orderly. They derive great satisfaction from successfully tackling and solving large new problems. The plus side of this trait is the energy with which such a consultant can be relied upon to approach his or her assignment and the imagination he can bring to your problems. The down side is your continual need to contain and harness his explosion of ideas and be sure he focuses on the purposes of the assignment.

Flexibility, Independence, and Variety

This common consultant trait is the appeal of continuing variety, change, novelty, and travel; the independence, flexibility, and avoidance of the so-called organization trap by being one's own boss. These kinds of motivations rank with intellectual curiosity as the most likely to describe a career consultant.

Of all the incentives to consult, you can perhaps rely most on the sustained interest of the careerist to pursue your project in a focused and deliberate way. He loves the work and has the interest and capacity to take on unfamiliar assignments. He is most likely to stay with the project to a successful completion, because he would like the ultimate gratification that can only come from solid results and practical implementation. He also wants you to retain him further and/or recommend him highly to your peers.

Training for Career Advancement

Some individuals enter consulting as a fun and challenging way to speed their climb to executive levels. They feel management consulting can help them escalate their experience with the policy and major decision levels of business; thus, they enter consulting with a career objective of someday returning to line work. They are interested in upgrading their salability for higher positions in management than they held previously or than they would command fresh out of school. They may be aiming for a position with your company at the end of an assignment.

There is no inherent negative in using this type of consultant. He will be highly motivated to do outstanding work for you and will be very responsive to your needs. If you have engaged him because of a gap in certain talents or traits on your staff, you get a wonderful opportunity to screen him in depth without having to make a permanent commitment.

Do not be leery of taking on a consultant with this motivation, but do not give him any long-term guarantees. You have a built-in leverage to get him to produce to the utmost, provided he has the experience and expertise you need.

Economic Expediency or Necessity

One of the first instincts of a person who has just been released from a job is to hang out a consulting shingle. The motivation, born of financial necessity, can be either to start a new career in consulting or to use it as a door-opener to other jobs in industry. In such cases, you should be careful to ascertain that the consultant has enough financial staying power to see the commitment through to completion. You risk not only a waste of fees and expenses, but also the time you and your staff spend on the project.

A major concern should be that the neophyte will stay around only long enough to be rehired in industry. If he leaves prematurely, or even after an initial assignment, it means that your investment in his learning of the business is lost. As a general rule, you are unwise to use this type of person unless he has direct and timely know-how to bring to bear directly on your problem. Lacking this, he is not a good bet if he has none of the other positive traits to drive him on your assignment.

Boredom With Retirement

The pool of seasoned, retired executives in all branches of industry will continue to grow. The availability of a competent

individual who wants to become more active again should not be
overlooked as a source of highly qualified consulting help. The
major cautions should include the level of energy and motivation
to tackle a tough problem, and whether the candidate has kept
abreast of the pertinent changes in your industry.

Fitting the Combinations of Motivations Together

Normally, such motivations as the foregoing are not solo
characteristics with an individual consultant, and a team situation can be counted on to have a number of both positive and
negative factors bundled together on your assignment. Their diversity can be a benefit but also can contribute heavily to the
difficult task of choosing the best consulting team from the
people point of view. In the end, the choice is still a judgment
call based on considerations that stem from face-to-face discussions with the candidates.

Results Orientation

Has your best candidate produced superior results for others?
What is his or her evidence of past accomplishments, particularly workable recommendations, an implementation track record, favorable results achieved for other clients? Does he or she
appear to be a realistic thinker? Has your candidate demonstrated an interest in developing answers to your problems not
just comprehension and excellence in the major functions of
your business?

In the broadest sense, your screening of consultants should
seek hard evidence of their success in producing what Mc-
Kinsey & Company says is its main goal, namely "performance
improvement" via recommendations and action steps characterized by realism, feasibility, quality, value, and reach.

When the stakes for your project involve significant change,
a seasoned consultant who can be visionary *and* practical rein-
forces your own confidence in such moves and adds credence in
the eyes of your organization. Then you hope he or she can help
you produce the results you need and the benefits you have
sought.

Whether the consultant you are seeking or considering is a major firm with several hundred professionals or is an independent, free-lance loner with no supporting staff, the nine critical selection factors apply. As witnessed in the City Museum situation, these people questions are as germane to follow-on assignments you give your consultant as they are to the first screening that led you to select him. The need continues for a sound matchup with your staff at all levels of contact.

PART FOUR

Structuring a Realistic Assignment

The Proposal is the first important step in structuring a realistic and controllable assignment. It can be considered a "friendly game of entrapment by the client."

Determining the need and timing for outside help and searching for and screening consultants to match them with your organization are usually difficult to bring into focus until you start the discipline of structuring the assignment. The first step and the catalyst or vehicle for providing such discipline is a well-structured project *proposal* and the various controls and *modus operandi* derived from it.

In his impressive wisdom, Rudyard Kipling set forth the embryo of such structuring with his Six Journeymen: What? When? Where? Why? How? and Who? Today's thousands of proposal types, in their almost infinite variety, must cope in one way or another with these generic questions if they are to provide an effective structuring, discipline and direction for both client and consultant.

You may find it useful to influence and specify the structuring of your consultant's proposal as a friendly, constructive game of entrapment. Use the discussions and development of alternative proposals as the final aid to your selection decision. Make certain the winning consultant has crafted a tight proposal designed to produce the perspective, focus, and action plans your best thinking indicates you will need in order to achieve substantive value and cost benefits from the assignment.

The scope of this book is concerned broadly with the kinds of advice and counsel employed by industry and other organizations in both the for-profit and not-for-profit sectors. Two principal types of proposals are applicable to these kinds of organizations: the proposal or bid that responds to a Request for Proposal (RFP) and the free form proposal.

The RFP response is a must form for consultants in many branches of government, as well as other not-for-profit organizations, and in certain aspects of industry. A major benefit to the client of the RFP approach is that it forces competing consultants to respond more uniformly to the client's defined needs, and it ensures that all proposals submitted will at least cover the items specified in the RFP. A number of excellent treatises offer in-depth instructions on how to use this type successfully, and seminars are held on the subject. The approach is not treated in this book, but the Bibliography contains references to sources for guidance in working with RFPs.

The free form proposal has been typical of the management consultant approaches for many years, and the forms it takes are almost as varied as the types of consulting practitioners. As with Kipling's Journeymen, however, a distinct pattern of the essential elements has evolved. Seeking proposals in free form has the advantage of giving the client a wider range of perspectives on his problem or opportunity and how to approach it. This is particularly helpful where his issues and problems are a bit unclear or where he is veering into unfamiliar marketplaces or other territory new to his company's experience. In its most classic style, the free form management consulting proposal deals with Objectives, Scope, Approach, Staffing (including Qualifications and References), and Time and Costs.

Part Four presents guidance in structuring a realistic assignment for carrying out the aims of your consulting venture. The five chapters err on the conservative side and present a thoroughgoing set of checklists and considerations for the first-time client. They are organized around the basic elements that structure a realistic assignment. Principles, guidelines, and case illustrations are used to amplify the presentation. An outline of the points emphasized in Part Four is presented in Building Block Diagram C.

Chapter 9 provides an overview of all of the elements, and the

Building Block Diagram C.   Summary factors: structuring a realistic assignment.

Implement Plans

Control Project

Achieve Perspective and Focus

Structure Assignment

Proposal Elements

Project Objectives:

- ▲ Effort stretching aims.
- ▲ Financially feasible.
- ▲ Friendly game of entrapment.

Scope:

- ▲ Focused, unambiguous limits.
- ▲ Monitor scope enlargement.

Approach:

- ▲ Survey plan and scenarios.
- ▲ Make reconnaissance studies.
- ▲ Limit the initial orientation.
- ▲ Make periodic progress checks.

Staffing, Time, and Costs:

- ▲ Qualifications and compatibility.
- ▲ Projected costs and benefits.

Match People

Determine Need and Timing

next four chapters deal with a proposal's Objectives; Scope of Study; Approach to its conduct; and Staffing, Time, and Cost considerations.

While Part Four consists primarily of guidelines and examples of a proposal's content and its elements, each chapter's overview is to address the challenges to an effective project. Chapter 10 augments the material of Part Two, which concerns the first challenge, setting clear and challenging purposes with sound timing. Chapters 11 and 12 are concerned with the ramifications of and solutions for challenge 3, defining the project's scope accurately and challenge 4, employing workable project approaches. Chapter 13 concerns staffing, time, and cost issues.

Two more key challenges are stressed in Part Four:

CHALLENGE THREE: DEFINE PROJECT SCOPE ACCURATELY

CHALLENGE FOUR: EMPLOY WORKABLE PROJECT APPROACHES

9

Elements of the Proposal

Kipling's Journeymen	Proposal Elements
Why?	Objectives
What?	Scope
How? When? Where?	Approach
Who?	Staffing qualifications
Client's Journeyman	
How Much?	Time and costs

If the people fit is "right," *if* the client knows exactly what he wants accomplished, and *if* a truly objective and independent consultant is in accord, a proposal of five or six pages, a single page, or a handshake can be effective to start an assignment on the right note. Such iffy conditions are extremely rare, however. Usually a client has at least a bit of confusion about his future and how he should proceed or he would not be considering outside help. Experience has proven the value of some degree of discipline to start an assignment.

The Roles of the Proposal

The role of the formal proposal can be of prime importance for all but the simplest of assignments. As a new client-to-be, you probably will find that rarely do any two consultants take identical tacks for addressing the problems you have outlined to them. Also, the potential variations in consulting purposes can be so great that, before commitments are made, extraordinary care is required to specify what is to be accomplished and what you, the client, expect.

A Game of Entrapment

From the client's viewpoint, the proposal stage is a game of entrapment, and you should insist on a formal proposal that sets forth a minimum declaration of and commitment to the assignment.

The greatest assurance for accomplishing entrapment centers on the preparation and acceptance of a written proposal, jointly hammered out and negotiated between the client and the consultant. In a complex situation, it is helpful to repeat this process with at least two competing firms before settling on the best one for your situation. It is a very formative process of negotiations in which you will gain insight for your project with each consultant "encounter."

An Aid to Screening

Working with several candidate consultants to extract proposals from them is a material aid to screening. It provides a growing awareness of which applicants best understand what you are seeking in outside help. Normally, reputable management consultants undertake such proposals without charge to you as a regular business-development or promotional cost of doing business. They are willing and ready to invest a reasonable amount of their own time and attention in pursuing you as a client.

Once you have obtained at least two drafts that feed back to you the consultants' understanding of the objectives and scope of your intended project, you begin to have a solid basis for making a choice, or deciding whether, in fact, you really want to go for outside counsel. This is the overwhelming argument for requesting a written proposal, no matter how brief it might be.

Negotiations: The Heart of a Realistic Proposal

The name of the proposal negotiating game is to interact with each consultant candidate on an iterative basis until both parties have the same clear understanding of the client's objectives for the project and how the consultant plans to proceed to meet them. Often a common perception of what is to be done can be reached through discussions and a handshake. However, with a first-time situation or a particularly tricky and complex problem, it is best to commit everything to paper. Even then, you cannot always be certain you have a meeting of the minds.

Essential Elements of the Proposal

Whether written or oral, the understanding reached between client and consultant should include at least the following six key elements:

1. *Objectives*. What is to be accomplished? With what basic timing and sequence?
2. *Scope*. What subjects, aspects of the business, and client organizational units are to be covered and what excluded?
3. *Approach*. How is the work to be undertaken? In what steps or stages? What client involvement will there be? What principal liaisons between client and consultant?
4. *Staffing and availability.* Whom will the consultant assign? Who will be in charge? When can the work be initiated?
5. *Qualifications and references.* What qualifies the consultant and staff to perform the assignment? What references can attest to the caliber of work expected?
6. *Time and costs.* How much actual working time will be

needed? Over what elapsed time period? At what cost? What provisions exist for changes in scope and cost during the course of the study?

Requiring one or more of the candidates for the assignment to commit all of the foregoing to a written proposal could be ponderous. Nevertheless, it is critical to establish a clear agreement on the six aspects. A tight, well-negotiated proposal can cover the essentials adequately in just a few pages if preceded by open and lively negotiations and effective communication.

It is useful to examine the elements of a proposal that was successful in securing a first assignment for a new client, and which formed the basis for a most satisfactory result for that client. As a guide to the would-be client, an abstract of the contents is presented here. Chapters 10 through 13 refer in greater detail to each element and to the key issues and questions you should consider in your negotiations.

Abstract of Proposal for Ultronic Systems Corporation

Ultronic was one of the early leaders in providing real-time stock market quotations and related financial information to stockbrokers and others in the investment community. Such information was transmitted over private telephone lines to computer terminals leased to the customers.

In the early 1970s, the company's first-generation brokerage terminal, the Stockmaster, was rendered technologically obsolete by a new system Ultronic developed for its primary markets. Since the first version still was not physically obsolete, Ultronic sought to identify secondary markets for the old product being retired whose applications would not require the advancements and sophistication of the new models. Competing proposals were solicited from consultants, and the winning bidder covered the subject matter outlined and paraphrased below.

Objectives

1. Define any attractive new secondary markets for the Stockmaster, and recommend product features, pricing, and marketing programs.

2. Determine the best way to set up a New Venture for each new market segment or business segment that appears viable.
3. Recommend whether Ultronic should proceed or instead abandon the old terminals as sunk costs.

Scope

For each potentially viable secondary market segment, determine:

1. New applications for the Stockmaster
2. Product features and services
3. Sales and marketing methods
4. Organization of the venture
5. Stockmaster business plan

Approach

Sequence of steps to be taken will emphasize all pertinent Ultronic knowledge prior to undertaking field marketing explorations.

1. Develop preliminary Business Plan outlines, using all appropriate Ultronic staff inputs to test viability and set up parameters for the later field investigations.
2. Review preliminary Business Plan and determine next study steps.
3. Conduct initial field market research.
4. Give progress report on initial field interviews.
5. As required, conduct and report on additional field interviews.
6. Develop alternative Business Plans and Recommendations.
7. Report on final Recommendations and Action Steps

Time and Costs

1. Completion of Scope and Approach as outlined is estimated to require twelve to sixteen elapsed weeks.
2. Consultant, working alone, would commit average of 60 percent of his time on this study.

3. Total professional fees would range from $_____,
   billing only for actual time expended, to a maximum of $_____, not to be exceeded.
4. Actual out-of-pocket expenses for travel and living
   away from home base would be billed in addition.
   Fees and expenses would be billed monthly.
5. If client terminates project early for any reason,
   only the actual time and expenses to that date
   would be billed.

Qualifications

(A resume was attached presenting relevant background
and experience in strategic planning, marketing research,
sales organization, and new-venture development, along
with appropriate references to other clients.)

The foregoing example is only one of many appropriate
illustrations of the specific form and content of a suitable proposal. The variations would far exceed even the range of alternative consulting projects suggested earlier in Figure 6, the
needs checklist. Nevertheless, the elements covered in the Ultronic proposal are generic to virtually any situation. You should
make certain your consultant addresses all of them in one form
or another in order to assure a soundly structured project.

Since the proposal will set the game plan for your project,
insist that its objectives call for more than conservative, realistic
results; press for effort-stretching, visionary goals that are tough
but achievable. The winning proposal's scope should sharply define and limit the "playing field." You should guard against an
impractical or unachievable approach and survey plan, in both
study methods and timing. Where you and your consultant have
major uncertainties about the scope and approach, specify that
a limited reconnaissance study be the initial project phase.

You should always retain flexibility and be alert to adjust the
proposal terms as the project's findings unfold. Do not put your
consultant into a straitjacket; that can be counterproductive.
Just construct a flexible trap with pressure to perform but not
frantic pressure.

10

Proposal Elements: Realistic Objectives

To dream the impossible dream, . . .
To reach the unreachable star.

Lyrics of "The Impossible Dream"
by Joe Darion, as they appear in *Man of La Mancha*

Shooting for the stars is not the monopoly of a Don Quixote or his creator, Cervantes. Consultants and unseasoned clients do well with the conception of far-reaching or blue-sky consulting objectives and then remain hopeful that the results will be truly outstanding. The trick is to set effort-stretching Objectives for the consulting assignment, without straining them to an unrealistic level.

President Kennedy could direct the initiation of a bold program to reach the moon; President Wilson could not have done so, because the technologies were nowhere in sight. Somewhere between these extremes is the realistic range for a new set of effort-stretching goals and strategic concepts. You should expect your consultant to assist you materially in clarifying that range. A former IBM associate and subsequent client, Tom Lawson, charged, "What I want is a tough but achievable plan."

Proposal Objectives: Great, but Not Too Great, Expectations

Clients and would-be clients consider consultants because they believe the outside advisor can do more than their staff or can perform other services not readily accomplished internally.

Some consultants have an affinity for framing lofty, effort-stretching, sometimes unachievable objectives for a study. They are optimists at heart and sometimes purists as well. They can take your most well-grounded purposes and translate them into flawless, hard-to-challenge conceptual aims. The "we can do anything" goal is what many of us dream we would like to make happen.

Some even argue, "What is so bad about an extraordinarily broad reach? A project is, in a sense, a low-risk dry run to serve as a learning experience before the full exposure of a major new commitment needs to be risked." Such aggressiveness is admirable in the right situation but also can waste management time and money and create problems for the client.

Common Problems With a Proposal's Objectives

The aims of a project may not always be realistic and consistent with what the client desires to accomplish and when. Several of the most significant and frequent problems and their causes follow.

Perceptions of the need can differ. The client comes into the negotiations thinking he knows what he wants. The consultant thinks he hears the client's meanings and frames his proposal objectives accordingly. However, his perception of what the client has been saying is off the target. In the preproposal discussions the client had perceived what he desired from the words the consultant was using. Often this is a matter of the two parties engaging in polite head nodding without focusing sharply on the language of the proposal or really listening well to each other. This chronic communication problem—missing real cues because of polite head nodding—exists in all walks of life.

A serious perception problem occurred in the situation of

Info/Universe, as detailed in Chapter 6, when the client wanted only "ripe" acquisition prospects, not an overhaul of his strategies.

The focus may be on the wrong problem. The project may be set up to chase symptoms of problems, not their causes or may be aiming at the wrong problems entirely. The owner of VanityWare, discussed in Chapter 5, faced this classic situation when he was focusing more on technical and production-system problems and solutions than on issues of achieving better-balanced general management, tougher-minded factory supervision, and more resourceful order scheduling.

It is important that the objectives of a proposal provide sufficient flexibility to allow for the discovery and treatment of hidden or unforeseen problems and their causes and solutions. Successful consulting practices have been established that specialize primarily in problem determination, and Chapter 15 deals in some depth with this art.

Strong natural disadvantages can pose a hurdle. The project objectives may conflict with strong natural disadvantages in the client's situation. Emotional and subjective considerations frequently lead people to pursue ventures that have two strikes against them from the outset.

A case in point is an entrepreneur who wanted consulting help and capital to introduce to the market a new extra-long-lasting lubricating oil for automotive and other internal combustion engines. He was hoping to emulate the success of the Mobil Corporation with its Mobil One. The entrepreneur had an associate with a presumably better formula, but little else; and they expected to buck the vast resources of a major integrated oil company. The prospective client was persuaded not to proceed with the project because of its obvious barriers to success. Several additional cases of seeking *natural* strategic advantages against heavy odds are presented in Chapter 16.

Objectives may be overly ambitious and premature. It is easy for client and consultant to be swept along by overly optimistic expectations for a burgeoning new market opportunity. Some endeavors are simply unrealistic or are overhyped about how quickly a new market can be developed for entirely new applications. For example, numerous organizations and their advisors have become enamored of the home electronic information business because of the apparently huge potential market to take advantage of "the PC in every home." This business, which has consumed substantial consulting time and effort over twenty or more years, has yet to become an established and viable major industry. It is reviewed in some depth in Chapter 14 as a prime example of unrealistic and unduly optimistic overconceptualizing.

Objectives may be too idealistic, conceptual, and overreaching. The impossible-dream syndrome predestines many studies of new business concepts to failure and blue-sky proposals to rejection. A client who headed a private foundation had been backing some highly successful R & D programs with laser technology, one a technique for removing red-wine birthmarks and another for burning out malignant tumors, both without having to resort to surgery. The research being sponsored by the foundation also had several significant classified laser-based projects for the military.

The client wanted to obtain funds to substantially escalate and diversify the foundation's programs, so he solicited a proposal for a broad-based strategic market study of "all" conceivable new applications. The proposal was comprehensive and wide-sweeping in its aims and scope, covering the entire known universe of established and experimental applications, as well as a number still in the nebulous idea, or science fiction, stage. It scared off the foundation board, who would not support a go-ahead on any scale. On hindsight, a few of the more commercially feasible applications should have been targeted for initial study by the client and his consultant with a modest reconnaissance effort as a first step.

High promises may be a proposal-selling technique. As suggested at the outset of this chapter, a consultant may construct an impossible objective in order to make his proposal stand out clearly above all others. His motivation may stem from wishful thinking and a genuine feeling he can accomplish the impossible. On the other hand, he may never consider he has a chance of delivering fully but feels that an extravagant promise can land the job and that he then will somehow be able to make enough of an accounting to satisfy the client.

The careful client need not be reminded that there truly are no miracles for hire. A too-good-to-be-true promise is virtually certain to lead to disappointment and wasted management time and effort.

An "old boy" relationship may be too unfocused. There is much to favor engaging as a consultant a close personal acquaintance, a long-standing associate, or a consultant who has performed many assignments for the client and is quite familiar with his managerial style. Too often in such instances, however, not enough attention is given to clarifying the specific project objectives or going beyond a verbal commitment to proceed. This situation may be suitable for general counseling or a retainerlike relationship with the CEO. However, it often falls short of the structure and discipline needed for a complex proposition that depends on frequent and significant involvement of the client's staff.

You should also be alert to a few additional problems that can arise in framing a realistic proposal.

- ▲ A proposal that does not stretch far enough
- ▲ A "me too" effort aimed at little more than copying a successful competitor's strategies
- ▲ A misfit with the company's basic purpose, mission, or strengths
- ▲ An intended purpose that is impossible to perform within the apparent market window of opportunity or within a client's own internal time constraints
- ▲ A hidden agenda with potential exposure to drastically negative consequences
- ▲ An unsolicited proposal and objective the client didn't realize he needed to pursue

Guidelines for a Proposal's Objectives

So much for the problems that can occur with a proposal's objectives. What should you be striving for? The short answer is: avoid the foregoing, and you'll know when it feels right. Specifically, there are several broad, commonsense guidelines that can be useful for assessing competing consultants and their proposals and for directing their efforts.

Insist on believable objectives. The study purposes should be understandable and credible, not just to you and your consultant but also to all in your organization who will be involved. Are the purposes in fact what you are asking for, as adjusted by any changes the consultants have convinced you should be made? Do you understand and agree with such changes? Do the objectives contain any ambiguities or unfamiliar concepts? Are they credible and meaningful to your key staff and/or your Board? Is the logic of the project's objectives clear, understandable, and realistic to all concerned?

Seek results-oriented purposes. First and foremost, the purposes should be consistent with the needs of your customers and your competitive marketplace. They should be aimed at producing results that are fully consistent with your corporate mission, Board directives, charter, and strategic directions, unless the study purpose is intended to refine, challenge, or change such directions.

Ascertain that financial implications could be met. The purposes need to be consistent with the realities of your financial performance, objectives, and resources. Assuming the project's basic objectives would be accomplished, could the resulting recommendations be funded? Can you reasonably expect to meet your company's hoped-for financial performance criteria over the planning period?

Resolve conflicting views in advance. Have all basic conflicts in definition of the project's objectives been resolved? Have all significant differences in purpose statements by competing consultants been clarified and rationalized in relation to what you want to accomplish with the project? Is your finalist candidate in accord with you and has he so adapted his purpose statements?

Assure that the needed scope and approach will work. As a key test of the reasonableness of your project objectives, you need to be comfortable that the scope and approach required to accomplish such purposes are feasible. You need assurance that knowledgeable staffing is available to work the approach and that the essential information sources are likely to cooperate.

Avoid or minimize unfavorable people impacts. All potential people impacts, including those on your own staff, your customers, your suppliers and middlemen, your shareholders, and the financial community must be evaluated. The objectives and the approach needed to accomplish them must be assessed carefully for their possible adverse impacts, and any such risks that must be taken rationalized to the fullest extent possible.

Representative Consulting Objectives

These illustrations suggest some of the ways a well-constructed set of objectives can serve the client.

Ultronic: New Markets for Old Products

The Ultronic study outlined in Chapter 9 was seeking to evaluate a number of individual and institutional investor markets that the company had not been serving as possible secondary markets for its obsoleted stock quotation terminal. The objectives, stated in full below, gave the consultant a relatively broad initial charter, because the client wanted to obtain and compare an unbiased outsider's view of the most attractive new markets as a check and balance against the opinions his own staff had been voicing.

Objectives

The objectives of the proposed assignment would be threefold:

1. Define the new markets for Ultronic's prospective Stockmaster venture; recommend product features, services, and pricing to be offered; and develop suggested sales, distribution, marketing and service methods for the new markets. (The defined scope was to include individual investors, banks, industrial concerns, insurance companies, tax-free institutions, and other categories yet to be determined.)

2. Determine the most appropriate way or ways to set up the organization. For each such approach, develop a

Business Plan for establishing the venture as a profitable, growing business.

3. Recommend whether Ultronic should undertake the new venture. If the recommendation is favorable, present a suggested plan of action.

These objectives could have been a license to survey many new markets for weeks and months, but the client stipulated an early staff review with the consultant. At that time the study was narrowed to just three market segments: commodities, bank and insurance trust departments, and so-called affluent individual investors. These represented the consensus of consultant and Ultronic staff as to the prime candidate markets to emphasize in depth. Thus, the client had started with a broad perspective to cover all possibilities and then quickly focused it onto the most appropriate alternatives.

Ideal Toy: A Marketing and Distribution Audit

In this situation, the client modified and scaled down an overly ambitious survey objective based on the consultants' early field survey findings.

Purpose

In general, the study will seek to determine how well prepared Ideal is today to meet its future challenges in comparison with other leading companies in the toy industry. It will also make comparative evaluations of the marketing concepts and methods used by selected, consumer-oriented companies in other industries, to determine their applicability for Ideal.

The specific purposes of these evaluations would be:

1. Refine Ideal's marketing organization and planning, advertising, promotion, sales programs, and management practices; and define what the future business should be. Recommendations in these areas would be aimed at helping the company to:

▲ Make near-term improvements in the distribution of its products relative to its major competitors.

▲ Continuously identify and act upon new opportunities and new definitions of Ideal's business as changes occur in markets and the industry over the long term.

▲ Attract, motivate, develop, and retain the caliber of marketing executives essential for achieving Ideal's growth potentials.

2. Introduce innovations in the Company's advertising, marketing, and distribution activities (with particular attention to the applicability of successful advertising, marketing, merchandising and distribution practices in packaged-goods industries such as toiletries and cosmetics, foods, drug products, and other mass-market lines)

As suggested by the above statement, the client was initially interested in emulating the best practices of other successful consumer-products companies and the other leading toy makers, particularly Mattel. However, the consultant's early efforts soon proved the statement of the audit's purposes to be far too broad and academic for the compelling needs of the client. The early field work revealed important policy issues in dealing with Ideal's retailers and wholesalers, personnel and managerial problems with the company's salesforce, and a compelling need for better-balanced product lines.

The latter issue, actually outside the original purposes and scope of the study, loomed particularly large in the trade, who considered that Ideal was emphasizing low-margin, TV promotional toys far too much. They hoped the company would place much more emphasis on developing staple product lines that could continue to sell without heavy promotional expense, and thus yield larger margins for all parties.

The client adjusted the study to the narrower purposes, and the consultants completed the assignment and performed additional follow-on work for Ideal over a number of years.

Universal Metal Works: A Complex Industrial Market Study

Market research on industrial products can be much more unruly than consumer-product market research. The latter can utilize sophisticated sampling, opinion-gathering, and market measurement techniques, and has become the forte of the focus-group consultants. The CEO of Universal Metal Works, a subsidiary of a larger company, commissioned a consultant to undertake a multimarket study and was successful in pulling off an unintentional entrapment with a simple and straightforward survey objective.

Objectives of the Survey

The major objectives of the proposed marketing survey would be twofold:

1. To identify, define, and measure the markets for the products and services of Universal Metal Works. (As you requested, this would exclude power press products.)
2. To develop a comprehensive market information file with prospect lists and establish an ongoing market research procedure for Universal to use. This procedure would assist you to:
   - Develop short-term (two- to three-year) marketing strategies and programs to enhance your position in your current business.
   - Evaluate the long-term soundness of the business for Universal and identify new directions from the present business base.

Universal was a versatile fabricator of a wide range of metal parts sold to original equipment manufacturers (OEMs) in many industries. These stamped and bent products included metal eyelets, bent tubing, bulbs, and unique wire forms for inclusion in products of such industries as automotive, instruments, plumbing and heating, air conditioning, appliance, hardware, and electrical equipment manufacturers.

Virtually no quantitative industry data existed on shipments, market forecasts, or applications. Ultimately, the consultants identified and quantified several hundred potential products and applications in over two dozen industries, with aggregate unit forecasts reaching tens of billions of small parts per year.

The consultants kept to the letter of their commitment, delivering market estimates, which they named a Speculative Forecast, to emphasize the absence of any prior market data. They also provided the client with a market prospecting workbook on the twenty principal OEM end-markets, containing the unit data, comprehensive prospect lists, and diagrams of end products showing some of the key applications that had been discovered during the course of the study.

The client acknowledged an outstanding and resourceful project but did not accede to the consultant's request that he share in their rather significant overrun beyond the maximum fee to which they had committed. The consultants hoped for additional work from the parent corporation, which unfortunately did not materialize but they did gain a learning experience in complex industrial market studies. The client received extra value from the entrapment, which benefitted Universal in its ensuing sales and marketing programs.

The Objectives of the Proposal set the basic parameters for its Scope. Definition of the study scope, considered in Chapter 11, helps test the soundness of the intended objectives.

11

Proposal Elements: Scope of Study

Objectives promise the future!
Scope limits it.

Scope: What Is to Be Studied; What Is to Be Left Out?

This section of the proposal tests the consultant's understanding of what aspects of your business you are expecting him to cover and what you do not want him to spend time studying. It may be particularly critical to specify certain exclusions that represent areas or issues the consultant might naturally endeavor to cover in his efforts to give you a broad, inclusive perspective. A tight scope definition reduces this risk and helps you to meet your time and cost targets.

The Focusing Role of Scope Definition

The proposal's Objectives promise the future; the Scope of the study places limits and parameters on that future. It is the role of scope definition to build boundaries for the project when client and consultant are thinking too expansively and to extend the boundaries when their perspective is unduly narrow. The outset of the study is the best time for such focusing, but adjustments should be made at any time during its progress when so indicated by the project work.

As the field findings for the Ideal Toy audit began to clarify, both the client and consultant found it constructive to shrink some parts of the original planned scope of study and expand or add to others. The planned comparative analyses of other consumer products companies' practices were virtually eliminated, and much heavier attention was given to recommendations for Ideal salesforce management and control procedures. Also, the consultants developed findings and recommendations for product line strategies and policies outside the original scope because of the compelling messages they were getting from the trade.

Except when you have given your consultant *carte blanche* to evaluate and make recommendations for your entire business, you need to take particular care to provide clear limits to the project. By so doing, the scope definition of the proposal provides a test and a check and balance on your consultant's understanding and interpretation of the objectives.

You also should be careful that your candidate, in his effort to submit a winning proposal, has not been unrealistically optimistic about what he can cover and accomplish. You are taking on the study to solve a problem or define an opportunity, not drive the hardest financial bargain you can extract.

Dangers of Loose and Overly Ambiguous Scope Definition

Defining an ambiguous scope of study leads to time wasted by both consultant's and client's staffs and can result in missed schedules, closing market windows, and failure to produce meaningful, workable results. Defining too ambitious a scope or allowing the consultant to get carried away with optimism about what realistically can be done within the client's budget and timeframe wastes money and time.

Often, this danger is the fault of an eager senior consultant, anxious to win the job by making a substantial promise of performance. Or, it might result from a client's unwitting pressure to get the most for his investment. Either way, it translates into excess fees and expenses to be absorbed by either client or consultant, or to be shared, depending on the terms of the proposal.

It is often difficult to estimate the ultimate scope required for market research surveys and strategic planning studies of new or emerging product/market opportunities. In these and other cases where the exposure of an open end is high, a preliminary reconnaissance study with precisely defined time limits is a wise initial move. This study can provide definitive findings for sharper scope definition, with the provision built into the proposal to renegotiate at the conclusion of the reconnaissance stage. This technique is discussed later in this chapter and also in Chapter 12. (See the Moderne Personal Care Products proposal in Chapter 12.)

Problems of Narrow Scope Definition

Quite often, scope has been too narrowly defined, and the full scope needed to accomplish the project purposes was not anticipated at the outset. It may only become apparent as the findings begin to develop, resulting in incomplete analyses, late reports, and cost overruns. You need to make certain you are not placing unrealistic demands on your consultant in your efforts to meet your budgetary and timing constraints.

Certain types of assignments tend to be more vulnerable than others to unduly narrow scope definition and consequently, too tight time allotments for the investigation. Among the most likely of such situations are the following:

- Situations where top management has not kept in very close touch with the needs of customers in its marketplace and the consultants are not intimately familiar with the particular industry concerned.
- Incomplete or inaccurate starter definitions of problems and their causes. A case in point was the VanityWare project reviewed in Chapter 5, which was initially envisioned

as mainly a technical and plant production system problem.

▲ Surveys of embryonic markets and technologies, where relatively few users are widely scattered geographically and little useful secondary information exists in the trade press.

▲ Assignments that depend heavily on the inputs and co-operation of the client's line executives who are under severe day-to-day pressures of their regular responsibilities.

▲ Projects that depend on coordination of inputs and agreements with parties outside the control of the client organization for success.

Adjusting the Proposal for Scope Enlargement

When either of you has initiated a definable, justifiable, and agreed-upon scope enlargement during the course of a study, it is only fair that you adjust the fees and expenses accordingly. Gross errors on the low side in the consultant's estimate of his survey work are another matter, and you have a right to hold him to his original commitment. Or, a scope enlargement may just "slip in" by mutual default through your insistence and his desire to please. In such cases, you probably should propose sharing the overage provided he is delivering you a high quality result. Both parties need to stay alert to major needed scope changes and negotiate new terms at the instant of agreement or recognition of the work enlargement.

Reconnaissance Stage to Reduce Scope Uncertainty

Any uncertainties about the desired scope for a project can run several companion risks. The scope might be based on perspectives that are too narrow or too ambitious, or you may not have focused on the critical aspects or dimensions of a problem. Erroneous time and timing estimates can result from either or both of these deficiencies. One of the most effective and efficient ways to reduce or eliminate such exposures is to start the project with a brief reconnaissance stage or pilot study.

The concept is not unlike a military scouting foray over unfamiliar combat terrain. A modest initial effort samples the various types of information sources and other inputs that have been envisioned initially for the full study. You and your consultant then can more readily determine what aspects to include, what to exclude, and how to balance the effort on each essential aspect. As a result, you are in a more informed position to readjust the scope of the proposal accordingly.

More often than not you will be able to reduce a project's time and costs. As in the case of Ultronic's project for its Stockmaster, you might learn that you can concentrate on considerably fewer market segments than originally contemplated.

The foregoing discussion has emphasized the importance of planning a realistic scope and the desirability of avoiding both narrowness and overoptimism. Overoptimism is perhaps the most disappointing to the client, but it seldom pays either party to "seek the moon," as the following situation suggests. This case is particularly useful, since it gives a seldom-glimpsed view inside a consultant's hallowed walls for a greater appreciation of the invisible things that can go wrong and that bear closer watching by the trusting client.

Centurian Steel: Same Scope in Half the Time

A managing partner took on a series of marketing research, organization, and management studies for Centurian Steel, a diversified manufacturer of heavy construction and industrial equipment, with the first key phase being a multimarket study. The survey scope involved diversified markets for products and services in highway construction and paving, chemical process industries, steel foundries, milling machine manufacturers, fabricated pipe, and chemical plant design.

A senior marketing associate was assigned to draft the proposal for the market study phase. Based on the staff available and his own vacation plans, he estimated nine elapsed months to complete all markets represented by the product scope. The senior partner ruled this timing unacceptable; he wanted completed findings in time for a national sales meeting the Centurian CEO had already scheduled for six months hence. Thus, he committed to the full original scope of study and staffing but with a due date in five months.

After warning that the timing was far too tight for the promised scope, the marketing senior and his team proceeded in earnest. Within four months they had made good progress, but still had three-plus months of additional field and analysis work ahead. The senior partner, who had not kept in close touch with the team's progress, was furious on learning that the final report would not be ready for the client's sales meeting. Nevertheless, his project leader left for his summer vacation as scheduled. Needless to say, the Centurian CEO was extremely disappointed that the work was not ready, and word got back to the senior consultant that his good client had aired his dissatisfaction at his downtown club. This club had been an excellent prior source of new prospects through the years. After the originally proposed studies were completed, no more client assignments were forthcoming.

This ended as a most embarrassing situation on both sides. It had many of the faults of a careless project scope definition: a senior partner anxious to meet a good client's needs; a CEO who had never been warned that his own time requirements could not be met; and a supervising consultant who failed to oppose his boss strongly enough about what he knew from the start was unrealistic in terms of staffing conditions and the proposal's commitments.

This situation is common in consulting, but is normally hidden from you, the client, who has every right to trust a reputable consultant to deliver as promised. Unfortunately, you still must do everything possible at the outset to assure yourself that the proposal is realistic and that there is a full meeting of the minds on the project's stipulations.

Representative Scope Definitions

Definitions of a survey's scope should not only establish parameters and boundaries but also indicate the content and any exclusions that need clarification. The survey content may touch upon products, markets, application categories, competition, business policies, timing parameters, the client's functions, managerial processes, economics and financials, or any other dimensions of the business that are critical to the particular project. A few of the myriad variations in scope definition for different types of projects are illustrative.

Ideal Toy: A Marketing and Distribution Audit

Chapter 10 presented the original objectives of a marketing audit for the Ideal Toy Corporation and discussed the ways in which they were changed based on the consultant's initial field findings. The target scope for an audit of this magnitude is quite comprehensive, and the proposed scope for Ideal was no exception. A schematic of the scope of subjects to be covered is reproduced in Figure 7.

With Objectives and Scope clearly established, the next critical element of the proposal and the structuring of a realistic and smooth-working assignment is the Approach your consultant plans to use. Chapter 12 acquaints you with some of the surprises that might be in store for you as the job proceeds.

Universal Metal Works: Industrial Market Study

The topics included in the scope of this industrial market study, whose objectives were presented in Chapter 10, embraced six subject areas, outlined below with highlights of each item. The proposed survey scope would cover the following aspects:

1. *Products and services* (market size, geographic distribution, and growth trends for each of four product classes; only applications with annual potential of one million or more parts; value-added engineering opportunities; product-category sales erosion)
2. *Markets and applications* (product-type demand within each end-market segment, classified as established, developmental, or potential using the company's existing production equipment)

Figure 7. Ideal Toy Corporation marketing profile.

Market Potential	Competitive Differentials	Ideal's Industry Position	Ideal's Assets and Potentialities

Business scope as defined by:
 	
▲ Ideal
▲ Competitors
▲ Distribution channels
▲ Consumers
	In scope definition
	
	In image in the trade
	
	In penetration by business segment
	
	In growth base by business segment
		(By business segment)
		
		Scope of:
		
		▲ Product lines
		▲ Distribution channels occupied
		   —Type
		   —Number
		   —Shelf space
		   —Seasonal
			Market standing:
			
			▲ With distribution channels
			▲ With consumers
			
			Image with financial community

Business segments: ▲ Product ▲ Consumer ▲ Distribution	In profitability by business segment In marketing objectives		People
			Product base
Growth potential (by business segment)	In marketing strategies and operations	Share of market Product introduction record	Distribution channels and organization
			R&D base
Profit potential (by business segment)	In marketing organization and management	Acquisition patterns Profit performance	Production base
			Financial and profit base
Marketing innovation potential		Relative growth potential: ▲ Profit ▲ Volume	Requirements for success
		Caliber of field representation	

(continues)

Figure 7. Continued.

Ideal's Marketing Objectives	Strategies and Marketing Operations	Marketing Organization and Management
(Related to overall corporate objectives) Business scope Growth: ▲ Volume ▲ Profit Marketplace image: ▲ With consumers ▲ With distribution channels ▲ With the financial community	Marketplace strategies of: ▲ Product lines ▲ Market segments ▲ Distribution channels ▲ Geography ▲ Strategy families of the above Marketing strategies and operating programs for: ▲ Marketing and distribution research ▲ Test marketing ▲ Advertising ▲ Sales promotion ▲ Packaging ▲ Pricing and sales policies ▲ Selling approaches ▲ Sales compensation and management Marketing participation with other Ideal functions	Organization goals: ▲ Penetration capability ▲ Market development capability ▲ Innovative capability ▲ Acquisition capability ▲ Attractiveness of company to top-notch people ▲ Continuity of organization for the above Definition of marketing work to be done (by functions by business segment) People requirements and inventory: ▲ Numbers ▲ Skill areas ▲ Experience ▲ Attitudes Organization structure and relationships Management practices: ▲ Planning approaches ▲ Leadership, motivation, direction ▲ Control and feedback ▲ Innovative approaches

3. *Competition* (significant competitors and reasons for their success; competitors leaving the business and why)
4. *Economics of order size* (guidelines and criteria for prioritizing products and market categories according to relative profitability)
5. *Market research procedures* (a starter market information file and prospect list; procedures for continuing market research)
6. *Sales and marketing practices* (secondary consideration of industry practices, roles of manufacturers' agents versus direct salesforce, and customer preferences)

The permutations and combinations of these six dimensions for four product lines and two dozen end markets should suggest why this client was referred to earlier as having effected a most advantageous entrapment of a consultant who had not previously studied his industry.

12

Proposal Elements: Project Approach

The Approach is the basic blueprint or game plan for the project. It establishes the events by stages; the players, their positions, and roles; and the governing schedule, timetable, and milestones to be achieved.

The *Approach* is the project game plan and the dynamic element of the proposal. It sets forth how your consultant expects to conduct the project. In evaluating this section of competing proposals, a variety of subjects and questions are relevant, depending upon the type of study to be undertaken. It is unnecessary to request that all such items be documented in the consultants' proposals, but you will need to think through their requirements and implications.

Requirements for an Effective Approach: Realistic Survey Plan, Timetable, and Events

▲ *Request consultant's project stages and sequence.* What stages or phases is the consultant proposing for the entire project? Does it appear that these planned steps will move the project from A to Z in the most timely, effective, and cost-efficient manner? Should the completion of any of these phases be decision points, times to determine whether the project should be continued or terminated?

▲ *Establish client/consultant liaison and communications.* Will you personally provide close, day-to-day surveillance of the project? Or, have you designated your representative to oversee the study and all liaison with your people? What are your plans for acquainting your people with the project? When and how should this be done? What specific procedures have been established for client communications, contacts, and progress reports? What is the probable nature and form of the interim and final reports, and what level of documentation do you desire?

▲ *Limit initial orientation and education of consultants.* What, if any, preliminary internal orientation and background study will be needed? Does the survey plan avoid excessive education of the consulting staff at your expense? Should this early stage include consultant contacts with a representative sample of your personnel in field sales and service, headquarters marketing, finance, at plants and labs? Is the consultant proposing seemingly excessive orientation time and tuning-up activity? Does this suggest that you should seek other candidates more familiar with your type of business?

▲ *Insist on New and Independent Inputs.* Any worthwhile and productively planned approach *must do more than* play back information already well known to client top management. In addition to identifying unsuspected internal attitudinal hurdles to teamwork, seek significant external inputs concerning your overall business environment and marketplace. Some inputs will come from the prior experiences of the consulting team. However, the approach also should provide exposure to your users' needs, demand trends, competitive activities, independent distribution and marketing channels, and your field sales and service organization.

What survey methods will be used? What plans are included for using your staff and resources in gathering information? What field survey contacts does the consultant plan to make with your personnel, customers and prospects, competition, suppliers, financial advisors? Are internal contacts planned to uncover prevailing attitudes and conceptions employees hold about the business that could well be part of the problem under study? How does the consultant propose to approach such aspects?

▲ *Prethink implementation expectations and plans.* What should be the consultant's expected implementation responsibilities and activities if the final recommendations so require? Have you asked him to build implementation assistance into his proposal, or will you hold this out pending the outcome of the study and as a "carrot" contingent on his superior performance?

▲ *Review compatibility of approach with objectives and scope.* All elements of the proposal are cumulative and interdependent. Thus, the needed approach should flow naturally from the defined Objectives and Scope and become the *modus operandi* and the control blueprint for reaching the desired results. It should reveal to you a combination of proven consulting and survey techniques and any innovative and creative departures the problem at hand dictates or could well use.

The foregoing scratch the surface on the detailed questions that need to be considered in evaluating the adequacy of a proposed Approach to your project. It is helpful to think of the Approach as a scenario or simulation of the way the consultant expects to proceed. Can you visualize clearly how each critical stage of his process will work, and does it seem workable in the aggregate? Also, what are some of the most typical problems that can creep into the conduct of a study? Can these be anticipated in advance and avoided?

Common Shortcomings of Project Approaches

Among the shortcomings of approaches and survey plans that have been most prominent in a wide variety of consultants' proposals are

▲ *Excessive start-up time.* One of the best ways to avoid this common occurrence is to press your consultant in the pre-proposal stage to develop definitive survey plans in more than a broad outline form. This gets considerable preplanning accomplished before the meter starts running and also gives you a greater credibility test on both his approach and your need.

▲ *Too little external marketplace exposure.* Most projects with strategic and marketing implications or purposes require considerable outside exposure. Normally, your problem will be unique enough that it needs more than the consultant's historical experience with your particular type of marketplace. If he argues against this, you may be considering the wrong choice.

▲ *Questionable survey techniques.* You need to be certain that the contemplated approach for obtaining essential inputs is workable, particularly if your project will be heavily dependent on external sources. A situation that posed such a problem is presented in the Walk Wear project later in this chapter.

▲ *Inadequate interaction with client staff.* In many types of projects, you will need your own associates' inputs to assure that you understand clearly their viewpoints, attitudes, and concerns. You also want all who will be instrumental in carrying out any recommendations to be attuned to the situation and to have "bought in" to the suggested actions as wholeheartedly as possible.

▲ *Too few planned checkpoints.* No assignment warrants the risk of initiating a project and then letting the consultant go for long periods without forcing him to pull together his findings and report progress to you. You should schedule frequent sessions for his informal presentation of progress reports, particularly in the early stages of the project. These normally should not be detailed written reports because you do not want the team to consume valuable billable time that could detract from unfinished information gathering and analysis. Lateness in conducting the initial progress report is particularly critical to avoid.

▲ *No provisions for go/no go reviews at key stages.* The approach to your proposal should have built into it two types of decision points for determining whether to proceed. One is a scheduled time to review whether the project appears to be doing what was intended or should be terminated. The second relates to any hierarchy of agreements needed; a new venture's first stage may be the issue of whether the basic direction should be pursued, with subsequent stages for developing alternative approaches to implement that basic direction.

▲ *Insufficient review of financial implications.* Make certain the project includes adequate testing against the critical financial performance requirements. It is too easy for both your consultant and you to become enamored with exciting new conceptual directions without sufficiently tracking their impact back to your balance sheet and the bottom line of your operating statement. As noted elsewhere, general financial feasibility of the proposition should be thought through even before deciding to take on a consultant. Then, as a study proceeds, periodically check the financial practicality of your consultant's recommendations as they are developing.

All of these shortcomings are important to avoid in order to execute a sound survey plan within budget and timing commitments. Among the worst, however, are faulty approaches for obtaining the desired information and insights. It seldom works out satisfactorily when a client insists upon or a consultant agrees to study impractical or impossible approaches as in the following experience.

Walk Wear: Don't Expect the Impossible

Walk Wear Enterprises, a venerable, family-owned shoe manufacturer, had enjoyed profitable private-label sales to the major U.S. mail order houses for many years. This was an adjunct to its own shoe brands sold through company-owned and independent retail stores. When Walk Wear's mail order business started to suffer from declining sales and margins, the company reluctantly called in a consultant.

Throughout the negotiations, the Walk Wear owners expressed extreme nervousness about the trade's attitude if they learned the company was turning to outside help with their problems. Yet this manufacturer wanted the consultants to go directly to the buying executives in Sears, Wards, and Spiegel (with the client's name withheld) to solicit their advice.

After much debate on this confidentiality issue, the newly promoted consulting partner, in order to get the job, assured the shoe executives that his staff could get the buyers' full cooperation without revealing who their client was. The partner had never worked with the mail order houses; and to the chagrin of the associate who was to do the lion's share of the work, he accepted the assignment on that basis. It was that partner's first sale!

Mail order houses buy with no holds barred, and the determined consultant was unable to get any of them to spend one minute talking with him incognito. In desperation, he revealed the client's identity to the Ward's shoe buyer, who reciprocated with a significant interview, and commended the client for seeking outside help. After also gaining entree to the Sears buyer "in the clear," he was able to complete a second highly productive session. Both executives, when they learned to whom they were really talking, were most anxious to help. They valued the shoe manufacturer as one of their more dependable and lucrative sources.

The consultant returned to the client to review the interview findings and to inform them of the action he had deemed necessary. They were most upset, immediately shut off the billings meter, demanded a complete documentation of findings to date, and terminated the assignment. Walk Wear abandoned any further use of consultants, and their overall shoe business continued with only mediocre results. Some years later they were acquired by another industry factor.

In the vast majority of cases, the trade views the use of a consultant to address a management's problems as a sign of strength. A company is just fooling itself when it places unrealistic or impossible demands on its consultant. From the consultant's viewpoint, committing to impractical or impossible conditions may make it easier to obtain a sale but virtually always places an insurmountable burden on delivering the promised results.

Safeguarding Against Negative Impacts on Client Personnel

There are relatively few effective ways to control impact on personnel. The best is through continuing, close communication with the involved individuals on both sides as the project progresses in order to understand whether the consultants are meeting their staffing commitments. Periodic in-depth but informal discussions should be initiated to assure that the staff's competences, analytical and communicating abilities, and relevant experiences are as promised.

Even the most meticulous precautions are not sufficient to meet some situations, particularly those where the objective of the project is clearly threatening to the client organization. Unless one of your project aims is to spread a little fear and uncertainty and force some soul-searching and introspection among your management staff, you should consider several ways to assure a positive impact from your project.

- ▲ Clarify to your organization why the consultants have been brought in, what you hope they will accomplish, and why you feel the project will benefit all concerned.
- ▲ Have an informal, social get-together between your key people and the consultants at launch time or early in the study.
- ▲ Make your key managers in all studied areas integral parts of the client/consulting team.
- ▲ Assign responsibilities for informal, continuing contact and communications to individuals in your organization at each of the consultant's responsibility levels.
- ▲ Request periodic, informal oral reports from your senior executive on the assignment about its progress.
- ▲ Except for sensitive, confidential feedback sessions from your consultant, include your key managers in all of the consultant's progress reports.

Prioritizing and Attending to First Things First

A long-standing debate among consultants concerns how much internal exposure to the client's thinking and experience should be undertaken before obtaining the objective outside viewpoints from the external environment, when that is a pertinent part of the assignment. At issue is a fear of becoming unduly biased toward the client's perceptions, thus damaging the consultant's ability to bring fresh and independent perspectives to the project. Several procedural questions are relevant to this issue.

- ▲ What sequence of subjects for the consultant's agenda will lead to the best possible perspective about the business?
- ▲ After his basic orientation to the 'facts' of the situation, should he concentrate initially on the markets and competition?
- ▲ Or, should his first in-depth probing be to master the client's financial history and the economics of the business so that he is better equipped to focus on the key marketplace issues in more realistic economic terms?
- ▲ Where new products or technology are involved, should such aspects receive the heavy initial emphasis, so that the consulting team is better equipped to relate any innovations to what they will find in the markets?

Some consultants argue that their obvious point of departure is field work and a thorough grounding in your external environment in order to ensure objective, independent perspective on your users' needs, market opportunities, and competition. They contend that any mainly strategic assignment should not be initiated with internal number-crunching or review of R&D programs, beyond a brief general orientation, in order to maintain maximum objectivity as outside conditions are studied.

The priorities for study should not be dictated by any of these preconceptions but rather by the nature of the project, timing considerations, and the extent of knowledge the client and/or the consultant already possess about the proposition. It often is faster and more economical use of your consultant's time to have him exhaust and soak up all internal sources of information and insight before going to the marketplace. He will then go outside with a sharper focus on the issues he must explore. A case in point is a proposal for a marketing audit where management felt the need for substantial external inputs as a basis for future strategic planning, but wanted in-depth preparatory steps prior to a reconnaissance study in the field.

Moderne Personal Care Products: Structuring a Competitive Audit With a Pilot Study

A manufacturer of personal care products for men obtained a proposal employing a two-phased approach, starting with a brief pilot or reconnaissance study.

Survey Approach

The proposed Objectives and Scope would be accomplished in at least two phases: first, a pilot study; and second, an in-depth study to be structured and tailored to the findings of the pilot study. The second phase could be divided into two or more stages to progressively hone in on the outstanding "tough" issues, and to allow for possible implementation of test policies and programs as future marketplace requirements and opportunities unfold.

Phase I—Pilot Study

1. *Develop internal background data* on the areas defined in the Scope section above. This would include pertinent historical data plus facts and opinions to be obtained from the key headquarters executives. About ten members of management have been tentatively identified for the initial round of internal discussions. They would be interviewed separately and confidentially to determine their best thinking on alternatives, priorities, and pros and cons of the present product lines.

It has been our experience in similar studies that this early step brings the consultants up to speed most rapidly and helps to avoid reinventing the wheel. It provides objective access to the creative thinking of management, which is not always available during the normal ongoing decision-making processes. It can be done effectively without risk of biasing or slanting the consultants' views.

2. *Develop a policy question structure.* As a result of the first step, a number of key alternatives would be identified. Supporting assumptions for each would be defined,

and the questions to pursue in the subsequent field work would be clarified. In close cooperation with the "client" management supervising us, we would then complete the decision structure by defining the kinds of information to be obtained and how we would effectively use it as the field study progresses. Jointly with your management, we would also establish priorities during this second step for the most critical items to emphasize.

3. *Conduct a field reconnaissance study.* Contacts would include regional sales managers, company salesmen and reps, distributors, large retailers, and field service stations. An adequate sample for the first field work would be about twenty-four completed interviews within these categories. The relatively small number of individuals to be contacted at this stage would expose us to all types of field survey sources in order to test the approaches and determine the sample mix for subsequent field stages.

4. *Make progress reports to management.* During and on completion of the field study, we would develop preliminary findings and conclusions and evaluate them against the policy decision structure. We would make informal presentations to you and your management, and would include in the wind-up of the pilot phase our plans for the next study phases and their objectives. Documentation of the findings would be in any form you prefer, with brevity as a major aim.

Phase II—In-Depth Studies

▲ The specific direction and scope of further field work and internal discussion would, of course, depend on the outcome of the Phase I pilot study. Assuming the survey should be deepened in all Scope areas, an additional 24, 48, or 72 field interviews plus further internal management discussions should suffice.

▲ We would undertake this second Phase in one, two, or three steps with a progress report at each step. At the end of the first additional set of interviews, your management would decide whether to one, terminate the field work and have us draw up the final report and implementation plans; two, postpone further field work until testing of recommendations; three, proceed to another round of field interviews; or four, terminate the study. We frequently use this approach to give the client maximum flexibility for timing and for shifting the direction and scope as critical issues develop or priorities change.

The preceding example is typical of a reconnaissance-type approach aimed at eliminating uncertainty about the total effort needed. It was designed to begin with a modest sampling of all input sources considered at the outset to be germane to a successful end result. More often than not, the reconnaissance approach turns out to be adequate for the overall study, thus shortcutting the sometimes expansive proposals of the consultant and resulting in time and cost savings for the client.

In your negotiations with candidates on their approach, initially you should be nondirective about how they would conduct the study. The most effective approach to an assignment is one of the key areas of expertise a competent consultant can bring to your situation. Their process can be as useful and innovative for you as the content of the work you expect from them. In addition to establishing confidence in your selection, you and your management can learn new ways to approach your ongoing managerial responsibilities after the consultants have completed their work.

13

Proposal Elements: Staffing, Time, and Costs

The purchase of consulting services is the most judgmental of all the executive arts. Every project is unique; every proposal is unique; and every staffing plan is unique.

You may be fortunate to have only one outstanding proposal among those submitted. If you have found a consultant who sees eye-to-eye with your needs, who is head and shoulders above any others you have evaluated, who can communicate effectively with you, and whose proposal gives you complete confidence to proceed, you are halfway home with your decision. You still should examine his staffing plans and terms for the people who will do the work and the timing and cost of their services. Always keep in mind that *the specific persons who will perform your assignment are the substantial portion of what you are buying from a consulting firm.*

If you do not have one outstanding candidate, you definitely need to solicit competing proposals, compare and apply judgment and feasibility tests to each element, and most carefully examine your feelings about the people involved. If the first two submissions for a complex or unique assignment are poles apart, obtain a third—and, if necessary, a fourth or how many more it takes—to reach your level of conviction.

Problems Comparing Alternative Proposals

Except in the world of RFPs, consulting proposals from multiple candidates are extremely difficult to compare strictly in terms of time and costs. Consultants' views of what the client needs can differ widely. As a result, alternative approaches to solving the same basic problem might be strikingly different. The caliber, experience, and intangible worth of consulting staffs to be assigned can vary significantly. In view of this, the number and types of consultants proposed to work on the assignment are likely to differ from one proposal to another. Your most critical initial task is to compare their all-important people dimension.

Three Major Performance Considerations

As you read through the final sections of alternative proposals that have been tendered, you should be seeking positive assurances to three key sets of questions:

1. *Staffing, qualifications, and availability.* How comfortable do you feel with each firm and the caliber of their staffing? Are the key staff members fully committed to you as proposed? Have you been assured you will have use of the "stars" you have met?

2. *Time and timing.* Does each consultant present realistic and reasonable estimates of total time to be spent on your project? Of time for each key stage? Are checkpoints built in for progress reports, appraisals, and go/no go decisions?

3. *Cost and benefits.* What will all this people power cost you? Do you have protection against overruns? Do you feel the cost will be money well spent, and can you relate it to promised and expected results and benefits?

Staffing and Availability: The Right People When Needed

The Staffing section of the proposal is an effective way to verify that the staff to be applied to the job matches the representations made in your discussions with the selling partner. Here you must assume that what you see is what you get. Timing of the staff's availability is also important, including when the consultants will begin work, and any currently known limitations to their continuing availability until the commitment is completed. Among the most common availability exposures are these:

▲ It probably will not be clear how much of the senior proposer's time, and that of other key staff, will actually be devoted to your project. Were they just brought in to impress you and sell the job, or will they, in fact, be on hand to apply their intellect to your assignment?

▲ Have you met all of the staff who will carry the heavy workload, and particularly those who are likely to be meeting with your underlings, your customers, distributors, and other outsiders important to you?

▲ What assurances do you have that if key staff have to be pulled away from your account, they will be backed up and replaced with at least the same caliber of substitutes? How will the consultant handle such transitions and at whose expense if more orientation is needed? In such instances, what assurances against schedule slippages can he offer you?

Qualifications of Consulting Staff

You may choose to ask your consultant to document the qualifications (backgrounds and experience) of the key people to be assigned, their pertinent prior experience in your type of business and other expertise that particularly fits them for this assignment. Hopefully, you have met all or most of these people during the screening and negotiating stages, so the paperwork will be backup verification.

Consulting References

References of other clients are also desirable and can be particularly helpful in checking out the people match—the caliber of the project leader, expertise of the supporting staff, and their apparent compatibility with your own people. If any doubts linger after all of the above, it may be wise to track down clients they have not mentioned. Even the quality consultants have some skeletons in the closet, and it is far better to clarify any misgivings before the fact.

Time and Timing: Well Phased and Tightly Scheduled

The Time and Timing section needs enough specific information to enable you to relate the consultant's estimates of staffing levels to the project's stages and major aspects.

If the Approach section of the proposal has not been sufficiently specific as to the project timetable, you should request that it include a summary of key stages and completion dates and any of your own "must" dates and pertinent milestones. This does not need to be a full-blown survey plan; usually that is not appropriate until a study has been officially launched and the consultants have had deeper exposure to your situation through initial orientation and interviews with your key people.

Several additional details should be pursued and clarified, if not in the proposal document, at least in its discussion with the proposer.

1. Has the proposed staffing schedule been carefully correlated with your company's pertinent schedules and commitments?

2. How much time has been planned for initial orientation and education of the consultants, and is this reasonable?

3. If after launching, the orientation reveals gross miscalculations in the time and timing requirements, how will you handle adjustments?

4. Does the proposal contain clear cut-off provisions and conditions? Has your right to terminate the project at any time, or after reasonably short notice, been documented? Virtually any reputable consultant should honor such a request at any time, but it saves misunderstanding to clarify this at the outset.

Costs: Questions of Time Utility and Cost Benefits

Assuming the Approach section of the proposal has established a convincing survey plan outline and acceptable timing for its major elements, the next step is to examine the pricing of those elements and their aggregate cost to you. A number of pricing considerations are of interest.

Determining what a given consulting project should cost and how long it should take still is a primitive art and is likely to remain so. Not unlike the old "beauty-beholder" cliche, a consultant's value truly is in the eyes of the beholder, his client. Results provide the only reliable benchmark but unfortunately cannot be divined at the proposal stage. This situation tends to argue for a client to choose someone who is already a known entity to him or a business associate, if at all possible to locate some such firm or individual.

Complex projects particularly, such as organization and management studies, business or marketing audits, strategic planning assignments, and information systems planning projects can have such unique conditions and characteristics that they defy useful generalizations about cost. A few of the facts of life about consulting charges illustrate some of the vagaries associated with concluding that a proposal is fairly costed.

Billing Rates Can Escalate Rapidly With Experience

Years ago a newly released airline cargo marketing manager decided to hang out a consulting shingle. When queried about his billing rate by his first prospect, he replied, ". . . at my normal rate of $25 per day." His response to his second client in the airlines industry was ". . . at my normal per diem of $35." Going strong after three years and seven client assignments he was quoting his "normal" rate of $40 per hour or $320 per diem! He had established a track record that warranted the escalation in his rates; he had also become realistic about what he had to charge to cover his overhead and downtime.

If You Must Probe for Cost Details, Don't!

At the other end of the scale, a previously quoted *Forbes* article
stated that McKinsey & Company "won't itemize a monthly bill.
We're not selling time and answers, like law or accounting firms.
We're selling a benefit called change. Change is where the value
is." and "Clients must trust McKinsey to set a fair fee." A common *modus operandi* is said to be "teams of four or five consultants being billed to the client at $120,000 to $130,000 per
month plus expenses."[1]

Those Expensive New MBA Grads

A manufacturer of specialty chemicals was contemplating the
need for a consultant and discussing the practice of the major
consultants to compete aggressively with high starting salaries
for MBA graduates from the prestigious business schools. He
could not accept the high fees required to employ, in his words,
"wet-behind-the-ears" MBAs on his tough problems.

Most consultants do not share McKinsey's enviable position
and reputation, and time and costs often are the most thoroughly
read sections of the consulting proposal. They price what has
been promised in the Objectives, Scope, and Approach. Methods
of charging for services normally relate to the predictability of
the assignment's workload, whether it is one-shot or continuing
advice and counsel, and the experience, standing, and reputation of the consultant.

Alternative Pricing Methods

Pricing methods include per diem rates for actual time spent;
annual or monthly retainers; and fixed amounts for a job, which
might be one figure, or a minimum-maximum range with the
top number an upset figure above which the client will not be
charged irrespective of how much extra time the consultant
takes. In studies where more than one consultant staff member
is to be used, the proposer will estimate the differing times and
per diem rates for each class of participant. If this mix of esti-

mates is not clarified in the proposal, the client should ask for such details.

1. *Per diem rates.* These rates require the least effort for the proposer to prepare and present but often are the most difficult for the client to evaluate and the candidate to defend. They are most common with a single consultant and a client who desires a continuing relationship with broader interests in the consultant's help than a specific fixed-term project.

If a per diem consultant needs to bring in additional professionals who will be in contact with the client, his normal practice is to arrange to bill for such individuals separately at the latters' rates. He may or may not be taking a markup on the associates. The per diem method is not confined to individuals. Frequently it is favored where a long-term relationship is developed and the client employs a team whom he views as an extension of his ongoing staff.

From the consultant's viewpoint, the rate level quoted derives from a combination of factors:

▲ What the consultant has been commanding from other clients, often not necessarily keyed to differences in the relative complexity of the work but what he thinks the market will bear

▲ Allowances to cover ongoing expenses during the consultant's downtime, or time required to develop client interest and prepare proposals to them

▲ Self-development expenses (professional conferences, dues, books and magazines, etc.)

▲ His overheads for rent, secretarial and other assistance, computer equipment and software, and report preparation costs (sometimes billed to the client);

▲ Direct marketing and promotion expenses, such as brochures and mailings, not usually high for the loner but becoming increasingly high for the major firms

▲ Provisions for health protection and retirement funds

From the client's viewpoint, the rate, of course, must be acceptable in terms of perceived future worth for outstanding results from the job yet to be performed. The difficulty of accepting the stated rate varies inversely with prior experience with the consultant, feedback from others who have used him, comparative rates and judgmental evaluations of several consultants who are bidding, and just plain, subjective gut feelings.

2. *Retainers.* Standard monthly or annual rates may be agreed upon, with the consultant committing to an average amount of time per month, quarter, or year. The rate is set considering basically the same factors as with the per diem approach. Retainers give the client and consultant more flexibility to vary the short-term workload with the specific timing of needs, and the accounting is simplified.

3. *Fixed-cost proposal.* In this method the consultant quotes a single figure for the job as proposed. For protection of both parties, he customarily quotes minimum and maximum dollar figures and time estimates (both total and elapsed), so that the max becomes an upset price on which the client can usually rely for his heaviest cost exposure.

The consultant develops his total by aggregating the specific time to be spent and billing rates for each person on the proposed team. If the proposal quotes only one weighted average figure, it is fair game to request a breakdown of the team. This breakdown should include their estimates of the amount of time the senior partner and other critical senior staff will be devoting to your project.

This long-established approach enables you to establish a more accurate budget of your cost exposure and gives you much more leverage to assure that the consultant will finish the job in the agreed-upon timeframe.

4. *Stock options.* A frequent approach with new entrepreneurial ventures or growth companies is to seek stock options in combination with per diem and retainer arrangements but less often with fixed-cost proposals. The consultant's aim is to defer income, build equity, compete at a lower cash-out level for the client, and lock in a self-motivating spur to excellent performance. The client goes along when he wants a longer-term relationship and his board and corporate by-laws permit, and when he feels the options will stimulate higher-quality consulting performance.

5. *Issues of contingency fees and commissions.* It has been a practice of some firms for years to contract for fees as a percentage of reduced expenses or increased profits, often in situations where a client is in dire financial condition. More recently, certain types of consulting businesses have charged commissions on products, systems, and specialized services provided to the client. This issue has developed particularly in the area of information systems consulting projects. For some time such practices have been considered unethical by many consultants; and they were not condoned by ACME or the Big Six accounting firms.

In the 1980s ACME lifted its ban on contingency fees but not commissions. The American Institute of Certified Public Accountants followed suit later by lifting its contingency fee ban. A number of the major firms still consider both practices professionally unethical. While the contingent-fee approach can offer tempting carrots to a consultant, it most often is an extremely high-risk approach wherein the client may fail despite the consultant's efforts before the latter can regain even his basic costs.

From your viewpoint, a major drawback to this method is an inevitable lessening of objectivity on the part of the consultant. You are well-advised to investigate the alternatives thoroughly before undertaking either a contingent fee or commission arrangement.

6. *Out-of-pocket expenses.* With all of the first five approaches, it is standard practice to bill all legitimate out-of-pocket expenses to the client at cost, in addition to the fees. Normally, these expenses are defined as travel, living expenses while away from home base, report preparation costs, attendance at conferences and meetings authorized by the client, and other items unique to the assignment, provided the client has agreed to them in advance. When the consultant is authorized to commission and supervise special outside studies or services for the client, it is best for such services to be billed or contracted directly to the client.

Normally, a one-time project that can be estimated with reasonable accuracy will be priced at a fixed range of amounts. Projects with highly unpredictable time requirements and significant speculative unknowns are more likely to be proposed and accepted on a per diem basis. In such instances, it is prudent to use the reconnaissance study approach or schedule into the proposal periodic checkpoints for deciding whether to proceed or terminate the effort. An arrangement for continuing, periodic consulting, or consulting on call, is more likely to be set up with per diems or retainers.

Additional Costs to the Client

The additional costs incurred by the client throughout the anticipated duration must be estimated and added to the maximum costs committed by the proposal. Normally, the most important of these is the time of client personnel who will be needed to support and participate in the project effort and must be replaced in the interim. Among additional items not to be overlooked in making such estimates are the following:

- ▲ Extra out-of-pocket expenses to be incurred for client people to travel with consulting staff
- ▲ Costs for any special meetings, conferences, retreats, and so forth that would not be required without the project
- ▲ Special computer time made available to the consultant
- ▲ Temporary support work, such as extra staff to generate background information, special analyses, market research, technical studies
- ▲ Added costs accompanying provision of on-site facilities for consulting team
- ▲ Report preparation, secretarial, telephone, and telefax expenses client has agreed to provide in support

Depending on the nature of the assignment, other exposures also should be considered. For example, in hopefully rare instances, unforeseen costs could be incurred as a result of controversies generated by the assignment. This became a significant cost exposure for the Majestic Mills CEO when his consultant's recommendations brought down the wrath of the sales agent fighting termination in the case reviewed in Chapter 6.

Cost Problems as a Study Proceeds

As Chapter 11 discussed, one recurring problem of the proposal relates to scope and directional changes that may be made during the course of a study. Often the effect is to significantly enlarge the consultant's workload. If this is at the client's initiative, the only fair treatment is to adjust the fee and staffing terms of the proposal accordingly. If done unilaterally by the consultant, the client should clarify where his obligation for additional fees stops. More importantly, he should determine whether the consultant is putting his effort into jeopardy with a budget and deadline squeeze that could adversely affect the quality of the all-important wrap-up stages of the project.

Another, but less common, omission is a failure to build in natural times and stages for implementation and for orderly termination of the consultant's work. If your consultant stays on and on either at your insistence or your inertia, do not just let the relationship drift. Determine whether his tenure is to your advantage and whether he is continuing to deliver time utility and cost/benefits.

Comparing the raw billing rates and project costs of competing proposals is easy, as is the separate comparison of proposed time and timing. The difficult part is to compare the time/cost package as an entity in terms of time utility and cost/benefits to be expected from competing consultants. Not very many would-be clients take a precise comparative approach in advance. They are much more likely to decide on a judgment of reasonableness against the promises made and particularly on their relative confidence in the people who will become involved.

During the course of a project, you need to ask yourself and your associates periodically:

▲ What value and what benefits appear to be materializing from the consultant's efforts underway?

▲ What should be done to escalate the chances of superior results?
▲ Do the emerging results appear to offer reasonable value for the time and costs expended by both the consultant's and my own staff's efforts?
▲ When the work is completed, do I believe I will be able to identify clearly, and possibly even measure, the cost/value and productivity benefits I will have received?

Issues Related to Terminating the Assignment

In addition to all of the classical project control requirements, the consulting project adds one very important new dimension that can present a difficult control problem. The consulting staff is not really under the day-to-day control of the client, even though the client can turn off the work at just about any time he becomes dissatisfied and convinced that the effort will not succeed.

Reaching a conclusion to terminate is made more difficult by several inherent characteristics of consultants and consulting. Most consultants by nature are optimists; and they usually possess great powers of persuasion and communications skills. They can argue convincingly that they are indeed making more headway than is apparent and the client needs to be a bit more patient or that the scope turned out to be larger than represented by the client and will take a bit more time than anticipated.

The consultants may request permission to finish the work satisfactorily at whatever cost, fully honoring the upset ceiling price of their proposal and absorbing the overrun. They may contend that they are building to a peak of insight, which needs a bit more time to season before a truly innovative recommendation will be presented. Or they may argue that the client has already invested so much time of his own staff that it would be a waste to lose the further experience, training, and sense of achievement of completing the work.

Or the rare ones may say, "You're right, let's just call it off at no further cost to you." Years ago a consultant's client, in the orientation briefing, gave him a prior McKinsey report to review for historical background. The transmittal letter stated that since the study's purposes were not achieved, McKinsey was charging him nothing!

Note

1. "We Don't Learn From Our Clients, We Learn From Each Other," *Forbes* (October 19, 1987), page 124.

PART FIVE

Assuring Sound Perspective and Focus

Realistic perspective and focus—the most elusive project aspects

The basic issues of perspective and focus, in addition to warranting attention as one of the six basic building blocks, are important considerations in all of the other five. Although specified early, perspective and focus cannot be predetermined with any assurance or finality at the outset or be built into the consultant's proposal and decreed in advance. They also require vigilant attention throughout the entire course of the assignment. Both need the new inputs and insights that can only be developed by you and your consultant as the assignment progresses. Often, they are not finalized until the recommendation stage.

Throughout the entire project, you face the crucial, ongoing challenge of managing its conduct, particularly the issues of perspective and focus. Successful plans and recommendations for implementation require:

▲ *Perspective: clarifying the "bigger" (or smaller) picture* that best fits your business situation and your opportunities. It is a realistic view of your company's basic aims, needs, and opportunities; of the major dimensions of your opportunity and how these dimensions relate to each other; and of defined

Building Block Diagram D.   Summary factors: achieving perspective and focus.

Implement Plans

Control Project

Achieve Perspective and Focus

Key Problems and Obstacles:	Guidelines and Principles:
▲ Thin marketplace inputs.	▲ Invite divergent views early.
▲ Loose problem definitions.	▲ Focus on market needs.
▲ Over-conceptualizing.	▲ Clarify causes of problems.
▲ Overstressing of technology.	▲ Stress "natural" strategies.
▲ Too many new programs.	▲ Test concepts against the "art of the possible" and
▲ Action steps undetermined.	financials.

Structure Assignment

Match People

Determine Need and Timing

breadth, scope, and strategic directions deemed most appropriate for your situation.

▲ *Focus: targeting the very best specific choices* for future emphasis and action culled from your array of opportunities. Focus means achieving a clear image and a sharp definition of your central aims, interests, and activities; the convergence of alternative objectives, strategies, and programs into your composite plans: all leading to sharply defined, selective, and prioritized recommendations for concentration and emphasis.

▲ *Counterbalancing of the two into action programs* that optimize the range of opportunities open to you with the art of the possible, those things you realistically can hope to accomplish profitably.

Whatever the scale of your project, you will want your consultant to assist you substantively to develop new perspectives and focus that will add value to your business through *profitable change*. Such change occurs through astute reallocation of resources and reassignment of responsibilities for them. New perspectives and focus are the major determinants of what that change should be.

Your consultant's role in this process should be to add new perspectives to your thinking in one or more of three basic ways: (1) solving compelling problems; (2) improving the competitive effectiveness of your present business; and (3) successfully pursuing new opportunities.

Part Five explores several of the most significant challenges to achieving sound perspective and focus with the consulting project and offers suggestions for dealing with such challenges. Chapter 14 concerns several key issues in these areas; Chapter 15 concentrates on focused problem solving; and Chapter 16 explores considerations with natural strategic advantages and disadvantages. Building Block Diagram D highlights a number of the key points considered in these chapters, which are concerned with the fifth challenge:

CHALLENGE FIVE: MAINTAIN SHARP AND RELEVANT PERSPECTIVE AND FOCUS

14

Issues of
Perspective and Focus

At the close of a consulting team's final progress report to their client, two of the client's vice presidents were heard to remark as they left the briefing

First VP: "Was he discussing the problems of our company?"

Second VP: "Yes, really! He's advocating strategies for a different ball game; and he's way out of sync with our competitive situation!"

First VP: Well, he's certainly not relating well to what we need now."

Second VP: "Let's just hope the final recommendations are a lot closer to the target."

Unfortunately, the above situation is not unique. Problems of perspective and focus in the conduct of a consulting project occur more often than they should. They can exist from the outset of the client/consultant discussions. Their origins might have been preexisting conditions in the client's *modus operandi*. They may stem from the way the consultant views his client's business and approaches his own work. They may be the result of faulty communications from either or both parties or lack of joint diligence in sharing views. They may represent either a consultant's or a client's myopia about the marketplace.

Breadth and consistency of perspectives between you and

your consultant need early and continuing attention in the course of the assignment. Then your consultant must focus on a selective package of realistic and workable objectives, strategies, and programs. The ultimate result sought should be an optimum and resourceful blending of the two.

At least seven classes of problems and issues in maintaining sound *perspective* and *focus* throughout the consulting assignment occur with considerable frequency. One of the most important of these is the failure to get to the main causes of problems the company may face. Another significant pitfall is overlooking the natural strategic advantages and disadvantages in your situation. These very major and pervasive issues are treated separately in the next two chapters.

This chapter reviews five other significant issues of perspective and focus, each of which can affect your consultant's effectiveness with problem solving and strategy development.

1. An unrealistic sense of strategic timing with new programs
2. Leaving the consultant's and client's perspectives out of sync
3. Indiscriminate study and recommendation of "everything"
4. Overconceptualizing and idealizing the new opportunities
5. Stressing technology over market and user needs

An Unrealistic Sense of Strategic Timing With New Programs

You need to monitor your project's progress to ascertain that new programs do not contain unrealistic timing expectations. You must be certain your consultant recognizes the time needed to put the fundamentals into place for a new program or project outside your experience or even for major enhancements or leapfrogging within your present business expertise.

The late Dr. Richard Hayes, while in charge of the Xerox Corporation's new venture areas, used a most useful sequence

of philosophical, but extremely practical, questions in screening
and evaluating the countless new opportunities to which he was
exposed regularly. He contended that in looking for that great
new winning proposition for the future you should start by assuming that "the world has no huge *gaps* of market opportunity
just waiting patiently out there for you alone to exploit." Dr.
Hayes raised a sequence of six straightforward sets of questions
to gain perspective and focus on your new propositions.

1. What kind of business are you in?
2. Who's the competition?
3. What's the technical situation? What was it three years
   ago? What is it now? What is it most likely to be three to
   five years hence?
4. Who are the leaders now? When did they get started?
5. What are the leaders doing now to move to their fifth-
   year-out position?
6. What do *you* need to do now to get there? In time? Before the present leaders?

Leaving Strategic Perspectives Out of Sync

It is both wise and normal to assume that you and your adviser
will begin an assignment with some key differences in perspective. Such differences are a healthy and highly desirable point of
departure for a study that seeks fresh and objective results.
However, as the conversation at the start of the chapter implies,
it is both wasteful and unsatisfactory if fundamental differences
and confusion still exist as a project reaches its termination or
implementation stage. A failure to achieve a common perspective and focus is one of the major reasons for poor consulting
results.

Among the most typical areas where the client and consultant are prone to start with gaps or differences in perspective are
the following:

▲ Perceptions of users' needs and the current and future
  validity of such perceptions

- ▲ Customers' loyalty for the client's products and services
- ▲ Opinions on the size and growth prospects for new markets
- ▲ Attitudes of the client's distributors and dealers toward his products, policies, and services
- ▲ Definitions of the bases for principal competitors' strengths and product attributes
- ▲ The pace and applicability of new technology relevant to the client's products and processes
- ▲ Managerial effectiveness of the client and his key executives
- ▲ Capabilities of the client organization for getting up to speed in new or unfamiliar aspects within the available window of market opportunity
- ▲ Economics of new programs and feasibility of meeting financial resource requirements

The foregoing are the tip of the iceberg for the many issues where differences in perceptions can be critical. Both client and consultant can have perfectly valid arguments for their respective positions based on their own prior experiences. Also, where one party is in error, it is at least as likely to be the consultant as the client, the consultant from unfamiliarity with the client's particular industry and the client from incomplete exposure to his outside environment.

A corporate executive may have been motivated to bring in an outsider mainly to obtain a fresh, independent view and innovative ideas. Or, he may have decided it was time for a hefty intellectual bout with a devil's advocate to test his own and his associates' convictions about the direction they are pursuing. You should always give serious consideration to choosing a consultant for his differing viewpoint. This consideration may even be the main reason for selecting a particular consultant. If you are lock-step with your consultant from the outset, then perhaps you didn't need to spend the time and money on him in the first place.

On the other hand, having deliberately sought contrary opinions, you should just as deliberately work at closing the debate. It is important that you and your consultant agree early about the assignment's approach, your company's business needs, and the eventual recommendations for action. Analyze your differences early in order to identify any significant can't-see-the-forest-for-the-trees blind spots and major issues so that the project proceeds effectively in the intended direction. Any critical differences certainly must be resolved before the findings and recommendations are set.

Hopefully, the new shared perspectives will be somewhat different and more realistic for each of you than they were when you started. The fresh interactions between client people and consultant staff can generate new combinations of opportunities and promising new strategic concepts and directions.

Indiscriminate Study and Recommendation of "Everything"

Often a failure to close the gap in the client's and consultant's perspectives and focus for the project results in great indecision on the part of the consultant. As a consequence, he or she may undertake indiscriminate fact finding and analysis of "everything," launch misdirected research, or pursue the wrong information sources. The consultant in this situation tends to cover all bases and include every possible issue and alternative action in sight without focusing on those aspects that will make a significant difference.

This problem frequently begins either with an unseasoned consultant who lacks the confidence to start separating the wheat from the chaff early in the assignment or with someone who has never experienced your industry before. In both instances, one important consequence is a fact-finding phase that encompasses every essential and nonessential aspect and issue of the client's situation without differentiating and concentrating on those items that bear directly on the issues and objectives of the project.

If allowed to go unchallenged, such a consultant is likely to try to wrap up his assignment with an indiscriminate array of recommendations that endeavor to "cover the waterfront." Obviously, both perspective and focus suffer in the process, and the final recommendations may turn out to be totally useless. In such situations, it is virtually guaranteed that neither the financial implications will be well covered nor the necessary considerations for preparing the organization to take action will be specified.

The Beguiling Dangers of Overconceptualizing

Of all the ways to define new strategic directions, stimulating new *concepts* are among those that can appear to offer the greatest promise and appeal. New concepts are exciting and forward-looking; they are optimistic about the future; and they provide a generalizing logic for what the company is doing or is about to undertake.

Consultants are among the very best at "the fine art of concepting." This often stems from graduate business school experience, where business policy courses and cases forced the student at a relatively early age to grapple with the "big picture," the overall viewpoint of all the functions. He developed analytical and communicative skills in handling major issues. Then, he often went directly into consulting without first experiencing the lower-level line and staff activities that help one relate more pragmatically to solid bottom-line result.

Whatever your adviser's particular educational experience, if he or she is a seasoned and competent management consultant, you should expect and want him to develop useful generalizations about your business. Hopefully, he can bring to you much applicable insight from his work with other organizations in the same or different industries. His application of the lessons of others to your new problems or opportunities is most readily conveyed through concepts, principles, and other generalizations, and he often will do this by reclassifying your business situation into his or her own frame of reference. However, going this far may be unnecessary and misleading.

The wisdom and value of the concepting approach has not needed to be debated for several generations of executives and consultants. It is expected as a matter of course and frequently is a basic reason for the client's decision to bring in someone with fresh, outside perspective. However, when using a "concepting" consultant's services, make certain that the conceptual directions being advocated are rooted in reality.

> *The persuasive power of concepts that are innovative and exciting but too much blue-sky need to be tested very pragmatically against today's competitive realities—against the more mundane and conservative-sounding "art of the possible and the affordable" and against the bona fide needs and economics of your marketplace.*

Particularly in the pioneering stages of a new "concept" market, risks are enhanced because the needs of the potential user are unclear, and the major requirements for success are not readily definable in advance. A dramatic example of the dangers is presented below with respect to the home electronic information industry.

Stressing Technologies in Search of Markets

> Here lies a brilliant product
> Based on state-of-the-art technology.
> It expired while searching for
> a market that did not exist!
>
> —Silicon Valley corporate epitaph

Silicon Valley has become synonymous with and conjures up the image of high tech—leading edge technology ventures in semiconductors, computers, electronics, and optical information systems; engineering teams spinning out of major technology firms; and "instant" millionaires. There have been phenomenal new start-up success stories in these industries over the years: Intel, Apple Computer, Microsoft, and Compaq Computer, to name a few.

Silicon Valley also has fostered its share of burnouts, new ventures that enjoyed more rapid and greater growth than their entrepreneur founders could cope with, and others that never got beyond the misdirected technology stage when the faith of their venture-capital providers expired. More often than not, the corporate epitaph should read as above.

Based on the track records of the most successful corporations, it is difficult to overemphasize the lasting advantages of focusing a company's objectives, strategies, and programs on the needs of the marketplace. The dangers of the internally focused and product-oriented corporate mission have been stressed periodically in this book. Any technology-based company is highly vulnerable to the rapid pace of innovation and change in today's business world, as are countless organizations involved with so-called mature products and services. The conceptual danger can be the same for the low-tech organization, as illustrated by a situation in the retail furniture trade.

Many years ago, two leading retailing consultants in a major firm advised a prestigious New York specialty retailer against taking seriously some upstart forays of Levitz Furniture and others into discount furniture marketing. They judged broadly that the discount retailing phenomenon would be short-lived and that it would end up being no more than a faddish and gimmicky effort by sensationalist operators who didn't really know their costs, much less the deeply entrenched desire of consumers for full service!

The Levitz furniture warehouse/showroom phenomenon caught on and did some heavy competitive damage over the years to other retailers in the lower end of the market where customers were willing to forego the full services of the traditional specialty retailers and department store furniture departments. In this situation, it behooved retail clients to discover early where their consultants stood in relation to the newest trends in their industry. Both the consultants and their clients were caught napping.

Several situations discussed in other chapters demonstrate the problems of achieving a balanced and outward-looking perspective in the strategic development of a business. For example, the Radio Technology case, presented in Chapter 4, illustrated the blinders of the emotional, subjective experiences of a client, and in that instance, his consultant as well. The two became unduly enamored with a new technology because both had gone through extended bouts with cancer in their respective families.

During the 1980s, a succession of companies and their consultants have endeavored to establish viable electronic home-information services. In most instances, their efforts have resulted in ill-fated ventures based on overly optimistic expectations by both clients and consultants.

Home Electronic Information Services: Operation "Over-Hype"

Starting in the 1960s and earlier, entrepreneurs and others established successful electronic information services that were based on clearly demonstrated needs for repetitive information. Such services grew because they could deliver significant savings in both costs and time to the information seekers.

Among the earliest were the providers of electronic stock quotations and credit information, such as Ultronic, Bunker-Ramo, Quotron, TRW, Dun & Bradstreet, and others. Markets for scientific, technical, legal, and medical information were established by Lockheed's Dialog service, the National Library of Medicine, Mead Data Central, which offered LEXIS to the lawyers, and OCLC with bibliographic information for libraries. All of these services were concentrating on niche markets comprised of serious, repetitive information seekers with a continuing and compelling need-to-know and the ability to cost-justify their purchases.

The conceptual, targeted strategies of the pioneers and their consultants have proven to be quite sound. However, the lure of the results being realized by the leaders, coupled with the tremendous growth of the personal and home computer industry ushered in a wave of overoptimism to start developing the so-called home information market segment. Expansive forecasts and claims of high potential among millions of home consumers led to a number of projects and joint ventures. None of these have achieved the promised revenue and profit potential.

Although its concept from the outset has been imaginary,

exciting, and challenging, the home market for electronic information has not been established as a viable, major industry. It has had relatively few successes to date, notably H&R Block's CompuServe and France's Minitel. The earliest U.S. and British ventures, The Source and Prestel, could not establish viable home-market businesses, and later the videotex ventures of Knight-Ridder and the Times-Mirror were abandoned after costly expenditures. Hundreds of millions have been invested in the latest entrant, Prodigy, a joint venture of IBM and Sears, but its success is by no means assured.

In brief, a formula of information offerings to home consumers has yet to be developed that will become habit-forming and keep them spending dollars repetitively for electronic delivery on a major scale for information they cannot do without!

Most entrants who have been pursuing so-called home information applications continue to be a prime example of overly ambitious projects that can devour substantial consulting fees and client resources to little or no avail. The business is still, to a considerable extent, a glamorous technology in search of a viable market.

A consultant's work on market focus is one of the most useful roles he or she can play for you. His utility resides in playing back to you an outsider's objective view of what you are telling him is your reason for being and what he sees as expanded or changed directions for you. Encourage him to challenge your scope of vision and your view of your role in your marketplace. Let him debate whether you are defining your mission with strictly a product-oriented or other internally focused reference point. Put him through this fruitful exercise at the outset of the engagement and during its progress; make it an integral part of his recommendations to you; and listen carefully and seriously to his divergent or contrary viewpoints.

A common theme that recurs throughout this book is to keep the organization and the consulting task *focused clearly on the company's marketplace and on its users' needs.* In today's global competition, it has never been more critical for the client and consultant to keep constantly in mind Peter Drucker's sage principle that "The purpose of a corporation is to create a customer."

You and your consultant must take every precaution to avoid getting trapped into pursuing a product or a technology in search of a market. The history of successful business growth is a history of the ever-changing and ever-expanding needs of consumers, which are being fulfilled in new ways and with new applications.

The principle of market focus is not confined to high tech, but holds equally for low-technology organizations. Virtually any type of organization will survive and continue to thrive to the extent it maintains its outward-looking perspective and is successful in focusing its strategies and programs on delivering exceptional value-added benefits to its customers. An outward focus on market needs and the added-value benefits that can be offered to one's customer and prospect base is the proven way to maintain viability and a profit stream over time.

15

Focused Problem Solving

We trained hard ... but it seemed that every time we were beginning to form up into teams we would be reorganized. I was to learn later in life that we tend to meet any new situation by reorganizing; and a wonderful method it can be for creating the illusion of progress while producing confusion, inefficiency, and demoralization.

Petronius Arbiter, 210 B.C.

Getting Problems and Their Root Causes Into Focus

Petronius was perhaps the first to observe the human tendency to solve problems by changing people and organizations rather than taking the time to identify fundamental causes of those problems. The earliest clients brought in consultants to define and solve problems and the art of addressing such issues as the following continues to be a prime aspect of the consultant's work.

- ▲ Do we clearly understand the problems we face and the hurdles to realizing our opportunities? Have we pinpointed all of their underlying causes?
- ▲ Have we defined these problems and their causes as external circumstances and a run of "bad luck" beyond our control?

▲ Or, rather, have we traced them all back to causes that clarify internal reasons and responsibilities for them in our own organization? To explanations that lead to clear-cut corrective action? And to when and by whom?

IBM: Conquering a Process-Control Marketing Dilemma

During the mid-1960s, IBM was striving to gain a market position with its large computer systems in process control applications. The target markets were big manufacturing facilities with continuous production operations, such as paper making, petrochemical products, plywood, and fluid foods and drugs. The principal competitors who were dominating those markets were Honeywell and General Electric, both of whom manufactured and marketed computer systems during that period.

With the assistance of internal consultants, IBM assigned some of its most successful sales executives, salesmen, and computer systems experts to the process control programs but with most disappointing results. During one two-year period, they completely reorganized the department three times and still could not achieve a satisfactory order position.

On hindsight, IBM and its internal, captive consultants had not been facing the fundamental cause of their problem. They could not match the expertise and experience of their principal competitors. They lacked people with in-depth experience in their customers' and prospects' operating processes, and particularly the control functions for such processes.

Both General Electric and Honeywell, by virtue of their long-standing positions in the manufacture, marketing, and service of control and instrumentation products and systems, were heads and shoulders above IBM in their expertise with the customers' processing operations. They understood what had to happen at each basic step in a customer's flow diagram of the production process and were much better prepared to design computerized operating and control systems. When IBM addressed the fundamental cause, process-control application expertise, they began to have significant success in that marketplace.

Understanding the Problem Hierarchy

"Problems are opportunities in disguise!" "Are problems obstacles or opportunities?" "If you are a part of the problem, then
you need to be a part of the solution!" These comforting cliches
put one back into the positive frame of mind needed to eliminate
the roadblock or the troublesome situation. But they do not take
one very far toward solutions. Consultants are supposed to be
experts at problem solving, starting with thorough digging for
the facts and careful evaluation of their causes. If the client gives
them a free enough hand to make their own objective determination of just what the problem and its causes are, or are not,
their assistance can be most constructive.

Problem solving should be viewed as one of the universal
managerial arts. Every executive and every worthwhile consultant, after being confronted with enough real-world problems to
resolve, either learns how to do so, or goes into some other line
of endeavor that does not require the skill, patience, or discipline
of careful problem solving.

One consulting firm that has made a specialty of training
managers in such an art is Kepner-Tregoe and Associates.
Among other services, this firm conducts on- and off-site group
training sessions of up to a week's duration. Impressive results
are obtained in imparting skills to the client's key managers and
professionals, honing their skills in problem analysis, decision
analysis, and potential problems analysis, and the whole deci-
sion/action sequence of follow-through that must happen. These
sessions for an individual client are tailored to the problem areas
that client's people are most likely to confront.

The Clutter in Loose Problem Definition

A foundation for problem solving is to clear up the clutter of
"apples, oranges, and bananas" so typical of many attempts at
problem definition. The clutter and the deterrents to bona fide
solutions occur most often:

When symptoms are mistaken for problems

When problems are confused with their causes and vice versa

When the analysis stops with the identification of external culprits beyond the company's ability to control

When the tracing from problems to causes never gets back quite deeply enough to the decision points where individuals could have either avoided the cause or taken action to modify its impact

When responsibility for taking the needed remedial action is not clearly or properly assigned

A typical symptom of the inability to see beyond the clutter of incomplete problem definition was the statement of a self-made entrepreneur who had just received a tutorial on his management style from his consultant: "What do you mean, I'm two-thirds of the problem?" This client had been unable to track his technology-problem analysis inward from his competitive marketplace to position its root causes at his own doorstep. He could not admit to his own failure to keep upgrading his originally brilliant technological innovation. His subjectivity and closeness to the situation prevented him from clarifying the internal factors that were causing or contributing to his difficulties. Significant among these was a complacency traceable to his initial invention and a failure to keep investing in further applied research and development.

The Problem/Cause/Solution Chain

Figure 8 is one representation of the general analytical process the entrepreneur cited above needed to apply in order to determine effective corrective action. This so-called problem/cause/solution chain can be most useful to reestablish both a *perspective* on the various factors contributing to a difficult situation and a *focus* on the root causes that must be addressed. The name of the problem hierarchy game is to move progressively from the

Figure 8. The problem/cause/solution chain.

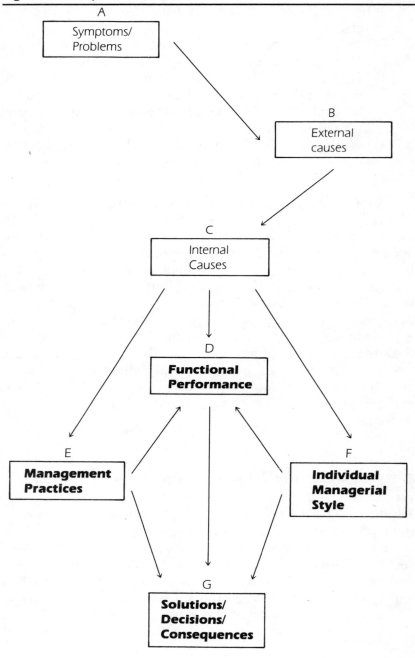

first Analysis Stage A through to Action Stage G of the figure and then to assess the seriousness of the consequences of not adequately addressing the problem and its causes.

Confusing Symptoms With Problems

Management faces numerous typical temptations or excuses for stopping the problem/cause analysis along the way before it reaches the moment of truth. One of the more frequent offenders is at Stage A where the line of least resistance can be mislabeling symptoms as the problems you are trying to attack. Several common classes of a problem's symptoms can show up in a superficial problem definition:

- ▲ Unsatisfactory financial and market performance data, such as declining revenues, losses, negative cash flow, and reduced market share
- ▲ Disappointing physical performance factors, including missed or late shipments, user complaints and dissatisfactions, and product malfunctions
- ▲ People problems, for example, poor employee morale, inordinate turnover and key employee defections, distributor and dealer resignations, and stockholder disenchantment

Any of these deficiencies arguably can be considered a serious problem, but none meet the test of explicitly clarifying their causes or suggesting actions to remedy them.

The Search for External Causes

After labeling symptoms as problems, the next easiest fall-guy is to search for the external causes (Stage B) of the company's difficulty. Any generalized random list might include:

Our customers' needs changed.
Materials costs rose.

Suppliers let us down.
Distributors lost interest.
Competitors gained market share.
Japanese imports stole our markets.
The dollar devalued.
The dollar overvalued.
New technology killed us.
The national union struck.

None of these kinds of statements tells us what we have been doing wrong or failing to do in response to such external phenomena. They just help us pass the buck to the outside world. Each item at one time or another may well have contributed to our problems and had a significant causal relationship. However, they should rarely be considered an *end-cause* in and of themselves. *Always* assume that some internal action or actions should have been taken, discontinued, or avoided in relation to them.

Identifying the Internal Causes and Their Consequences

With the exception of wars or Acts of God, virtually no external explanation, such as competition, changing technology, material supply shortages, or the value of the dollar, should be considered the root cause of the problem. The internal causes should be traced as deeply as necessary to the point of accountability in the organization where the root of the problem resides.

Where and when should someone in the organization have anticipated or foreseen a troublesome internal or external situation and then met it with action or relayed the warning to the appropriate management along with corrective suggestions? The purpose should not be principally to discipline but rather to identify who should be charged with, and who has the resources for, taking the necessary remedial steps.

The action decisions in the problem/cause/solutions process rest with client management. However, a consultant often is in a better position to work through the tricky analytical stages of problem definition and the isolation of causes. He can bring his

objectivity and outside independence to bear; and he is not burdened with the day-to-day pressures. He can be particularly effective when he has earned the confidence and respect of the
client staff, and, as a result, gets them to open up freely to him.

Differentiating Your Internal Causes

Figure 8 shows three principal categories of internal causes of
problems: functional performance deficiencies, management
practices and process deficiencies, and weaknesses of individual
managerial style. Figure 9 outlines a selection of the multitude
of generic internal causes of problems in these three categories.

   The point of Figure 9 and the three-faceted distinction is to
emphasize another tempting way to dodge full and final responsibility for the ultimate causes of the company's difficulties. It
often is easiest and most opportune to stop with functional performance deficiencies (D). These kinds of weaknesses frequently are much easier to attend to than those represented in E
and F in Figure 9. The D-type concerns usually can be addressed much more expediently and decisively than matters of
the management process and leadership. Moreover, they are less
likely to point the finger as far up the company's hierarchy as
causes in the E and F categories.

Solutions That Fully Close the Loop

Application of the problem/cause/solution chain to a company's
major difficulties never should be allowed to stop with the D
level. "Fixing" the overall managerial process may well be the
only effective longer-term and longer-lasting way of assuring
that functional performance problems do not rise again in the
same or other forms. *Always trace a significant problem and its
root causes as far up the line of command as the analysis leads
you or your consultant to a point of authority for a solution.*

   An impressive generalized formula for closing the loop from
problems to solutions was presented by Metzger in reporting on
the work of Tom Cummings and Susan Mohrman at the Univer-

Figure 9. Generic internal causes of business problems.

D—Functional Performance Deficiencies:

- ▲ Fuzzy definition of users' needs and applications
- ▲ Inadequate scanning of competitive environment
- ▲ Failure to market test conclusively
- ▲ Poor and sloppy product engineering and testing
- ▲ Faulty estimating and pricing
- ▲ Obsolete technology
- ▲ Weak order scheduling and production control
- ▲ Inattention to user feedback and customer service needs
- ▲ Thin technical and service support to field sales and customers
- ▲ Recruiting breakdowns and failures

E—Management Practices Deficiencies:

- ▲ Marketing myopia; weak market research
- ▲ Unclear corporate purpose and strategic directions
- ▲ Failure to communicate sound purpose and goals
- ▲ Expedient, intuitive choice of markets and strategies
- ▲ Frequent change of organization and personnel
- ▲ Unclear career paths and work alternatives
- ▲ Lack of definitive policies for risk/reward/penalty
- ▲ Limited incentives for risk taking
- ▲ No planned management and supervisory development programs
- ▲ Inconsistent performance measurement against plans and goals

F—Individual Management Style Weaknesses:

- ▲ Uninspiring and unmotivating leadership
- ▲ Immersion in details; poor delegation
- ▲ Undue stressing of favorite functions and people
- ▲ Obsession with volume over profit
- ▲ "Not-invented-here" syndrome
- ▲ Disruptive and confusing signal changing
- ▲ Mistrust of written plans and procedures
- ▲ Turf-building and political infighting
- ▲ Ineptitude at coaching and training subordinates
- ▲ Failure to groom successors
- ▲ Creative fatigue from "workaholism"

sity of California Center for Effective Organizations.[1] Their work on employee self-design programs led to a problem-solving technique called *innovation adoption,* which, in brief, works very well whenever there is a clear cause and effect, a clear set of implementable steps, a clear set of instructions, and a straightforward learning process.

Four factors should be foremost in your mind when selecting a consultant, while overseeing his project work for you, and when evaluating and implementing his recommendations.

1. Does your consultant evidence ability at objective and thorough analytical expertise in defining and developing relevant solutions for your problems and their causes?

2. Are you putting aside your own subjectivity and preconceptions about your problems as your consultant's analyses take shape? Are you particularly endeavoring to avoid bias in reviewing his analyses that trace back to matters of managerial processes, managerial styles, and leadership?

3. Have your consultant and you carefully weighed all of the identifiable consequences, both of failing to attend to the problems and of adopting corrective solutions for them?

4. Does the result of the exercise ring true in terms, not only of the facts of the situation, but also of your intuition, knowledge, and experience concerning your business situation? Have a sound and credible perspective and focus been achieved by the entire exercise?

Role of Imagination and Perspective in Problem Solving

The late Dr. Richard Hayes, while director of systems engineering for NASA's Apollo moon landing project, was struggling with the problem of removing 600 pounds from LEM, the lunar landing module. The objective of the weight reduction was to enable enough additional fuel to be carried for an added 15 seconds of safety margin for the reascent to the space capsule. In the finest problem-solving fashion, he combed through all components and operating procedures of the lunar module, but the alternatives fell far short of his objective. Finally, his solution came to him one day while riding the New York subway. As he stood in the aisle hanging onto the strap, he found his answer. His solution was to remove the astronauts' chairs from LEM; they were unnecessary for the short journey to the moon and back to the spaceship.

Note

1. Robert O. Metzger, *Profitable Consulting: Guiding America's Managers Into the Next Century* (Reading, Mass.: Addison-Wesley, 1989), page 104.

16

Natural Strategic Perspectives

"Natural" strategic factors, both inside your company and in your external business environment, will rank as significant determinants of performance improvement.

Neglecting natural strategic factors and forces is tantamount to mediocrity or even failure in your business situation. You and your consultant need to focus sharply on identifying your natural strategic advantages and disadvantages early and then clarifying the competitive opportunities or problems they may represent. Your strategic response should always encompass a combination or interlinking of the two. A CEO who enjoys important natural strategic advantages must make them touchstones of his overall strategic plan.

Natural Strategies: The Power of "Water Seeking Its Level"

Natural strategies are those major resource-allocation decisions that are based on significant inherent advantages your company may possess and on fundamental conditions and trends in your business environment. Both internal and external advantages, and particularly the latter, are almost like water seeking its level. The same is true if they are natural disadvantages for you; however, they call for different strategic responses and initiatives.

205

206 ASSURING SOUND PERSPECTIVE AND FOCUS

Bases for Natural Internal Strategic Advantage

Natural internal strategic factors usually are well within your control and influence as long as you monitor and nurture them regularly. They might stem from a secure patent position, a stable and dominant market share, or significant economies of scale in production, marketing, and distribution. More specifically, some of the more common internal bases for strategic advantage are the following:

- A company possesses superior, seemingly unbeatable product features and user benefits with significant patent protection, refurbishing it periodically with successions of new supplementary patents to extend the protected life.
- A company that was first in its market still owns a dominant share of that market, with offerings possessing an array of superior user benefits. Market share is based on a long-standing reputation for superior quality performance throughout its customer base that commands great brand loyalty.
- A relatively small newer company has a "quickly" established position in a small, highly specialized and unique market niche within its overall market based on its in-depth application know-how and astute assessment of latent needs of users.
- A company's unit sales are at high enough volumes to provide lucrative economies of scale, make it a low-cost producer in its industry, and afford significant levels of R&D effort.
- As a pioneering force in its industry, a company may have developed clear superiority in marketing, sales, and distributors, in terms of both numbers and depth of expertise, resulting in dominant distribution, service, and support capabilities.
- A company has developed superior supply and sub-contracting resources and relationships, and expertise in engineering, production, processing, and just-in-time manufacturing.

▲ A company enjoys a headstart and a timing advantage with upgrades, enhancements, or innovations to its product lines. Its competitors are faced with windows of market opportunity that are too short to prepare and introduce matching competitive market entries.

Certain of these factors may have been natural strategic advantages almost from the start, as with innovations and patents. Most often, however, they only emerged and became significant natural strategies as a company worked hard and resourcefully to develop its competitive prowess over time.

Natural External Factors That Can Present Strategic Opportunities or Problems

Natural external factors are those fundamental forces and conditions in your business environment that provide the base for complementing and reinforcing your company's internal strategies and resources. Among the many types of conditions in your business environment which can favor you *or your competitors* strategically are the following that you and your consultant should consider:

▲ Emerging applications and rapidly growing new market demand represent natural opportunities for those who are quickest to offer the best product solutions.
▲ Limited user experience and know-how with complex, new products and services can offer potential advantages to those products with the "friendliest" operating features and companies with outstanding user training.
▲ A limited installed base of costly equipment or installations may be needed to use a new product or service. This provides an early entrepreneur with an opportunity to beat competition with equipment (possibly offered on lease or at cost) that will give users their original capability to use the new service.
▲ Scarce critical supply sources provide lead time to those with the most dependable initial access to such supplies.

- ▲ A scarcity of trained and skilled people available for research, development, and engineering affords the nimble, leading-edge entrepreneur with a get-there-first opportunity.
- ▲ Early innovative technology to support entirely new application capabilities can either facilitate an early lead in the market or constitute an Achilles Heel leading to failure of the venture.

Basic Issues of Strategic Advantage

Some consulting projects start with two or three strikes against them. They contain fundamental requirements for success that cannot be met, whatever the resources, managerial acumen, and effort to be applied. The key questions to be answered by both you and your consultant throughout the course of the project are:

- ▲ What are all of the key strategies on which your present levels of performance and profitability are dependent?
- ▲ Are the dominant strategies that got you to your present position now passé or ineffectual in the face of changing conditions in your environment?
- ▲ What are all of the critical strategies that must work if your objectives are to be realized and your future programs are to succeed?
- ▲ Could your objectives be accomplished if any one of these strategies could not be carried out?
- ▲ Of those doubtful but possible plan elements, what is the probability of failure, or success, of each? Do you have capabilities to control them that offer a reasonable likelihood of success?
- ▲ In the early stages of a new venture that has passed the above tests, does additional information or insight raise new and serious obstacles to success not identified earlier? Is there serious cause for terminating your venture at such a point?

▲ Will your window of market opportunity stay open long enough to complete prototype development and testing, to introduce a superior competitive product or innovation to the marketplace, and to gain an early beachhead market share?

These questions usually cannot be answered clearly in the beginning, and some of their underlying issues do not even surface in the early stages of an unfamiliar venture. Moreover, the euphoria or optimism of an exciting new program tends to obscure or bias the decision makers toward thinking positively about all aspects. Intuitive entrepreneurial direction is most commendable when it works. However, it normally is more prudent to work with your consultant in seeking out those powerful natural forces in your situation that constitute fundamental advantages or disadvantages for you. The concept of natural strategies can be helpful.

At any given time many combinations of forces could explain the present rankings and differences in competitive standings within your industry. You should endeavor to analyze such improvement possibilities or competitive disadvantages critically to determine the odds and risks for improving your competitive performance. As with the above industry characteristics, these could work to your advantage if they describe your situation or could work seriously against you if describing competition. All represent strategic positions to convert into natural advantages.

The natural strategy concept almost always involves significant risk taking. The entrepreneur/executive is either moving to capitalize on strategic advantages that he hopes will give him a natural edge in his market, or he is flying in the face of one or more natural hurdles. More often than not, he has done his homework mainly on the positive side and approaches such a venture with great enthusiasm and conviction. In relation to natural disadvantages, however, he unfortunately is prone to view them too optimistically, or ignore them, or not even be aware of or focus on their existence until he has made major commitments of time and resources. Dortech Incorporated and its consultant faced just such a situation with a new venture in the air cargo industry.

Dortech CATS: Bucking Natural Strategic Obstacles

Dortech was a small systems engineering group in a large industrial corporation that had been quite successful in the design, development, and installation of major U.S. missile site launching systems. They spun their unit out of the parent company to start a pioneering business in automated freight handling systems for commercial airlines. Several major international airlines engaged Dortech to design cargo terminals and develop and install sophisticated automated storage and handling systems. Dortech quickly became a leader in large container handling, providing the entire system of conveyors and loading vehicles that interfaced the airplane and freight cargo warehouse.

In the mid-1960s, the Port Authority of New York and New Jersey (PONYA) offered Dortech a lease option on fifteen choice acres of airport land adjacent to a key runway at JFK Airport. The purpose was to develop and promote an automated air cargo terminal, which Dortech would then run as a consolidated service for multiple "member" airlines. The potential benefits included sharing the costly and scarce airplane parking ramp space and getting substantial cost benefits from the shared, automated warehouse handling of their cargo. The airlines would retain their own customer identity with separate sales and marketing activities, but common warehouse and ramp service people would be used in the new service to be called CATS (Consolidated Aircargo Terminal System).

PONYA gave Dortech sixty days to persuade some representative airlines to tender letters of intent to seriously consider participation. Dortech brought in a consultant to serve virtually full-time as the CATS project manager. Proposals were made to a number of airlines and letters were soon obtained from six participants who represented a workable mix of domestics and internationals with well-staggered flight schedules to avoid aircraft ramp congestion. Under the consultant's direction, Dortech staff began developing plans for warehousing, ramp layout, handling processes, pricing, and policies.

Efforts continued for some time without success to seek final accord among all participants. Then Dortech formed a joint venture with a major refueling and baggage handling service that was well established at the New York airports. This linked Dortech's strong systems and engineering capability with a proven airline service organization that hopefully would be capable of convincing the airline participants it could manage the union operating personnel effectively.

The venture partners tried to commit the participating airlines to break ground but were never successful in overcoming all of the objections and concerns of every interested airline, each of whom had invested significant time of their own to making the venture work. In the end, the major cause of the project's failure was inability to work out an acceptable solution for staffing the operation. One severe problem was the cargo handlers' potential loss of airline privileges, particularly free air trips, once they would sever their airline employment to become CATS employees. Also, every combination of airline participants had at least three different unions representing the respective crews who would be merged into one new operation. Staff reductions were inherent in the concept, and no airline was ready to bite this bullet with its own union.

The airlines, PONYA, and the venture partners stayed with the CATS project for so long because of powerful potential benefits for all parties. However, hindsight suggests that there was always a substantial natural strategic hurdle that could doom the project—the union compatibility problem. It might have been foreseen that no otherwise compatible combination of airlines, *all* having contracts with the same cargo handlers union, was likely to be assembled. In the end, this issue stood out well above all others. Earlier and more objective evaluation by both client and consultant could have saved considerable management time and expense for all parties.

A highly successful case of capitalizing on significant inherent strengths is afforded by IBM's reorganization of its domestic computer marketing operations into industry-specialized sales and systems branches and districts. This case provides an example of outstanding perspective and focus in exploiting a critical mass of resources.

IBM: Focusing on Natural Strategic Advantages

By the early 1960s IBM's domestic computer marketing forces in its Data Processing Division's branches had been specializing individual sales territory assignments by type of industry or line of business wherever enough of a branch's accounts in the same industry existed. This had been happening naturally at the branch level, because sales success was proving to be clearly related to the depth of understanding of a prospect's unique business, applications, and terminology.

The Data Processing Division launched a marketplace-oriented task force, in part to contribute marketing planning inputs to overall corporate studies but primarily to further its own domestic strategic planning. Assigned to this task force, and headed by a senior executive, were members of group and division line management, the corporate marketing staff, and several captive consultants in IBM's corporate organization department.

From the outset, the team concentrated on the fundamental characteristics of IBM's markets and focused on making maximum use of natural strategic advantages. They determined that their customers and prospects were heavily clustered within a 50-mile radius of the major U.S. metropolitan centers. This was the furthest distance away from any account they wanted a sales, systems, or customer engineering (equipment servicing) person to have to travel from a branch (an hour's drive or less) to reach the customer. They estimated that 70 percent of IBM's domestic potential resided within a 50-mile radius of the top twenty U.S. market areas.

Center by center, the task force then determined the extent to which accounts and prospects were clustered by industry type. From this information, they made up workload-balanced sales territories of single industries, grouped common territories under an industry-specialized data processing (DP) manager, and same- or similar-industry DP managers into an industry-specialized branch wherever the numbers warranted. They then assigned the requisite number and types of systems engineers and managers to each branch and the supporting cadre of customer engineers and administrative personnel for order processing and other office services. Branches in the remainder of the country retained geographic assignments with industry-specialized territories wherever possible.

As a result of this planning, for example, the New York metropolitan area, which had had some specialized branches before, now had twenty viable, industry-specialized branches, including banking, insurance, retailing, education, government, manufacturing, and petroleum processing. The number in the other nineteen metropolitan areas scaled down, but none had fewer than two specialized branches, and all had significant numbers of industry sales territories. A few industry branches in the East were assigned to an industry district; and one industry region was formed. The industry region was headquartered in Washington, D.C., comprising a national organization of geographically-dispersed branches serving the federal, state, and local government accounts, educational, medical, and other not-for-profit institutions throughout the United States.

IBM's situation was unique in terms of number of employees, dominant market share at the time, financial strength deriving from the rental revenue base, and the insatiable demand for computerization in its marketplace. But the principle they employed is broadly applicable. They utilized a task force of seasoned executives and consultants to step back and look objectively beyond present ways of doing things. This enabled them to identify the basic characteristics of their marketplace and competitive environment and then match and team these with their superior natural internal resources and capabilities.

PART SIX

Controlling the Project

> "The best laid schemes o' mice and men
>   Gang aft a-gley;
> An' lea'e us nought but grief and pain,
>   For prom'sed joy."
>
> "To a Mouse,"
Robert Burns

At one time or another, every practicing consultant has disappointed his client with schedule slippages, missed project goals, unsatisfactory findings and recommendations, or unfavorable impacts on the client's people and his outside constituencies. While such problems frequently are traceable to deficiencies in the consultant's approach and performance, both parties usually contribute. However, the burden of avoiding them always rests with the client, not the consultant. The client has the ultimate accountability.

The client must live with the consequences after the consultant has departed—or been sent packing. Failure to focus on this consideration often leads a client to entertain unduly high expectations for his consultant's results and follow-through.

The two chapters of Part Six probe the sixth significant challenge:

CHALLENGE SIX: CONTROL PROJECT QUALITY
AND SCHEDULE RIGOROUSLY

They are concerned with control of the schedule and its critical milestones; control of quality and relevance of the findings and recom-

Building Block Diagram E.   Summary factors: controlling the project.

_____Implement Plans_____

_____Control Project_____

Control of Study Schedule:	Control of Content Quality:
▲ Use single client liaison. ▲ Clarify goals at start. ▲ Monitor for slippage. ▲ Adjust for scope change.	▲ Promote client/consultant interactions and partnering. ▲ Make surprise quality and content checks.

_____Achieve Perspective and Focus_____

_____Structure Assignment_____

_____Match People_____

_____Determine Need and Timing_____

mendations; control of costs, both the direct project fees and the implicit costs associated with recommendations; and perhaps most importantly, control of the impact on your people, including your own employees, your customers, middlemen, suppliers, the financial community, and other constituencies who might be affected adversely (or hopefully positively) by the consultants' approach to your project.

How can you best cope with or avoid problems of deadlines and consulting cost overruns? How do you assure the consultant's pursuit of end targets and cost/benefits versus his preoccupation with functions? What must you do to prevent his excessive attention to the managerial process as against astute identification of strategic directions and the *content* of your business?

Chapter 17 deals with the logistical aspects of a project, which involve control of the consulting schedule and the process. Chapter 18 is concerned with control and supervisory considerations for achieving superior quality and relevance in the content or substance of your consultant's findings and recommendations. Building Block Diagram E outlines the key points to be covered.

17

Managing the Process

I treat project slippage as inexcusable; otherwise, it would become habit-forming. I tolerate no buck-passing of responsibility
for it, and start preaching to guard against slippage from the
moment I launch a complex assignment.

CEO of a major multidivision company

Overall control of the consulting project involves two principal
aspects: control of the *process* and control of the *content* of the
findings and recommendations. Both aspects contain the seeds
or potential causes of project slippage. Chapter 17 considers the
key logistical and supervisory elements of the process. Content
control issues and guidelines are the subject of the next chapter.

Conditions for Effective Control of the Process

Given the building blocks of a realistic proposal and selection of
a qualified consultant who matches your need, you are in position to concentrate on the key operational tasks of achieving and
maintaining effective project control. Five aspects of the ongoing consulting process deserve your attention:

1. Assigning to one of your key, senior people concerned
   with the area to be studied the responsibility for the project's control and all liaison between your people and the
   consulting team

2. Launching the assignment with the full understanding of both the consultants and those on your staff who need to know the project's objectives, scope, and approach
3. Establishing a requirement for monitoring and updating the consultant's survey plan and for continuous tracking of progress against the schedule, staffing commitments, and key benchmark events
4. Taking special precautions whenever indicated to determine whether there is significant slippage in the schedule and survey steps, and, if so, what action is needed
5. Staying alert for the need for scope and/or approach changes or modifications in the project's objectives as the study progresses

Each of these aspects contains challenges to effective conduct and control of the undertaking.

Designate Unified Project Control and Liaison Responsibilities

Depending on the nature of the consulting assignment you are undertaking, you may decide to retain the responsibility for control and liaison in your own office. This could be preferable in several situations: when you are embarking on an extremely sensitive and confidential situation; when you have employed an adviser for general guidance, with an indeterminant project agenda and time period; or when the project is quite small and close to your interests. You also might be wise to retain direct control in the initial stages of an unfamiliar proposition while you shake out its ultimate scope and test alternative approaches to its conduct.

On the other hand, with a significant, well-defined project involving a number of your key people and departments, you can benefit significantly from designating a control and liaison officer. This enables you to delegate all logistical matters of setting up interview schedules; arranging for reports and information requested by the consultants; introducing the consulting team to suppliers, middlemen, and customers; and countless other support activities needed to orient them quickly to your situation. You will also be able to keep a more independent arms length from the conduct of the study so that you can more objectively evaluate and critique its progress in terms of both process and content.

The focal point afforded by one control and liaison person assures greater consistency, both in your staff's understanding of the study's purposes and in application of the ground rules under which it is to be conducted. Depending on the magnitude of the project, you may wish to assign your control officer to full-time temporary duty.

Establish a Clear Target at Launch Time

At start-up time, make certain that everyone knows and understands the task ahead. This requires:

- ▲ Emphasizing and clarifying the target; reiterating expectations and the commitments of the proposal or in the absence of a written document, crystal-clear understanding between you and your senior consultant
- ▲ Identifying and introducing the participants for both parties and clarifying their respective roles; assigning the liaison responsibilities between them; and establishing communication and feedback procedures
- ▲ Setting up the benchmarks and achievement milestones (who, what, why, how, when, where, etc.); reaffirming completion and closure dates
- ▲ Agreeing on the ground rules, such as setting reasonable limits to the consulting staff's start-up orientation and education
- ▲ Airing any special considerations which, at the outset, seem to be the most critical determinants of ultimate success for the venture

Often the seeds of control problems are planted before the actual job begins. One of the principal upfront exposures is the crafting of a sloppy or overly ambitious proposal. Taking on an

unrealistic scope of assignment is a frequent offender. It becomes particularly critical when the client commits his own organization to significant follow-up dates for presenting project
results. Such was the situation in the Centurian Steel case cited
in Chapter 11.

Require Regular Monitoring and Updating of the Survey Plan

All of the classic skills, techniques, and practices of corporate
project control apply here: regular monitoring of compliance
against the schedule and its key events; assuring that the intended scope and approach are being observed; promptly inves-
tigating the causes of missed deadlines, variances, and time and
expense overruns; insisting on periodic progress reports to sense
whether the work is achieving its benchmark tasks and beginning to yield relevant findings.

You should use early, informal progress reports as an opportunity to take the pulse of the consultant's performance. The
more informal you keep these sessions, the more sensitive will
be your feel for what he and his team have been able to accomplish. You should be probing for clues as to whether they are
getting adequate exposure to all of the internal and external
sources of information germane to the project's objectives.

You should invite dialog to bring out the extent of conclusions they are starting to reach about your problems and opportunities. You should be looking for gauges as to the caliber and
freshness of their ideas about your alternatives. Most importantly, you should try to get impressions as to the impact their
work seems to be having on your people and your outside constituencies.

Check Periodically for Slippage in the Complex Aspects of a Project

One of the most important project control problems is slippage—
slippage of time, slippage in getting to all aspects of the planned
scope, slippage in coverage of content, slippage in meeting dead-

lines, slippage in completing milestone tasks. Slippages have many causes, not the least of which is failure of a client's own staff to live up to their commitments or obligations to support the consulting team.

An effective way to determine if you have such a problem with your consultant is to call impromptu review sessions to discuss progress informally with him or her. Ask discerning questions to test his facility with various areas under study, to draw out his preliminary conclusions about your problems or opportunities, and to see if he is identifying alternative courses of action.

A frequent control problem is *scope change*, and most of the time this means that a broader scope creeps in than the proposal authorized or the consultant thought he was committed to. Scope changes can become necessary because of implications neither the client nor the consultant anticipated at the outset. The client may have after-thoughts about additional results he would like. Or, the consultant may initiate scope enlargement in the hopes of making a better showing or expanding billings and angling for continued business. Whatever the reasons, this issue needs careful attention at the moment of the scope change to avoid jeopardizing the overall results desired or piling up significant cost overruns.

Avoiding slippage with complex consulting assignments requires diligence beyond the normal monitoring procedures discussed above. At the outset and during the course of an involved study, you should be particularly alert to project characteristics or conditions such as the following, which can easily suffer slippage.

- Unrealistically ambitious project goals or objectives moving the study into largely unfamiliar or uncharted territory
- Overelaborate survey plans and overemphasis by the consultant and your own staff on preliminary planning of study steps
- Excessive reliance on client people; need for periodic and frequent interviews, group meetings, and planning exercises by a significant number of your people
- A requirement for extensive information from outside

sources where consultants' schedules are often overly
ambitious about its availability

▲ Inordinately tight project completion schedules, either
arbitrarily set or necessitated by the situation

▲ Unforeseen losses of critical consulting talent to the project and the consultant's substitution of key staff in midstream

▲ Limited and late attention to, or neglect of, the critical financial criteria and requirements of the project, which
may be the final determinant of the feasibility of the recommendations

▲ Sloppy problem definition leading down blind alleys or
otherwise obscuring the directions the project should be
taking

▲ Too few progress reports or interim review dates for you to
keep informed of what the consultants are finding and
the trends of their conclusions and recommendations

One facet of a major strategic planning exercise undertaken
at a university school of business demonstrates some of the slippage problems when a project is complex and depends upon numerous inputs for its success.

Southern States University: Complexities = Slippage

Some years ago a consultant had an opportunity to help develop a marketing strategy as part of a unique planning program for
the dean of a prominent school of business. The dean was developing a brilliant new total educational concept, an *Action Learning System*, comprised of three interrelated pedagogical approaches:

▲ *Subject areas* (wherein groups of faculty and students would
jointly design learning programs in certain business specializations)

▲ *Institutes* (which would focus on the application of knowledge to specify industries, such as retailing, financial administration, insurance)

▲ *R&D centers* (to research new ideas for solving tough business problems, for example, in asset management, diversifi-

cation strategies, the management of change, productivity improvement)

In the Dean's vision for the school, the students would participate actively in the design of their own degree programs. A key element would be their "employment" by the Institutes and R&D centers for hands-on experience in their chosen fields or subject areas.

Multitalented task force. Virtually the entire business faculty was involved in this summer project as well as the current class of MBA candidates, who would get summer credits for their participation. Aided by a significant grant from a regional industrialist, the dean also recruited experts and specialists from industry to help plan curricula incorporating "live business problems" and entrepreneurially related programs and to develop specifications for advanced audio/visual systems and methods, as well as computer and peripheral applications for learning. One group was planning a TV network as a key part of the dean's remote campus and open university concepts targeted at working people and continuing education beyond graduation. An architect was enlisted to develop new concepts of space utilization to stimulate learning and to execute a conceptual building design for housing the multifaceted programs being planned.

Marketing strategy project. The school's marketing strategy was one of the more intertwined and interdependent projects. In the dean's bold plan for the future, it depended on in-depth understanding of each of the school's markets or "customer" categories. He had defined nine such segments, which he envisioned broadly as including current and prospective students, current and prospective faculty and administration, alumni, funding support organizations and sponsors, a wide range of outside industry supporters and participants in the learning process, and, for various reasons, other educational institutions and government agencies.

Faculty participation in marketing strategy definition. In view of this complexity, the dean anticipated that the marketing consultant would want significant planning input from the faculty and Institute department heads. On this basis, the consultant proceeded to research and define the school's marketing strategy. He developed a market profiling exercise for each of the above market categories, which was to be completed by every department head and key staff administrator. The dean's overall timetable was extremely tight, and all projects were to be readied within three weeks for a first full plan review at a retreat to be attended by every team.

Nine market profiling tasks were assigned to the appropriate faculty and staff heads, and the consultant withdrew to await their completion. It would have been preferable for him to work individually with each profiler to develop a joint product, but funds were limited and the dean felt confident his staff would produce. Very few finished the profiling assignment by retreat time and the marketing consultant's recommendations were embarrassingly incomplete.

A few other multifaceted projects suffered from similar problems, as well. However, with a lot of anguish and scrambling, a fully developed plan, including a marketing strategy for the school, was completed by the dean's overall deadline. Unfortunately, the missed deadline for the marketing strategy project had prevented its getting the benefit of a review and challenge by the full assemblage of retreat participants.

Critique of consulting approach. In this complex and tightly scheduled program, several optimistic assumptions were critical. Both the dean and the consultant had assumed that the consultant would get up to speed much sooner in understanding the various traditional and new "markets" of the School of Business and the unique products of his bold new concept. On hindsight the dean should have brought the consultant in earlier and budgeted more funds for his role. Also, the dean had not focused on how heavily the consultant's work depended upon the responsiveness of the faculty and staff, which was not forthcoming.

Maintain Flexibility for Scope and Approach Changes

Coping with complex studies is made easier and less expensive by determining carefully in advance what is most likely to be the shortest distance between the desired points of the assignment and then building in flexibility to change the scope and approach as the early findings materialize.

One technique is to structure the proposal with a limited initial reconnaissance phase. A second is to schedule early, informal progress reports when it is unclear how to limit the scope of a reconnaissance exercise precisely. A third method is to analyze the critical financial aspects of a project before rushing out into the marketplace. This analysis can help to focus a study's key issues significantly and thereby reduce the potential waste and amount of field work needed.

The Ultronic Systems Corporation, whose proposal elements were used as examples in Chapters 9 and 10, combined these second and third approaches successfully. Their consultant focused on the financial performance factors and requirements before initiating heavy field research on a prospective new venture for the company. They then kept close touch with the early field work to narrow the market scope further based on the consultant's initial external findings.

Ultronic: Focusing on the Economics Early

The Stockmaster was Ultronic's original terminal for delivering real-time electronic stock price quotes. It had served the subscribers well until a redesign became necessary because of increasing competition and advances in small computer state-of-the-art. This first terminal was very heavy and slow and had a tiny viewing screen. Its functions were limited to current price and trading data on individual stocks.

In the early 1970s the company designed and introduced a far superior terminal incorporating the latest technologies and offering many new functions and additional information of interest to their market, including display of a multistock portfolio and latest market news.

The original model still was not physically obsolete, however, so the CEO engaged a consultant to research potential secondary markets for it. The objective was to discover where the old terminals that were being returned might be used online by subscribers who did not qualify to receive instant transaction information but would be satisfied with a Securities & Exchange Commission-mandated 15-minute delay in accessing security price data.

The proposal's first steps called for a brief initial review of a half dozen or so new potential classes of markets and development of a preliminary financial pro forma for the new venture. Based on the experience of client personnel and a few preliminary field interviews, the scope was quickly narrowed to just three potential secondary markets for field study. One group consisted of the trust departments of smaller banks and insurance company investment departments; another, small commodity traders and the commodity departments of processing and manufacturing concerns; and a third, so-called affluent individual investors. If any of these markets showed promise, the consultant was to evaluate the profit potential and develop an appropriate Business Plan.

Concurrently with the very small initial field interview sample, the consultant developed a starter pro forma P&L and balance sheet for the venture working with client people to establish assumptions. Unless this preliminary financial analysis clearly indicated that the idea should be abandoned and the residual values in the old terminals written off as sunk costs, he would then proceed with a more intensive schedule of field work. The pro forma approach brought the field study requirements into much sharper focus.

The ensuing field activities were not conclusive and the client decided to have a telephone survey undertaken in two of the markets to enlarge substantially the original sample called for in the proposal and to contain the higher costs of personal field visits. This unanticipated work was performed by a professional from another part of the client's parent company, and its findings were evaluated by the consultant. The additional findings contributed to the overall recommendation, which was that the old terminals be abandoned.

The decision to concentrate on an early pro forma exercise and relatively few initial customer interviews forced a better focus and perspective for both the client and consultant almost from the outset of the engagement. It clearly avoided excessive field work, had that been undertaken as the first step.

18

Obtaining a Quality Result

Quality: A characteristic or attribute of something; property; a feature; the positive or negative character of a proposition.

The Illustrated Heritage Dictionary

The consulting process needs to be controlled on two levels: the logistical aspect, reviewed in Chapter 17; and the content-quality aspect. The name of the game is not a tight logistical process per se, although that takes you to your destination, but a superior quality result. The result needs to be relevant to the company's situation and its opportunities, timely, implementable, and hopefully achievable with lasting benefits to the client.

This chapter presents four sets of control and directional considerations that can be instrumental in achieving an outstanding consulting result of superior quality and relevance.

1. Fostering ongoing interactions in depth between client personnel and the consulting team
2. Monitoring findings for their quality and integrity
3. Striving for positive impacts on the people involved
4. Insisting on a realistic, workable, action-oriented focus

Fostering Ongoing Client/Consultant Interactions

A healthy, ongoing program of information interchange between client and consultant needs to continue through three key stages: (1) conveying information to the consultants; (2) interactions about their findings and conclusions; and (3) discussions, brainstorming, debates, and arguments about the emerging alternative courses of action and recommendations. Each stage has different, but vital, effects on the quality, relevance, practicality, and timeliness of the end result you are seeking.

Initially, your organization is conveying background information the consultants will need in order to relate their experiences to your situation accurately and realistically. Most consulting assignments require substantial input from the client organization as background and a frame of reference for launching and proceeding with the study. Too often most of the healthy interchange takes place mainly in the orientation stage with briefings, key interviews in each aspect under study, product presentations, plant tours, and examination of voluminous reports, financial statements, market studies, product literature, policy and organization manuals, and the like. Then the consultants explore the outside world and counsel among themselves.

For several reasons, it is essential in most assignments that you start a new project by encouraging and promoting a pattern of periodic communications between your staffs and the consultants. Open exchange is important to clarify your policies and programs, performance experience, and case analyses of innovations you may have tried in the past that did not work as intended. The consultants can benefit from learning firsthand at an early date who in your organization are the most realistic sources of experience and expertise on the various pertinent facets of your situation and who are the most imaginative and provocative thinkers.

As the consultants digest and synthesize their findings, periodic interchanges of views should continue in order to ensure that they are drawing relevant conclusions. Also, the dialog can have major on-the-job training and development benefits for your staff as they face new questions, issues, and challenges raised by the outsiders and as they learn of approaches other companies have taken in similar situations.

Perhaps most importantly, as the iterative process begins to yield definitive alternatives and narrow the choices to the final recommendations, you and your people need to become sounding boards and devil's advocates. This process tests the relevance and workability of the consultants' position. It also starts your staff's "buy in" to the recommendations, making them an integral party to them and easing the path toward implementation and initiation of action.

Monitoring Findings for Their Quality and Integrity

It is always sound practice to begin early to assess the quality of the findings your consultant's team is developing. More specifically, in the processes of interactions described in the previous section, what should you be looking for?

- ▲ What perspective and focus are they beginning to reflect?
- ▲ Are they covering all of the essential information and opinion sources?
- ▲ Do they recognize the biases and blind spots of client people? Are they objectively assessing what they are discovering?
- ▲ How sharp are the consultants' problem definition skills; are they tracing back to root causes?
- ▲ Is there a meeting of the minds on preliminary conclusions; if not, what additional avenues of investigation are required?

Part Seven explores the issues concerned with the all-important implementation of a consulting project. The essential prelude to implementation and follow-through is to assure that the consultant is developing practical and implementable recommendations. Ninety-nine percent of the time, the client can tell a realistic recommendation after it has been presented to him. The problem is that while it is still in the work-in-process phase the client may not have stayed close enough to the project to realize whether the consultant's final package of proposals is likely to be feasible.

Questions and issues that you should probe during the wrap-up stages of a study include:

- ▲ Consistency with and sensitivity to the realities of your external business environment and the needs of your customers
- ▲ Consistency with and relevance to your corporate mission, objectives, and strategic directions
- ▲ Consistency with the project proposal and completeness in terms of the intended scope of study
- ▲ Quality versus quantity of conclusions and recommendations; avoidance of a textbook or primer about the client's business, seeking instead a report characterized by brevity, clarity, and communicability
- ▲ Results-oriented, effort-stretching; and workable recommendations; a good balance of content versus process and management practices; creative approaches to the client's business opportunities
- ▲ Concept recommendations directly trackable to specific actions for executing them
- ▲ Ability to reach closure on the assignment, in terms of the commitments made by the consultant and within the agreed time and cost

In addition to determining whether a project is moving effectively and efficiently toward its objectives, it is wise to double-check whether it is being undertaken in a desirable and approved way. One case in point was an electronics manufacturer who was in the midst of a consulting assignment and wanted to gain additional insight about his competition, which was beyond the agreed-upon study scope. He reasoned that he could save time and money by backing up his consultant with a market researcher, a corporate employee serving as a captive consultant, who could be made available for a short period.

This young man was a self-starter who was bucking for promotion, and it soon became clear that he was not one to encourage supervision from either the client or the outside consultant. He plunged into the task energetically and in a matter of less than three weeks was ready to report back to the client with comprehensive findings. He distributed fat notebooks to each attendee at his competitive briefing session and proceeded to reveal an amazing amount of information about the competitors. Several were privately held companies and, therefore, normally released little confidential information to the outside world.

The client was so intrigued with the thoroughness and the new "inside" information uncovered that he quizzed the market researcher at some length on his methodology. The young man unabashedly admitted that he had cultivated new acquaintances at key radio or television stations in the vicinity of each private competitor, and had "hired" them to go after human interest stories about the client's competitors. The approach the market researcher used was that, after appropriate review, the stories would be aired at some future date as public relations items for the concerned companies. The broadcasters would get useful program material, and the market researcher had full access to all of the information obtained.

The client blanched when these revelations surfaced and immediately ordered the confiscation and destruction of all notebooks and charts on the competitors. He sent the market researcher packing and directed both his staff and the consultant to avoid using any of the new competitive information that had been obtained through misrepresentation.

Striving for Positive Impacts

As a consulting study proceeds, continuing attention needs to be given to the impact it is having on the client's own people, as well as his customers, suppliers, outside directors, or other constituencies. This issue preoccupied the executives of Walk Wear Enterprises when, as discussed in Chapter 12, they insisted that their identity not be revealed in the consultant's discussions with their key customers, the mail order chain shoe buyers. They had concluded erroneously that the impact would be negative, when, instead, the buyers took their employment of the consultants as a sign of strength.

Among the objectives and areas of possible problems that need to be monitored regularly from the viewpoint of personnel impact are:

- ▲ Maintenance of positive working relationships between the client's and consultant's staffs
- ▲ Client's assurance that the consultant's contacts with customers, suppliers, the financial community, and other outsiders leave positive, constructive impressions
- ▲ Consulting staff's ability to protect and evoke confidences with client people in order to elicit their full cooperation
- ▲ A spirit of participation, which finds the client and consultant partnering closely in the pursuit of sound findings and recommendations
- ▲ Consultant's ability to communicate in the client's language and business vernacular
- ▲ Avoidance of proselytizing of the client's staff by the consultant

A positive impression is the normal overriding objective, but this cannot always be maintained, especially if there are explicit or implicit threats to the concerned parties, which can stifle cooperation by client staffs. Whenever projects give off an aura or suspicion that the performance and competence of key players or departments are being evaluated critically, they need to be carefully orchestrated to avoid undue disruptions or morale problems. Directed studies with concealed purposes or predetermined decisions and outcomes should receive the same consideration.

This book has stressed the people dimension of your consulting project throughout. Bringing in outsiders can be analogous to the alien rejection phenomenon with organ transplants. It can approach the apprehension, insecurity, and even terror of a turnaround specialist, a new broom sweeping clean. It can unleash imaginative speculation on the motives of top management, and encourage "underground" debate on prospective key firings, mass layoffs, sale of unsatisfactory divisions, and a host of other negatives. If not handled carefully, the advent of a consultant also can raise questions and concerns in the minds of the client's outside constituencies—customers, suppliers, middle-men, bankers, shareholders.

Insisting on a Realistic, Workable, Action-Oriented Focus

A fairly common problem of project control is the consultant who is obsessed with thorough and scholarly results to the neglect of, or underemphasis on, results.

The consultant's prime role is to help you effect profitable change, not to develop brilliant, flawless, and scholarly understanding of your situation. He should, of course, strive for such insights and perspectives as inputs for his recommendations but not to the exclusion of his principal mission, developing workable action programs to benefit your company.

Consultants, by nature, strive to be perfectionists and to impart such perfection to their clients. They are concerned with bringing the utmost possible order to a disorderly situation. In this pursuit they can be too idealistic and too scholarly in their approach to your assignment.

Hopefully, your senior consultant can be relied upon to carry much of the burden of practicality and feasibility for you. Although such a burden is always an implicit obligation, monitoring practically any project of large enough scope to require a team of advisors is not that easy. However, you cannot afford to assume that implementable recommendations will always follow merely because of reputation and the high level of fees being expended. The situation outlined below illustrates some of the behind-the-scenes problems in developing practical results and how the consulting partner in charge righted the ship in time, with a bit of prodding from his client.

Meadowlands: Functional Scholarship vs. Action Focus

Meadowlands Corporation, a major food and dairy products company, engaged a consultant to study its general management process and its strategic directions and strategies. The senior partner who sold the job assigned the supervising partner who had drafted the winning proposal to direct the work. The latter assembled a team from the firm's management and marketing divisions and was authorized to bring in special outside talent as needed. The collective internal and external staff included experience and expertise in organization planning, management processes, accounting, sales management, advertising, promotion, distribution, and production engineering. Several on the team had relevant consumer packaged goods experience.

Only the supervisor, a fanatical stickler for detailed planning, had participated with the senior partner in the preproposal client interviews. The supervisor's first step before bringing his full team and the client together was to direct his three functional leaders to review a mountain of historical documents provided by the client and prepare in-depth study plans. The starter game plans were to be based solely upon the initial working papers. Each set of plans was to include interview guides, additional information request lists, and tentative staff schedules for their respective functional areas. True to Parkinson's thesis (work expansion to meet the time available for its completion), redundancies and excesses developed in direct proportion to the four weeks spent on these exercises, with the staff still mostly in the dark about the dynamics of the client's situation.

The team was not exposed to Meadowlands management until the fifth week, when an intensive schedule of interviews finally was launched at corporate and group headquarters. By this time the team faced an imminent date for an initial progress report to the client. Critically, the senior partner had been out of touch with both his staff and the client once he had obtained the account.

At his first internal meeting with the team, he blew his stack because of the slippage in preparation for the initial client session. He also was critical of a lack of focus to the team's early findings and chastised his staff for their preoccupation with historical fact gathering and data massaging. He viewed the first four weeks to be largely an elementary educational exercise at the client's expense and was disturbed that the team had not yet identified any preliminary strategic alternatives.

The limited progress was evident to the Meadowlands CEO at the initial meeting, and he insisted that the senior partner right the situation immediately. The latter directed his project supervisor to set up without further delay several days of intensive field work with a representative sample of the client's direct salesforce to join them on their sales calls. These were retail salesmen who worked on shelf space allocations and point-of-sale promotions and delivery sales-men who followed regular store routes.

The senior partner participated with the entire team in these ex-ercises, riding with a delivery salesman, sitting on a milk crate, and visiting stores with him. The Meadowlands CEO had been per-suaded by the senior's rationale that if he/they could understand and focus clearly on the requirements of the salesman's job, sound stra-tegic directions would be forthcoming.

This grass-roots approach succeeded in breaking through the supervisor's obsession with functions and quickly focused the project on the important issues. As the client had insisted, the senior partner now stayed untypically close to the engagement until its satisfactory, although much-delayed, completion and reported back to the client CEO regularly. He led in developing some brilliant and substantive recommendations, which the client accepted as fully meeting the objectives and scope of the assignment.

The senior partner's belated attention to the end-point was what the Meadowlands CEO had assumed all along he was paying for. Clients who fail to keep tuned in from the start of the project aren't always that fortunate. From the beginning of a strategic-direction-seeking assignment, a client should make every effort to verify that his consultant is identifying strategic opportunities and pursuing end results and cost benefits, rather than remaining preoc-cupied with history, process, and functions.

You cannot begin too soon after the "meter starts running" to ascertain that your consultants have their eye on results and are not lingering through an "education" stage with you paying the tuition. Monitor for results orientation by insisting on early and frequent communication directly with the senior consultant to whom you awarded the assignment, by teaming your own people with the consulting crew, and by informal progress re-ports at key intervals. Also watch for critical impacts on your people.

PART SEVEN

Achieving Sound Implementation Plans

For every Future, identify a current Action. Identify a Person with the Action. Attach a desired Result to the Action. Define Incentives, Rewards for achievement.[1]

Michael J. Kami,
Strategic Planner

Mike Kami is a pioneering strategic planner who assisted IBM management during the late 1950s and early 1960s when they were establishing dominance with the electronic computer. He subsequently has consulted to many companies of all sizes in diverse industries.

Kami insists that every sentence of every plan be allowed to stand only if it has an Action attached to it and if someone specific is designated to take the necessary steps. You should find this test most illuminating and constructive as you review the recommendations and action plans your consultant has presented to you.

The client and consultant share the challenge of achieving useful end results from the engagement. Their procedural goal for wrapping up every consulting assignment should be a set of realistic, but effort-stretching, recommendations and an implementation plan, containing action steps, responsibility assignments, timetables, and scheduled follow-ups. Without these elements, all the good work and benefits of the prior phases can be dissipated or lost.

Even when the actions to be taken are well detailed, there are

Building Block Diagram F.   Summary factors: implementation planning.

_____Implement Plans_____

Plan Acceptance Steps:	Action Readiness Tests:
▲ Resolve internal politics and opposing views early. ▲ Heed contrary consultant recommendations. ▲ Assure key client "buy-ins." ▲ Clarify responsibilities for action steps.	▲ Concept/action linkages. ▲ Realistic project development goals and timing. ▲ Offers competitive gains, performance improvement. ▲ Compatible with situation, capabilities, finances.

_____Control Project_____

_____Achieve Perspective and Focus_____

_____Structure Assignment_____

_____Match People_____

_____Determine Need and Timing_____

additional challenges to be met. One is to make certain the client is convinced the recommendations should be followed. Another is the matter of who will be involved in the implementation and whether the consultant should be included. Overriding all of these questions is the need to determine that the final recommendations and action plan are realistic, workable, consistent with your organization's preparedness to undertake them, and offer the prospect of significant performance improvement.

Part Seven addresses the seventh major challenge in the use of consultants:

CHALLENGE SEVEN: ACHIEVE SOUND IMPLEMENTATION PLANS

Chapter 19 discusses a number of basic considerations for establishing the conviction and confidence you and your staff will need in order to accept the recommendations and action plans and to prepare your organization to implement them. Chapter 20 presents several tests of critical factors for the successful application and implementation of your consultant's final recommendations. Building Block Diagram F highlights these points.

Note

1. From a presentation to corporate executives by Michael J. Kami. Also see Michael J. Kami, *Trigger Points: How to Make Decisions Three Times Faster, Innovate Smarter, and Beat Your Competition by Ten Percent (It Ain't Easy)* (New York: McGraw-Hill Book Company, 1988).

19

Building Your Acceptance

I've read your report, but you've taken me by surprise. What have you given me and what do I do with it?

The conscientious consultant hates most to hear "You haven't really done what you said you would, so I'm not authorizing payment of your latest statement." His second most hated message is the one above.

This chapter presents several definitive cautions you and your consultant should heed to assure your organization's acceptance of the recommendations and to avoid ineffectual implementation and follow-through. Executives' bookshelves are filled with thick reports gathering dust because the client was not convinced or did not know what to do with them for lack of a workable action plan.

Are the Internal Politics Addressed Up Front?

No organization with more than a handful of people can avoid addressing this pervasive people dimension. Internal politics, turf-protection, the defensive motivations of insecure managers, the inevitable power conflicts—all can be a hurdle to successful implementation if not carefully addressed.

You may not always have a complete and current reading on the political implications of a new program. From the earliest stages of the assignment, you should charge your consultant with feedback that can clarify significant opposition, confusion, or indifference concerning the proposed moves, without asking him to betray individual confidences.

Is Your Consultant Obtaining Acceptances of His Findings and Recommendations En Route to His Final Position?

You need to make certain that the emerging findings and recommendations have been considered critically along the way by those in your organization who will participate in their implementation. One ever-present concern is the polite head nodding that so often occurs in exchanges between consultant and client.

At the outset of an action program, it is critical for your consultant to have obtained all of the essential buy-ins from your people who will make or break the program. This battle is partially won in advance if the individuals who will be needed to support the new program had a definitive role in developing the recommendations. The consultant should be including all such individuals in the analysis stage, but you should be monitoring him to be certain he does so.

For the balance of the organization, and particularly for the likely opponents of a planned move, it is imperative to present and communicate the most persuasive case possible for the recommendations to be installed. Demonstrating the benefits to the various affected units can flush out remaining opposition and help considerably to presell its implementation. Use trial balloons in advance of finalizing your position wherever appropriate.

Have You "Listened" to and Heeded Your Consultant's Contrary Recommendations?

Pay serious, thoughtful attention to your consultant's confirmable findings. Grapple intensively with credible conclusions and recommendations that may run counter to your instincts and desires. To protect yourself in advance against your own biases, make your consultant vow to "die hard" on any controversial position he may take.

Do not reject credible opposing views until you have reached complete conviction and confidence about your position. This gives you a better chance to consider thoroughly all of the key issues before locking in to a plan of action. The natural reluctance to take one's consultant's advice extends into many different aspects of a client's experiences. Since much has been said on this subject elsewhere, a digression from the normal business situation may be in order. The principle is exactly the same.

Not long ago the chief executive of one of America's top corporations was taking a well-deserved respite from his CEO responsibilities with some golf in Scotland. He and his friends were playing the tough and challenging links course at the Royal Dornoch Golf Club.

CEO had hit a long, booming drive to the left of the fairway on the sixteenth hole. A fairly high hill rose above him, completely obscuring the distant green and the flagstick. Just to his left and as far ahead as he could see was a sheer drop to the ocean beach, which paralleled the course. Both temporary and permanent caravans (or house trailers) filled the beach. CEO sent young Kevin, his caddie, to the crest of the hill to give him the distance and a sighting for his second shot into the green. CEO, nervous about hooking down onto the beach, challenged the direct line of flight that Kevin had established, but Kevin said, "No sir, that's the line you want."

After four of these exchanges, CEO's playing partner, standing at the crest with Kevin and seeing Scottish twosomes closing in behind, said "For gosh sakes, Kevin, give him another direction!" With that, Kevin moved to a line about twelve feet to the CEO's right, and the latter confidently settled in to a massive well-struck delivery, straight as a die from the clubface of his low iron. Highly pleased, CEO yelled up to Kevin for the result. "Pin high, sir, but ninety feet right of the green!"

While differences in perception often underlie a client's reluctance to follow a seemingly sound recommendation, the situation also can stem from the consultant failing to effectively demonstrate the need or, as in this case, not establishing his client's confidence in him.

Many years ago at the outset of President Eisenhower's interstate highway-building program, a marketing research firm was surveying a number of markets for a major heavy machinery manufacturer. Among many findings, the researchers recommended the acquisition of Euclid, the premier producer of super heavy-duty trucks. Unfortunately, the idea was lost within the massive report, which contained many other findings and recommendations. General Motors later moved to acquire Euclid and a significant opportunity was closed out for the client.

A client can never afford to dismiss lightly proposed solutions with which he does not agree. He has spent management time and out-of-pocket funds to invest in new perspectives and to test challenges to his strategic commitments. His exposure is compounded if his consultant does not fight hard to get him to focus seriously on the contrary positions.

Too often, the consultant takes the "selling" of his recommendations to the client too much for granted. As he winds up his work and locks in on a course of action, he assumes that his own new perceptions of what is needed will be self-evident to the client. Sometimes, he misinterprets the client's polite head nodding as clear evidence of assent. So he neglects his responsibilities, (1) by not "forcing" the client to grapple with all of the fundamental issues, and (2) by not following through on the client's responsive action to them.

A situation from the toy industry illustrates the dangers, where the client and consultant accomplished many constructive moves together, but one recommendation turned out to be the client's Achilles heel some years later.

Ideal Toy: Subordinating Needed Actions

The toy industry is exciting, fun-filled, innovative, faddish and fickle, severely seasonal, fraught with high rates of product obsolescence and new-product failures, and altogether, a very high-risk business.

Balancing a mix of promotional toys and staples. A balanced product-line strategy is one of the most critical and fundamental keys to generating consistent profits. The most successful companies pursue a strategy of balancing a mix of TV-promotional toys, games and dolls on the one hand with carefully-positioned staple lines on the other. Markets for the staples must be sustained over time until they become institutions, traditions or habits for repeat purchase of new versions.

Among the industry's most successful staples are two brand franchises owned by Mattel, the Barbie and Ken doll line and Hot Wheels, both of which have continued to sell profitably for many years. Hasbro's GI Joe line has been another long-living phenomenon. Staple games with long market tenure include Monopoly and Scrabble. A much more recent entrant, the TV game, Nintendo, has the earmarks of a long-lasting staple game line, subject to the dangers of losing ultimately to other contenders who will continue to exploit the advancing state-of-the-art in electro/optical information and computer technology.

Advantage of staple lines. The advantage of getting a product line into a staples status is that it then can be sustained in the marketplace with relatively little advertising. The manufacturer can concentrate instead on product enhancements, long production runs, key-account selling, support services to distributors, retail detailing to maintain good shelf position, and point-of-sale promotions.

The high risk of TV promotional toys. In contrast, TV promotional toys often are a huge "crap shoot" with a very short market life. The manufacturer spends large sums to excite the children, their parents, and grandparents through heavy television expenditures. If the product looks appealing and catches the consumers' fancy, the wholesalers and retailers are forced to stock it, frequently having to price-discount it to match their competitors or use it as a loss leader to draw people into the store. They may only carry and support it as long as their customers demand it. If it sells, the consumers and the manufacturer are the big winners, but the latter runs the risk of alienating his retailers and losing shelf space for his slower moving lines.

Marketing audit of Ideal. Ideal Toy engaged consultants to perform a comprehensive marketing audit. (The project objectives and scope were outlined previously in Chapters 10 and 11.) In the course of this work, the consultants assessed strategic product line directions and objectives from the perspective of the marketplace and competitive offerings, although the product planning and development functions had been outside their proposed scope of study.

Trade concerns about lack of product balance. Interviews with the wholesale and retail trade revealed the very strong opinion that the company was "heavily disproportionate" in its emphasis on TV promotional toys, games, and dolls. The trade felt Ideal was neglecting efforts to establish staple lines. The Ideal Toy founder's initial success had been based on a stuffed teddy bear that emulated a White House toy popularized during Theodore Roosevelt's presidency. This bear was the backbone of sales and profit growth through Ideal's early years; it became a highly successful staple product and was widely copied by others.

Ideal's initial success with MouseTrap. In the late 1960s, Ideal pioneered the toy industry's TV promotional strategy with a game, MouseTrap, which they advertised heavily on national television. This action game was a great success, and it encouraged Ideal and other toy manufacturers to continue to exploit their new advertising medium aggressively. Significant rewards went to the winners, but these were far outnumbered by the losers. Frequently, such products survived no more than one, two, or three years at the most, not long enough to amortize and recover the hefty front-end outlays for product development and costly national TV advertising.

Recommended emphasis on staples. As one aspect of their proposals, the consultants advocated that Ideal place a high priority on developing or acquiring some significant staple lines to balance the TV promotional efforts. Top management seemed to agree in principle with this position, and placed particular credence in the consultants' feedback from Ideal's wholesalers and retailers, although they were surprised at the trade's vociferousness on the point. However, a move into staples is easier said than done; it takes considerable time and effort to develop and requires more than a bit of luck on the product innovation and development side. Moreover, viable acquisitions are not that plentiful or easy to effect.

Some staple product planning and development efforts were initiated, and acquisitions of established staples lines were considered on a modest scale, but the memories of the earlier successes with MouseTrap and other TV-promoted items were too strong. Ultimately, little was accomplished with staples and the main focus continued to be TV toys.

Ideal's acquisition by CBS. Later, the company was acquired by CBS and merged into a leisure and recreational group that included other toy lines. A number of these lines were spun off subsequently by CBS. Some individual Ideal Toy brands continued to be available in the marketplace, but at a fraction of the sales level in the prime years.

At Ideal, neither party recognized at the time that the staples strategy issue ultimately could become a key make-or-break consideration. The consultants were unable to make a compelling enough case for a strong staples strategy and did not persevere with the point throughout the implementation of other recommendations. Although management exerted some serious effort in trying to add staples lines, that policy ran too counter to their perceptions about the TV-product strategy and the memories of their early successes with it.

The hindsight lesson for the client is clear. If you are paying substantial fees for objective, outside perspective, if that judgment is confirmed by the opinions of your own middlemen and some key people within your organization, and if the issue looms as a natural strategy in your industry, heed it and exercise its pros and cons diligently. In such situations, your consultant also assumes an obligation to follow through and to convince and motivate you to act.

Have You Expended Extra Efforts to Salvage Projects With Missing or Inferior Action Plans?

Some consultants overrun the earlier phases of the study and stop before developing an adequate action plan in order to avoid further overruns or to meet a final deadline. Surprisingly, others just do not emphasize implementation unless the client insists; both sides make the assumption that somehow action will happen in the normal course.

Recommendations that are not tendered in an implementable condition pose several obvious and serious problems. Significant fees and expenses may end up having been largely wasted. The client's key people may become disillusioned and confused about their overall leadership. Major strategic management opportunities may be lost.

Numerous first-time users of consultants face these possibilities each year when bringing in outside consultants to do major studies. One *Fortune* 100 company engaged a prestigious consulting firm to undertake a comprehensive review of its worldwide organization and management practices. The consultant brought in a team for about a year, rendered a "scholarly report" of recommendations, and then left to pursue assignments with others. The report was thick and impressively packaged, but it had some controversial recommendations and lacked a readily usable action plan.

The client CEO and his top management had great difficulty perceiving from the report the practical implementation steps they should take. However, the CEO authorized his executive assistant to recruit a small number of consultants from several firms (other than the original consultant) to assist in implementation measures. The logic was that the exercise had stimulated the managers to think in constructive new ways about the power of proven organization and management practices, and that the company should not lose the benefit of this by closeting or discarding the report.

From the outset, the captive group was helpful in counseling top management and the divisions, beginning with their review, revisions, and installation of the consultant's pertinent recommendations. Periodically over the years, a few outside consultants continued to be brought into the group; some went on to a variety of key jobs in other parts of the company.

Management embraced the new approaches wholeheartedly and momentum grew to innovate with their managerial processes in all areas. The original consultant's work had proved to be beneficial and even the doubters acknowledged that it gave management an agenda for refining their organization and management practices, and initiating constructive new programs and policies.

This client had chosen the best of two worlds for salvaging its substantial investment in the project. They took advantage of the broad exposure their managers had received concerning the managerial and strategic planning processes of the "outside" business world which the consultants had brought to them. They took steps to implement the recommendations and sustain such momentum by establishing an ongoing corps of "captive" or internal consultants to continue to assist top management with the process.

Can Your Consultant Help You Prepare and Install Incomplete Implementation Plans?

Another solution to filling out gaps in and undertaking the implementation plan is to retain the consultant who made the recommendations. However, it is unwise to assume categorically that the consultant is adept at practicing what he preaches. Some of the best conceptualizers and advisors frequently are weak at, and uninterested in, the "grubby" work of implementation and follow-through.

You should carefully check the consultant's previous track record in comparable situations. Even when he checks out with high marks, you should pick the strongest person available from your own team for overall leadership and liaison with the project, and you should consider a number of critical questions:

- ▲ Has the consultant presented practical and workable recommendations? Are they complete and consistent with your objectives and conclusions?
- ▲ Are they realistic in terms of your marketplace and competition and of your organization's capabilities and potential for introducing and employing them?
- ▲ Has your consultant "sold" you on his recommendations and helped you obtain "buy-ins" from your key management people?
- ▲ Did he present a credible action plan with compelling reasons for proceeding? Or, are you faced with prolonging the debate and acceptance?
- ▲ Has he helped ready you to move on all those action steps with which you agree? Has he offered a sound timetable

with such action steps? Responsibility assignments? A plan for measuring or assessing the results?

▲ What relationships has he established with your people? Will this facilitate or deter their cooperation in making needed changes?

▲ Does your consultant appear practical in action planning and implementation? Do you feel he would sustain a high interest level in the implementation?

▲ Conversely, do you have complete confidence that your staff could move ahead on their own? Would this hasten shifting the responsibility back to those who must effect the changes and live with them?

▲ Do your key people need further training, orientation, and coaching? Would this consultant be highly qualified to carry out the programs, or should you seek such follow-on help elsewhere?

▲ Do you have other areas where the consultant might be helpful and would the implementation experience heighten his understanding of your business as a basis for his increased future effectiveness?

▲ Do you have an adequate budget for retaining him further?

Only after you have positive answers to such questions should you determine whether to retain or terminate the consultant. Rarely should acceptance of the starting proposal already have guaranteed that he participate in the follow-through; this opportunity should be kept contingent on his performance.

If you are a client who has received an incomplete package of recommendations and implementation plans, you have several basic options. You may have confidence that the consultant can remedy the problems and thus help salvage the consulting fees and expenses and also the experience of your own people who have been involved. If so, send your adviser back to the drawing board, but not without assigning your strongest available executive to work on the project with him until the revision is completed.

Alternatively, you may terminate the consultant and set up your own internal team to rework the recommendations and implement them. Under only the rarest circumstances should you immediately bring in another independent outside consultant.

If the consultant's proposals are acceptable and ready to implement, then you face the commonsense decision whether to proceed with his help or implement with your own staff. In either case, you may want or need to supplement the effort by hiring new key people.

20

Tests of
Implementation Readiness

*Keys to performance improvement via your consultant's
recommendations*

- ▲ New concepts linkable with specific actions
- ▲ Actions that enhance competitive advantage
- ▲ Action steps compatible with your situation
- ▲ Adequate time for new project life cycles
- ▲ Focused processes and stimuli for innovation
- ▲ Organization ready for recommended changes
- ▲ Allocations for investment-spending risks
- ▲ Convincing performance-improvement prospects

As you near the moment of truth with the impending completion of the consultant's work, you need to test his or her proposed action plans for their feasibility for producing significant *performance improvement*. The final proposals should aim at believable costs and profit benefits, increased productivity in operations, stronger managerial processes, and greater values for your customers.

The challenge is to ensure that your consultant's recommendations are timely, relevant, action-oriented, and cost/value effective, with specific action steps and responsibilities clearly designated. To that end, as his or her recommendations near their final stages, you should check their soundness against such tests as the keys noted above, which are the subject of this final chapter.

Are Recommended New Concepts Clearly Linkable With Specific, Workable Action Programs?

Mike Kami's advice to identify a current action with every future, and assign a name responsible for it[1] is perhaps the best sniff test of the practicality of new concepts.

Profound and exciting concepts are the lifeblood of the competent consultant. More importantly, they can provide you with an extremely useful intellectual perspective to clarify and communicate to your people the basic directions you desire to take. However, they are just one-half of a well-constructed *recommendation set*. That set, to be implementable, must always contain a match of *concepts* and *specific actions*. The link between the two must be clear and unchallengeable, and responsibility for the action half must be assigned. Moreover, those designated people must believe in their assigned actions and understand how they relate to and support your overall mission and game plan.

All too often, a consultant's recommendations fail to leave the concept stage and thus offer little more than dreams, wishes, ideals, or the broadest of goals and directions. They ignore the proverbial one step at a time needed to climb the mountain. Your consultant is not fulfilling his responsibility if specific action steps and responsibilities are not defined and clarified.

One very serious consequence of leaving a gap between fine concepts and specific actions can be a failure to come to grips with the needed investment spending. Most broad, conceptual strategies of competitive commitment cannot be executed until you have recognized, planned for, and readied the foundation skills and programs that support the essential development strategies. In a high-tech application you might be involved with a three- to five-year time span between implementation of development projects and marketplace commitment.

The very real and serious problem of stopping at the sometimes-stratospheric concept level makes it worthwhile to reiterate a concept advanced years ago by Peter Drucker, namely "the futurity of present decisions." In his view, all key decisions are only valid in the present. Concept-only recommendations are akin to the idea of long-range plans and future strategies. They are not meaningful to the result you are seeking from your consultant except as an agenda of alternatives or possibilities for future reconsideration. Today's strategic plan of commitment and development decisions that clearly support such concepts is what should govern your allocation and use of resources. If your resource-building programs are valid and viable, they will prepare you for the longer term and will keep you flexible for needed changes along the way.

One useful approach is to insist on your consultant's development of scenarios that simulate his or her most essential alternatives and recommendations. The main stipulation for constructing such scenarios is that they try to portray all of the key assumptions that relate such recommendations to your market, competition, planned policies and programs, and timing decisions.

The scenario-building process can reveal unrealistic assumptions and clarify investment-spending programs and capabilities to be put in place as essential first steps for the full project. Finally, it helps to set up contingency planning for all types of "what if" situations. Its potentialities are limited only by the imagination and ingenuity of your consultants and your own team.

Will the Recommended Actions Enhance Your Competitive Advantage?

The prime purpose of most consulting assignments is to improve performance and enhance your competitive advantage, whether with your present business or new ventures. You should always critique your consultant's final recommendations from this perspective. Are they merely fine-sounding but "soft" concepts and programs, or do they truly constitute significant new measures for strengthening your present situation and/or diversifying advantageously into new opportunities?

There are numerous commonsense ways to test a plan's contribution to your competitive advantage, and the aforementioned scenario approach certainly can shed light on this issue. Another comprehensive discipline for directing and evaluating your consultant's contributions is Michael Porter's concept of the enterprise's *value chain* (see Chapter 3).

His dynamic scenario critically examines the numerous steps where value can be added in your product-flow process from your supplier, through the nine functions he defines for your enterprise, and on through your channels of distribution to your buyer. Such a discipline can provide valuable new perspectives and focus for testing your competitiveness comprehensively and can be applied for your total business or discrete aspects of it.

Are Your Consultant's Proposed Actions Clearly Compatible With Your Situation?

Relevance always is an essential criterion of well-matched recommendations. Irrelevance is not as likely to creep in when you and your staff have been working closely with the consulting team throughout the project's progress or when the subject is deeply familiar to you. New and unfamiliar areas can pose the greatest dangers, one of which is the burgeoning practice of information systems (IS) integration, which has become the particular forte of the consulting arms of the major accounting firms.

Especially for a corporation involved in widespread operations, integrated information systems is becoming a powerful managerial and competitive capability. However, the IS consultant can be overly zealous in recommendations to clients. In one instance, the implementation of some outstanding IS work was jeopardized by a recommendation that the information vice-president should report directly to the chief executive as *the* senior managerial function. All of the major line functions were to report, in turn, to the information executive. The basic organizational proposal was not adopted by the client, and implementation of some otherwise quite sound information integration steps were delayed.

In this day of mergers and acquisitions, another area that can be overdone if it is too inflexibly applied is the use of central-

ized organization and control in a multiunit company. The situation of Mid-Continental Industries shows how one chief
executive reversed a direction his company's board had taken on
the recommendations of a prior consultant.

Mid-Continental Industries: Don't Destroy the "Fine Jewels"

The directors of Mid-Continental, a heavy steel foundry, determined that they should diversify to balance the extreme cyclicality of
their base business and engaged a consultant to assist them with
diversifications and acquisitions.

After evaluating many industries, the consultant targeted the injection molded plastics business, and Mid-Continental was successful in acquiring four small and profitable regional custom molders,
mainly serving the U.S. automotive and appliance industries. Since
the four used basically the same manufacturing materials and
processes, had some commonality in markets, and all used manufacturers' agents, the consultant recommended a unified group organization for higher synergy and profits.

During consummation of the acquisitions, the board employed
the senior consultant to become Mid-Continental's president. One of
his early moves was to form a plastics group and bring in a seasoned
vice-president with automotive engineering experience to head the
group. The latter began to install a series of groupwide policies and
procedures with the objective of a standard modus operandi for his
four units.

All had been purchased from their entrepreneur founders, and
in each case, either the founder or some key managers had stayed
on to run the operations. The four managements resisted the new
restrictions and controls, contending that each of their businesses
was too different from the others to be subordinated to centralized
day-to-day direction. Over a number of months, confrontations between the group executive and his unit heads increased, and the
latter balked at accepting or cooperating wholeheartedly with the
group procedures.

Because of unrelated circumstances, a new president was
brought in during this period to run the company. One of his early
moves was to eliminate the plastics group structure, reassign the
vice-president to a staff role, and have the four plastics units report

directly to him. This dramatically reduced the friction and freed the unit heads to focus fully on their respective operational and competitive problems in their own managerial styles.

The president redirected the vice-president's attention to a staff support agenda for capturing some of the hoped-for synergy. The latter proved to be quite resourceful in his new staff role, with constructive projects and programs in resin and other raw material sourcing, plastics technology forecasts, and process studies.

On a gradual schedule, several common functions were integrated, starting with raw material supply and injection molded process engineering. Also, in collaboration with the director of planning, the vice-president developed and installed an automated information system for coordinating plant scheduling in an online link-up with the major automotive and appliance accounts' order departments. Eventually, manufacturers' agents' assignments were partially consolidated.

What the directors and their original consultant had failed to recognize, and the new chief executive had correctly diagnosed, was that each little plastics company was a somewhat unique "fine jewel" developed in individualistic style by its entrepreneur founder. Even the work flows and production machinery in each plant, although of the same general types, had been configured differently reflecting the different characteristics of their customers' product specifications and subcontracting policies as well as each founder's contrasting operating style. Teamwork and productivity were elicited in quite different ways at the four plants.

The basic entrepreneurial and profit responsibilities of the four small businesses were restored and encouraged. In so doing, this company worked itself away from exposure to the dire results of other conglomerators of small businesses and their consultants who have destroyed countless "fine jewels" by mistakenly assuming that strong, centralized direction *per se* would produce better results.

Has Adequate Time Been Allowed for Undertaking New Project Life Cycles?

Recommended changes involving new products and/or processes inevitably pass through several stages before they can be considered ready for commitment to your marketplace. Two concerns should be foremost in your mind when evaluating your consultant's recommendations in such areas. One is the odds against success with the brand new venture. The other is failure to anticipate all of the unavoidable steps the new idea must go through, with the risk of underestimating the time, cost, and special skills required.

In the first instance, the odds against ultimate success for an entirely new proposition run quite high and argue for extreme caution when evaluating your consultant's recommendations for new concepts and ventures. General Electric's new venture screening division found that for every one hundred new propositions with which that office was deluged, only about three were deemed worthy of further analysis. Moreover, the chances for survival of any of the remaining three following detailed evaluation were quite remote.

The second concern, underestimating a new project's requirements, also has both operational and financial exposures, not the least of which could be slippages that cause you to miss your market window. This can be appreciated when you consider that the project life cycle for a relatively novel and embryonic new proposition should entail as many as eight or more distinct and time-consuming stages: idea generation; screening and prioritizing; preliminary business evaluation; research and/or development; prototype evaluation and testing; market evaluation; business plan and analysis; implementation and commitment. Each stage is critical, but the three earliest are most subject to such problems as imprecise market measurement, faulty perspective and focus, prematurely buying a concept lacking a finite or tangible form, and inadequate economic analysis of feasibility and profit potential. Whether this early, formative work is done in-house or by your consultant, it requires your rigorous evaluation.

In a proposition foreign to your experience, consultants with the requisite background and expertise can be most helpful at any or all stages of the life cycle in two ways: (1) They can assist you in setting up the process, and (2) they may be qualified to bring new approaches into its actual conduct. For example, you should consider using consultants familiar with the new *concurrent engineering* approach to collapse the cycle time significantly. This method eliminates the traditional serial process and calls for a multidivisional team or task force working concurrently on concept, design, engineering, prototype testing, process planning, and production engineering.[2] As a general rule, your goal should be to become largely self-sufficient in the process at the earliest possible time.

Have Focused Processes and Stimuli for Innovation Been Recommended?

You should always hope that your consultant will come up with truly innovative ideas for programs, policies, strategies, even significant product enhancements. Do not hold your breath, however; not all innovation comes with a flash in the night. Nevertheless, you should push him, not only to produce innovative *content* but also to help you improve your *process* of innovation. Whenever it is within the scope of your project, explore with your consultant how best to set up processes and policies to generate and encourage the innovative idea stream. Test his recommendations against such questions as the following:

- ▲ Have one or more of your functions been designated the responsibility for identifying and evaluating new opportunities in each of your market segments and with each product type?
- ▲ Are the innovators concerned with these areas focused adequately in their efforts or are they scattering the company's scarce resources by chasing new ideas helterskelter?
- ▲ Are procedures recommended for authorization and monitoring of innovative probes? For adequate control over the time and resources being devoted to new projects? Is a screening and prioritizing procedure proposed for early focus on the flow of suggestions and proposals?
- ▲ Are there safeguards against individuals or departments initiating new projects and explorations on their own agendas without checks and balances on consistency with the overall corporate directions?

Is Your Organization Well Prepared to Take the Indicated Action Steps?

Lack of conviction to implement obviously occurs when the consultant has not developed a sound and logical set of action steps. He may have run short of time in the wind-up stage or failed to spell out step by step how to move from conceptual recommendations to specific strategies and action-specific programs. Or, he may not have presented recommendations and action steps best suited for the managerial style and structure in your type of operation.

Particularly with new ventures or significant changes in management processes or leadership, both the client and consultant may fail to perceive or admit that the client's staff is not well prepared or qualified for the implementation work. It may be a lack of expertise in an area that the client has not needed before. It may be only a shortage of manpower and less time than it will take to recruit and staff a full complement of the needed talents.

Alternatively, the implementation snag may be caused by more subtle hurdles that have been receiving new labels and increasing attention in recent years from some consultants and management scholars. For example, you may face such issues as needing to establish a clearer sense of mission throughout your organization, or redirect your "driving force," or effect a change in the "culture" of your company and undertake a program of basic "work redesign."

▲ *Corporate sense of mission may be unclear and unfocused.* This issue involves matters of content, communications, and control. In terms of strategic *content,* the consultant and client may have failed to address decisively whether the corporate mission, its prime purposes, and its objectives, are realistic, challenging, effort-stretching, worthwhile, and consistent with the company's total business environment and opportunities.

A companion question is one of *communication* and an issue of whether the client's basic viewpoint and mission are shared by all throughout the organization in a compatible and consistent way. Is there a problem of inconsistent understanding of mission? Is the corporate leader projecting and inspiring adoption of the attitudes required for continuing success in that environment? Do the company's personnel throughout the organization understand what its leadership is trying to accomplish? If so, do they accept this as worthwhile, and can they relate their own assigned responsibilities and performance standards to it? Is there teamwork, harmony, a pattern of shared values among all of the employees?

Control is another problem of unclear and unfocused missions. Client and consultant may have established a solid conceptual mission for the company but failed to develop action plans for assuring focus on and control over its implementation.

▲ *The company's "driving force" may be misdirected.* Among the most common problems is an emphasis on products and technology rather than markets and users' needs. Is the company product-driven or market-driven? Is it dominated by technologies in search of a market? Is the overriding philosophical viewpoint of the company's leadership and its top management fully attuned to the mission and environment?

▲ *The client's "culture" may not be ready.* Recommended actions may constitute so great a departure from a client's present planning and operating approaches that they dictate broad changes in the way the company is positioning itself in industry and the way its leader, management, and staffs go about their work. This requirement could well be an order of magnitude or more beyond the sense-of-mission and driving-force issues.

All of these broad corporate-level concerns have one trait in common. Each endeavors to describe an aggregate state of mind of an organization. Some executives and consultants tend to view them as recent-day fads or clever gimmicks conceived to generate new sources of consulting billings. Yet behind them all are fundamental conditions that can measure the extent and quality of a staff's understanding, consistency and harmony of individual and corporate goals; their degree of teamwork; and what overarching emphasis their efforts should have, for example, an organization that is market driven versus one that is product/technology driven.

A basic issue of concern to you and your consultant should

be to determine whether you have hurdles or blockages to motivation, teamwork, and direction in your company. If you have determined that you do have, you will eventually need to eliminate them. The question of how you go about the task is secondary. It may be as simple as sharpening communications and working harder on a continuing basis to keep the lines open in all directions—downward, upward, among peers, and interdepartmentally. Or, at the other extreme, it may warrant bringing in one of the newer experts who specialize in such areas. Among these are Noel Tichy and David Ulrich from the University of Michigan, and John D. Adams, an organization development consultant. A reputable and objective consultant who discerns your need for a culture overhaul and yet does not specialize in such work should suggest suitable expertise for you to consider.

Have the Major Recommendations Recognized and Allowed for the Necessary Investment-Spending Risks?

Changes that eliminate major problems or launch important new directions, approaches, and products inevitably require significant risk taking. Substantial investments in dollars and the scarce time of key people and facilities can be required before the recommended end goals can be realized.

Sometimes the effort involves seeking to salvage sunk costs, as when Ultronic invested in a consultant to identify and develop secondary markets for its first-generation stock quotation machine. In other instances, it is a matter of innovating and breaking new ground. Investment spending concepts of opportunity costs, risk/return tradeoffs, cost/value benefits, and present and future values of your alternatives may be germane. You have a right to expect your consultant to be conversant and facile with all of these considerations and to present recommendations consistent with their application in your case.

In order to investment-spend for the future, some things, such as near-term performance results, obviously must be foregone or sacrificed in the short run. You will need an understanding board, a clear public relations message for your shareholders and the financial community. You also may need a consultant who is capable of helping you optimize and reduce the impact between the new investment spending and the slippage in shorter term financial results.

Reflecting on the time requirements of the new-project life cycle, you should make certain that your consultant has factored in all key investment-spending implications. His final recommendations, to be complete, should recognize specifically what you will need to undertake in development programs *now* in order to be able to commit the essentials of his recommended programs in competition at the "right" later date.

Does the Final Action Plan Convincingly Promise Substantial Added Value and Superior Performance Results?

This last test brings this book full circle to the subject matter of the first part—the values and benefits you have a right to expect from your consultant's work. His or her final recommendations, when fully implemented, should offer the expectations of delivering at least three broad classes of benefits:

1. *Measurable performance improvements soon,* and/or establishment of solid foundations for realizing them in the future in the form of finite cost and profit benefits, increased productivity in operations, and greater values to be passed on to your customers
2. Significant companywide *improvements in managerial and operating functions* needed to sustain and extend the foregoing performance improvements through time
3. An *expanded awareness* of your objectives and strategic emphasis and an increasing cohesiveness and *sense of teamwork* and contribution throughout your organization. These culture-type improvements, if to be worthwhile, should be expected to facilitate improvements in functions, and ultimately, performance.

To whatever extent appropriate for your particular project, you need to be convinced that the final plan you have received presents a highly credible and realistic roadmap for achieving important results of these three types. Obviously, consulting projects vary widely in their influence on the overall business, and in the nature and extent of their *value contribution.* However, your target for every assignment should be at least some improvement in each of the three classes of benefits. If you, your associates, and your consultant can accomplish this, then the dire poetry of the fictional Bertie Ramsbottom, as expressed in his "Ballad of the Business Consultant" (see Chapter 1), can be superceded by:

An Ode From the "Experienced" Client

I brought consultants in to mend
My faltering business—end to end.
They questioned me and all my minions
Uncovering numerous new opinions!

They tore down fences I had erected,
To start communications previously deflected.
I even got inputs on my marketplace
Which not since my sales days I'd chosen to face!

They didn't quite perform the way they spoke,
But fresh, new approaches they did provoke.
And some of their words had to be translated.
When that was done, it mostly related!

Their grandest ideas sounded stupendous
And executing them could have been horrendous!
On many things we compromised.
Others I accepted, and was well advised!

The worst was when they challenged me
To defend the things I sought to be.
Those super-confident young ladies and men
Had the gall to do my sacred precepts in!

But when all was done they quietly left
Just before my coffers became bereft.
I might even use them another day
If things work out the way they say!

Building Block Diagram G summarizes the major considerations presented in *No Miracles for Hire.* The book has endeav-

Implement Plans

Plan Acceptance Steps:

- Resolve internal politics and opposing views early.
- Heed contrary consultant recommendations.
- Assure key client "buy-ins."
- Clarify responsibilities for action steps.

Action Readiness Tests:

- Concept/action linkages.
- Realistic project development goals and timing.
- Offers competitive gains, performance improvement.
- Compatible with situation, capabilities, finances.

Control Project

Control of Study Schedule:

- Use single client liaison.
- Clarify goals at start.
- Monitor for slippage.
- Adjust for scope change.

Control of Content Quality:

- Promote client/consultant interactions and partnering.
- Make surprise quality and content checks.

Achieve Perspective and Focus

Key Problems and Obstacles:

- Thin marketplace inputs.
- Loose problem definitions.
- Over-conceptualizing.
- Overstressing of technology.
- Too many new programs.
- Action steps undetermined.

Guidelines and Principles:

- Invite divergent views early.
- Focus on market needs.
- Clarify causes of problems.
- Stress "natural" strategies.
- Test concepts against "art of the possible" and financials.

Structure Assignment

Proposal Elements

Project Objectives:

- Effort stretching aims.
- Financially feasible.
- Friendly game of entrapment.

Approach:

- Survey plan and scenarios.
- Make reconnaissance studies.
- Limit the initial orientation.
- Make periodic progress checks.

Scope:

- Focused, unambiguous limits.
- Monitor scope enlargement.

Staffing, Time, and Costs:

- Qualifications and compatibility.
- Projected costs and benefits.

Match People

People-Matching Problems:

- Staff mismatch with client.
- Poor communications skills.
- Motivations lacking.
- "Unknowns" assigned to job.

Key Screening Steps and Criteria:

1. Identify potential consultants.
2. Screen several firms in depth.
3. Test against selection criteria.
4. Seek multiple formal proposals.

Determine Need and Timing

Key Consulting Roles and Benefits:

- Solve problems.
- Seek current competitive advantages.
- Pursue new options.
- Facilitate change.
- Improve performance.

Problems Determining Need:

- Fuzzy, unclear project purpose.
- Wrong problem focus.
- Myopic aims and options.
- Differing perceptions.
- Hidden agendas.
- Missed market window.

Clarifying the Need:

- Situation analysis.
- Needs definition.
- Matching needs and opportunities.
- Go/no-go criteria.
- Project objective.

ored to help you exceed the "experienced" client's level of satisfaction through the suggestions underlying the challenges and building blocks throughout. Hopefully, they can help guide you to productive teaming with your consultant, not to achieve miracles, but rather to obtain significant and lasting performance improvements with his or her support and counsel.

Notes

1. Paraphrased from a presentation to corporate executives by Michael J. Kami. See also Michael J. Kami, *Trigger Points: How to Make Decisions Three Times Faster, Innovate Smarter, and Beat Your Competition by Ten Percent (It Ain't Easy)* (New York: McGraw-Hill, 1988).
2. Otis Port with Zachary Schiller and Rosa W. King, "A Smarter Way to Manufacture," *Business Week* magazine (April 30, 1990), page 110.

Appendix

Information Sources on Consultants

Types of Consulting Practices

Greiner and Metzger have classified consultants into eight distinct types of practice:[1]

1. *National (and international) general management firms.* This category includes the early post–World War II leaders—McKinsey & Company; Booz, Allen & Hamilton; and Cresap (formerly called Cresap, McCormick and Paget), now a unit of Towers Perrin.

2. *National (and international) CPA firms with consulting units.* These burgeoning practices include Andersen Consulting of Arthur Andersen, who leads in the design and installation of information systems and the conduct of studies to produce management information for clients; KPMG Peat Marwick; Ernst & Young, who offers information systems, financial and cost management, strategic planning, marketing, operations, and other senior management services to a wide range of industries; Coopers & Lybrand, with consulting services in three main areas—information systems, strategic and financial planning, and resource productivity, including just-in-time approaches; Price Waterhouse, in strategic management counseling, information resource management, executive information and control, and manufacturing and cost management; and Deloitte & Touche, whose consulting is involved in all basic areas of management and operations.

3. *Functionally specialized firms.* Handy Associates (a unit of Science Management Corporation) which performs executive search and compensation consulting; Alexander Proudfoot in manufacturing; The Hay Group (of Saatchi & Saatchi) doing compensation and human resources work; Hewitt Associates, consulting in total compensation services; and the strategic planners, including The Boston Consulting Group and Bain & Co.

4. *Industry specialized firms.* These firms include Kurt Salmon Associates, which focuses on the consumer goods and services industries and A. T. Kearney, which started by emphasizing production and engineering consulting in manufacturing-based industry and subsequently diversified into service organizations, government, and health care.

5. *Public sector firms.* Greiner and Metzger cited PRC (Planning Resources Corporation) and Charles River Associates involved in a wide range of government contracts.

6. *Think tanks.* These firms include Abt Associates, an applied research and consulting organization offering analytical and problem-solving services in such areas as economics, statistics, marketing research, strategic planning, and sociology; Arthur D. Little, a prestigious technology and management firm serving a range of industries and government areas; and SRI International, founded as Stanford Research Institute, for basic research, new technologies and management consulting.

7. *Regional and local firms.* These firms include a host of smaller firms who limit their geographic scope but are active in a wide range of consulting services to small business. Many of these organizations are profiled and cross-indexed by industry, functional specialization, and geographical locations in two comprehensive directories noted below: *Dun's Consultants Directory* and *The Directory of Management Consultants: 1990.*

8. *Sole practitioners.* Tens of thousands of individuals are involved in consulting. They include college and university faculty serving part-time or embarking on full-time careers; former consultants with major firms performing many types of consult-

ing services as individuals; and a host of former executives replaced by mergers, acquisitions, and dissolutions, who prefer not to retire or rejoin industry, or who may be consulting as a stop-gap measure.

Two additional classifications not categorized by Greiner, which also fall into several of the foregoing groupings, are turnaround consultants and multibusiness firms.

▲ *Turnaround consultants.* These organizations specialize in helping ailing companies or those threatened with or entering bankruptcy. They are particularly resourceful at severe cost-cutting via personnel reductions and other drastic operation-paring measures. Many have entered this field from successfully turning around their own corporation or some of its troubled units or from their involvement in venture capital firms. Among the more well-known turnaround consultants are Q. T. Wiles of Hambrecht & Quist, Victor Palmieri, Multi Financial Services, Inc., and Sanford Sigoloff.

▲ *Multibusiness consultants.* These firms include Towers Perrin, the parent of Cresap and Tillinghast, and the huge advertising conglomerate, Saatchi & Saatchi, who announced intentions in 1989 to spin off its management consulting units.

Among other successful multibusiness firms is Science Management Corporation (SMC), which provides professional services in three principal areas. One is its management services and human resources group, which includes the aforementioned Handy Associates, productivity-related consulting, and contract, temporary and permanent placement businesses. A second SMC group is information technology, which serves federal, state, and local governments; offers systems engineering services; and provides publications marketing help to publishers and magazine agents. The third group, engineering and technology, is involved in stress and structural analysis, mechanical engineering, procurement and construction services, and environmental consulting.

Associations

A number of associations provide information on their member consulting organizations and usually have pertinent referral suggestions concerning expertise you may be seeking. Among the most important of these are:

- ▲ ACME (Association of Consulting Management Engineers, Inc.), 230 Park Avenue, New York, N.Y. 10169. Phone: (212) 697–9693. Was the first organization formed by the major consultants (excludes CPA members) to establish ethical codes of conduct and a common body of knowledge in which their members should be expected to become proficient. Publish an annual *Directory of Members* (numbering 54 firms in 1989) with descriptions of services. Considered by many to be the leader in setting the ethical tone for the industry.
- ▲ ACL (American Consultants League), 2030 Clarendon Boulevard, Arlington, Va. 22201. Phone (703) 528–4493. Has 1,000 full- and part-time consultants with varied fields of expertise. Publishes *Consultants Directory* annually and a bimonthly newsletter, *Consulting Intelligence*.
- ▲ AICPA (American Institute of Certified Public Accountants), 1211 Avenue of the Americas, New York, N.Y. 10036. Phone: (212) 575–6200. With 280,000 members and a staff of 700, this association is a comprehensive source of information on all aspects of the accounting profession, including the information systems and other non-accounting services the major members have been developing over recent years.
- ▲ AMC (Association of Managing Consultants), 19 West 44th Street, New York, N.Y. 10036. Phone: (212) 921–2885. Is a college of IMC having 400 members. Was formed to represent smaller firms and individuals serving all types of business. Operates a client referral service and publishes a *Directory of Membership* and the *Journal of Management Consulting* periodically.
- ▲ AIMC (Association of Internal Management Consul-

tants), P.O. Box 304, East Bloomfield, N.Y. 14443. Phone: (716) 657–7878. Was formed to represent so-called captive consultants employed fulltime in industry and government. With 240 members, seeks to develop and encourage the professional practice of internal management consulting.

▲ IMC (Institute of Management Consultants), 19 West 44th Street, New York, N.Y. 10036. Phone: (212) 921–2885. With a membership of approximately 2,000, serves individuals and firms meeting the Institute's requirements. Grants a certification of proficiency, CMC (Certified Management Consultant), to the professionals of member firms who meet certain qualifications of expertise and experience. In 1988, IMC absorbed SPMC (Society of Professional Management Consultants). In 1989, IMC and ACME were in the midst of merging the two organizations for a more concerted effort to achieve a truly unified professional status for management consulting.

▲ INTERMAC (International Association of Merger and Acquisition Consultants), 200 South Frontage Road, Suite 103, Burr Ridge, Ill. 60521. Phone: (312) 323–0233. Members (numbering 35) specialize in working with medium-size firms primarily.

▲ PATCA (Professional and Technical Consultants Association), 1330 South Bascom Avenue, Suite D, San Jose, Calif. 95128. Phone: (408) 287–8703. Members (about five hundred) are independent consultants active in supporting business, industry, and government. PATCA serves as a referral aid to members and publishes an annual *Directory of Consultants*.

Publications

Publications that also represent comprehensive sources of consultants with details about their practices include the following:

▲ *Bradford's Directory of Marketing Research Agencies and Management Consultants in the United States and the World*. Published irregularly by Bradford's Directory, P.O. Box 276, Fairfax, Va. 22030.

▲ *Consultants and Consulting Organizations Directory*, 1988. Published by Gale Research Company, Book Tower, Detroit, Mich. 48226. Phone: (313)961–2242.

▲ *Consultant's U.S. Statistical Guide & Source Finder*, 1986. The Consultant's Library, available through FIND/ SVP, 625 Avenue of the Americas, New York, N.Y. 10011. Phone: (212)645–4500. Contains information on sources, fees, and billings.

▲ *Consultants News*, a monthly newsletter. Published by Kennedy Publications, Templeton Road, Fitzwilliam, N.H. 03447. Phone: (603)585–6544. James H. Kennedy, founder, editor, and publisher.

▲ *The Directory of Management Consultants: 1990*. Kennedy Publications (see address above). This major source directory is a 680-page compendium with profiles of over thirteen hundred firms and consultants.

▲ *Dun's Consultants Directory*. Published annually by Dun's Marketing Services, Three Century Drive, Parsippany, N.J. 07054. Phone (800)526–0651. This annual publication lists twenty-five thousand consulting firms in the United States, alphabetically and cross-classified by geographic location and specialization. (Two hundred specialization categories including Consultants/General.)

▲ *Encyclopedia of Associations*. Published annually by Gale Research, Inc. (see address above). This vast compilation of virtually all associations in the United States lists 175 associations that represent consultants of many types. Profiles include brief descriptions of the emphasis of their memberships, and note any directories and other publications issued by the associations.

▲ *Management Consulting 1988–90*. Published by the Harvard Business School Press, Cambridge, Mass. 02163, in cooperation with the HBS Management Consulting Club. It is designed mainly to inform its MBA candidates interested in consulting careers, and contains profiles provided by more than fifty of the larger management consulting firms.

▲ *Research Services Directory,* 1987. Published by Gale Research Company (see address above). Covers research and development firms, contract laboratories, and consulting firms.

Two additional major sources of consultants are local telephone directories and special trade directories for most industries published by trade associations and/or trade publications.

Note

1. Greiner, Larry E., and Robert O. Metzger, *Consulting to Management* (Englewood Cliffs, N.J.: Prentice-Hall, Inc., 1983), page 12.

Bibliography

Albert, Kenneth J. *How to Be Your Own Management Consultant.* New York: McGraw-Hill, 1978.

Association of Consulting Management Engineers, Inc. (ACME). *Common Body of Knowledge Required by Professional Management Consultants.* New York: ACME, 1957.

Beniger, James R. *The Control Revolution—Technological and Economic Origins of the Information Society.* Cambridge, Mass.: Harvard University Press, 1986.

Cannon, J. Thomas. *Business Strategy and Policy.* New York: Harcourt, Brace & World, 1968.

Cohen, William A. *How to Make It Big as a Consultant.* New York: AMACOM, 1985.

Drucker, Peter. *The Practice of Management.* New York: Harper & Row, 1954.

————. *Innovation and Entrepreneurship: Practice and Principles.* New York: Harper & Row, 1985.

Easton, Thomas A., and Ralph W. Conant. *Using Consultants: A Consumer's Guide for Managers.* Chicago: Probus Publishing Company, 1985.

Economist, The. See the February 13, 1988 issue for a definitive discussion of consulting history and issues.

Greiner, Larry E., and Robert O. Metzger. *Consulting to Management.* Englewood Cliffs, N.J.: Prentice-Hall, Inc., 1983.

Guttmann, H. Peter. *The International Consultant,* revised edition. New York: John Wiley & Sons, 1988.

Hamermesh, Richard G. *Making Strategy Work.* New York: John Wiley & Sons, 1986.

Higdon, Hal. *The Business Healers.* New York: Random House, 1969.

Holtz, Herman. *Choosing and Using a Consultant: A Manager's Guide to Consulting Services.* New York: John Wiley & Sons, 1989.

Johnson, Kathleen M., editor. *Management Consulting 1989–90.* Cambridge, Mass.: Harvard Business School Press, 1988.

Journal of Management Consulting. Journal of Management Consulting, Inc., New York. Published quarterly.

Kami, Michael J. *Trigger Points: How to Make Decisions Three Times Faster, Innovate Smarter, and Beat Your Competition by Ten Percent (It Ain't Easy).* New York: McGraw-Hill 1988.

Kennedy, James, editor and publisher. *Consultants News.* Kennedy Publications, Fitzwilliams, N.H. Monthly newsletter.

Kirby, Tess. *The Can-Do Manager.* New York: AMACOM, 1989.

Kubr, M. *Management Consulting—A Guide to the Profession.* Washington, D.C.: International Labor Office, 1986.

Magaziner, Ira, and Mark Patinkin. *The Silent War—Inside the Global Business Battles Shaping America's Future.* New York: Random House, 1989.

Management Practices Quarterly. Management Practice, Inc., New York.

McVay, Barry L. *Proposals That Win Federal Contracts: How to Plan, Price, Write, and Negotiate to Get Your Fair Share of Government Business.* Woodbridge, Va.: Panoptic Enterprises, 1989.

Metzger, Robert O. *Profitable Consulting: Guiding America's Managers Into the Next Century.* Reading, Mass.: Addison-Wesley, 1989.

Parker, Marilyn M., and Robert J. Benson. *Information Economics— Linking Business Performance to Information Technology.* Englewood Cliffs, N.J.: Prentice-Hall, Inc., 1988.

Pendray, John J., and Ernest E. Keet. *Strategic Development for High Technology Businesses.* Wilton, Conn.: Value Publishing, Inc., 1987.

Peters, Tom. *Thriving on Chaos—Handbook for Management Revolution.* New York: Alfred A. Knopf, 1987.

Pinchot III, Gifford. *Intrapreneuring.* New York: Harper & Row, 1985.

Poppel, Harvey L., and Bernard Goldstein. *Information Technology— The Trillion Dollar Opportunity.* New York: McGraw-Hill, 1987.

Porter, Michael E. *Competitive Advantage—Creating and Sustaining Superior Performance.* New York: The Free Press, 1985.

———. *Competitive Strategy.* New York: The Free Press, 1980.

Roethlisberger, Fritz J. *Management and Morale*. Cambridge, Mass.: Harvard University Press, 1946.

Schaffer, Robert H. *The Breakthrough Strategy*. New York: Harper & Row, Ballinger Division, 1988.

Shenson, Howard L. *The Contract and Fee-Setting Guide for Consultants and Professionals*. New York: John Wiley & Sons, 1990.

Steiner, George A. *Strategic Planning*. New York: The Free Press, 1979.

Weinberg, Gerald M. *A Guide to Giving and Getting Advice Successfully*. New York: Dorset House Publishing, 1985.

Index